# 100个热门话题汉译英

## Chinese-English Translation of 100 Hot Topics

王逢鑫 著

### 图书在版编目(CIP)数据

100个热门话题汉译英/王逢鑫著.—北京:北京大学出版社,2010.1
ISBN 978-7-301-16127-2

Ⅰ.1… Ⅱ.王… Ⅲ.英语－翻译 Ⅳ.H315.9

中国版本图书馆CIP数据核字(2009)第198377号

| | |
|---|---|
| 书　　　名: | 100个热门话题汉译英 |
| 著作责任者: | 王逢鑫　著 |
| 责 任 编 辑: | 宣　瑄 |
| 标 准 书 号: | ISBN 978-7-301-16127-2/H·2367 |
| 出 版 发 行: | 北京大学出版社 |
| 地　　　址: | 北京市海淀区成府路205号　100871 |
| 网　　　址: | http://www.pup.cn |
| 电　　　话: | 邮购部 62752015　发行部 62750672　编辑部 62754149 |
| | 出版部 62754962 |
| 电 子 信 箱: | zpup@pup.pku.edu.cn |
| 印 刷 者: | 世界知识印刷厂 |
| 经 销 者: | 新华书店 |
| | 880毫米×1230毫米　A5　11.5印张　320千字 |
| | 2010年1月第1版　2011年1月第2次印刷 |
| 定　　　价: | 24.00元 |

未经许可,不得以任何方式复制或抄袭本书之部分或全部内容。
版权所有,侵权必究
举报电话:(010)62752024　电子信箱:fd@pup.pku.edu.cn

# 作者简介

王逢鑫,1939年生于山东省青岛市。1957年考入北京大学西方语言文学系英国语言文学专业,攻读英国语言文学。1962年毕业后留校任教,任北京大学外国语学院英语语言文学系教授、博士生导师。1973年,赴英国埃塞克斯大学短期进修。1981年至1983年,在英国爱丁堡大学中文系教授中国文学、语言和文化。曾三次在巴黎联合国教育、科学和文化组织工作,1979年担任同声传译,1990年担任笔译,1999年担任审校。1992年赴加拿大从事加拿大研究。学术领域涉及:语言学(应用语言学、语义学、词汇学、词典学、句法学、语言测试等)、英美文学(诗歌、小说、散文等)、跨文化研究(美国研究、英国研究、加拿大研究等)、及翻译(口译与笔译)理论与实践,在这些领域均有著述。毕生从事教育事业和中外文化交流。主要著作有:

1)《英语意念语法》,北京:北京大学出版社,1989

《英语意念语法(修订版)》,北京:外文出版社,1999

《王逢鑫文法语义篇》,台北:台湾经典传讯,2004

《王逢鑫文法形式篇》,台北:台湾经典传讯,2004

2)《英语情态表达法》,香港:香港商务印书馆,1990;台北:台湾商务印书馆,1991;北京:商务印书馆国际有限公司,1996

3)《活用英语动词》,香港:香港商务印书馆,1990;台北:台湾商务印书馆,1991;北京:商务印书馆国际有限公司,1996

4)《英汉意念分类词典》,北京:北京大学出版社,1991

《常春藤 TOEFL 分类式字汇》,台北:台湾常春藤解析英语杂志社,1991

《英语词汇分类联想学习法》,北京:外文出版社,2000

5)《汉英口译教程》,北京:北京大学出版社,1992

6)《英语词汇的魅力》,北京:北京大学出版社,1995

《英语词汇的魅力(修订版)》,北京:外文出版社,2003

《繁星组合英文学习法》,台北:台湾经典传讯,1999

《王逢鑫词汇繁星篇(日常用语)》,台北:台湾经典传讯,2004

《王逢鑫词汇组合篇(自然万象)》,台北:台湾经典传讯,2004

7)《英语构词的玄妙》,北京:北京大学出版社,1997

《英语构词的玄妙(修订版)》,北京:外文出版社,2003

8)《汉英饮食文化词典》,北京:外文出版社,1998

9)《英语同义表达法》,北京:外文出版社,1999

《王逢鑫进阶文法同义表达(词汇&句法)》,台北:台湾经典传讯,2004

《王逢鑫进阶文法同义表达(逻辑&特例)》,台北:台湾经典传讯,2004

10)《英语模糊语法》,北京:外文出版社,2001

11)《英汉比较语义学》,北京:外文出版社,2001

12)《汉英旅游文化词典》,北京:北京大学出版社,2001

13)《高级汉英口译教程》,北京:外文出版社,2004

14)《英语文化》,北京:北京大学出版社,2004

15)《中国人最易犯的汉译英错误》,北京:中国书籍出版社,2008

# 前　言

　　这是我继《中国人最易犯的汉译英错误》（北京：中国书籍出版社，2008）之后，又一本关于汉英翻译的结集。一百篇文章绝大部分在《环球时报》上刊登过，时间是从 2007 年 4 月至 2009 年 3 月。在这两年里，我们的祖国经历了许许多多不平凡的事件。这一百篇文章反映了我国在这两年里的热门话题。其中的关键词，有些是新生的词汇，另有些是原有词汇赋予了新义。如何将这些热门词汇译成英语，是译界、词典界、媒体、英语教师和广大英语学习者共同关心和探索的问题。我紧紧地追逐我国日新月异的发展形势，敏锐地捕捉不断出现的新词与新义，冥思苦想如何用地道的英语表达这些热门词汇，并不失时机地写成文章发表。我提出自己的译法和见解，以抛砖引玉。

　　有些热门词汇是从英语借来的，外来语比较好办，翻译回去即可。然而，翻译土生土长的汉语原生词汇，却是件麻烦事。译界学者常常讨论"不可译性"，有些热门词汇确实是不可译的。但是，在翻译过程中不能留空白，明明不可译的东西也要想方设法表达出来，因此实际上不存在"不可译性"，而这恰恰是对翻译家的挑战。语言本身具有模糊性，一些汉语热门词汇带有多义性，在不同语境中有不同含义，很难在英语中找到合适的对应词以概括汉语的丰富内涵。"折腾"一词，就是例证。"折腾"是个多义词，"不折腾"的意思更是五花八门，译成英语可以说是仁者见仁，智者见智。不同的译者在不同的上下文里会有大相径庭的理解，再加上语言知识和能力的差异，会产生形形色色的译法，很难找到一个放之四海而皆准的答案。可是在篇幅有限的译文中，总要提供一个比较可信的译法。我的做法是：广泛搜集相关语料，进行精心的选择，寻找尽量符合英语习惯的翻译方法。

　　我一生从事英语教学与研究。可能是出于职业特点，译文要求尽量对齐，即使稍微罗嗦一点，也要让学习者容易接受。这种路子和风格不同于职业翻译家。他们追求文字华丽，格调高雅，而我更希望朴

# 100个热门话题汉译英
## Chinese-English Translation of 100 Hot Topics

实无华,平易且忠于原文。在近50年的英语教学生涯中,我体会到精选例句有助于学习者准确理解、掌握和运用英语。但是,过去我国的英语教科书所使用的例句,有些是从古典名著中摘录的,虽然文字优美,可是往往内容脱离实际,或者语言陈旧。还有一些是编者为配合某个语言点教学而自己撰写的,虽符合教学要求,但是由于编者水平有限,造成语言生硬,枯燥乏味,甚至是"中国式英语"。再有一些例句抄自国内外出版的词典。诚然,词典具有规范性,但仅仅是以往用法的梳理与总结,不能反映语言的最新变化。更何况现成的词义和用法不一定能回答如何将这些汉语热门词汇翻译成英语。例句应有典型性,学会了可以举一反三、触类旁通。例句还应该具有真实性,是来自生活中活生生的语言。现代网络给我们提供了海量信息,提供了丰富的语料资源,提供了方便的搜索工具任我们选择和使用。但是,我们在网络上搜索到的素材,都是未加工的原始资料,充满有用信息,却也谬误百出,不能直接拿来就用,需要我们进行去粗取精,去伪存真的选择和加工,方可为我所用。我常常在浩瀚的网络中冲浪,浏览,搜索,寻觅所需的语料、词汇和用法。为避免"中国式英语",我尽量不采用网上由国人写的英语,而从英语国家网站或博客中寻找所需的语料。当然,我不排斥我国权威媒体新华社和中国日报的译法。语言是反映社会生活的。我认为不仅需要对语言敏感,更需要对社会现象敏感。我们需要关注发展,更需要关注民生。我们需要关注媒体的报道,更需要关注草根的观点。

  以上是我最近两年从事汉英翻译的点滴心得体会,愿与读者共享。

王逢鑫

2009年4月16日于北京海淀区蓝旗营小区

# 目 录

一、发帖子 ……………………………………………… (1)
二、清除小广告 ………………………………………… (3)
三、出专辑 ……………………………………………… (6)
四、发烧友 ……………………………………………… (9)
五、追星族 ……………………………………………… (13)
六、空巢老人 …………………………………………… (17)
七、啃老族 ……………………………………………… (20)
八、炒股 ………………………………………………… (22)
九、理财 ………………………………………………… (26)
十、选秀 ………………………………………………… (29)
十一、作秀 ……………………………………………… (32)
十二、换客 ……………………………………………… (35)
十三、打工族 …………………………………………… (38)
十四、泡沫 ……………………………………………… (43)
十五、作弊 ……………………………………………… (46)
十六、桑拿天 …………………………………………… (49)
十七、中暑 ……………………………………………… (52)
十八、义工 ……………………………………………… (55)
十九、八卦 ……………………………………………… (59)
二十、短信 ……………………………………………… (62)
廿一、忽悠 ……………………………………………… (65)
廿二、漫游 ……………………………………………… (69)
廿三、倒计时 …………………………………………… (72)
廿四、房奴 ……………………………………………… (75)
廿五、写真 ……………………………………………… (78)

廿六、遗产 ……………………………………… (81)
廿七、继承 ……………………………………… (85)
廿八、人质 ……………………………………… (88)
廿九、主持 ……………………………………… (92)
三十、主持人 …………………………………… (96)
三十一、第三者 ………………………………… (99)
三十二、拓展 …………………………………… (102)
三十三、科学发展观 …………………………… (106)
三十四、小康社会 ……………………………… (109)
三十五、飙升 …………………………………… (112)
三十六、晒工资 ………………………………… (116)
三十七、拼车 …………………………………… (118)
三十八、恶搞 …………………………………… (121)
三十九、违章 …………………………………… (125)
四十、上市 ……………………………………… (128)
四十一、瓶颈 …………………………………… (131)
四十二、潜规则 ………………………………… (135)
四十三、盘点 …………………………………… (138)
四十四、膨胀 …………………………………… (141)
四十五、枪手 …………………………………… (144)
四十六、雪灾 …………………………………… (148)
四十七、高峰 …………………………………… (151)
四十八、基石 …………………………………… (155)
四十九、草根 …………………………………… (158)
五十、重建 ……………………………………… (161)
五十一、接轨 …………………………………… (164)
五十二、排行榜 ………………………………… (168)
五十三、造假 …………………………………… (172)
五十四、怀疑 …………………………………… (175)
五十五、形象 …………………………………… (179)

五十六、事业 …………………………………………… (182)
五十七、架子 …………………………………………… (185)
五十八、摩擦 …………………………………………… (190)
五十九、出轨 …………………………………………… (193)
六十、妖魔化 …………………………………………… (196)
六十一、地震 …………………………………………… (199)
六十二、第一时间 ……………………………………… (203)
六十三、救灾 …………………………………………… (206)
六十四、断层 …………………………………………… (209)
六十五、加油 …………………………………………… (212)
六十六、搜索 …………………………………………… (216)
六十七、干预 …………………………………………… (219)
六十八、封杀 …………………………………………… (222)
六十九、领养 …………………………………………… (225)
七十、疏导 ……………………………………………… (228)
七十一、公害 …………………………………………… (231)
七十二、泛滥 …………………………………………… (234)
七十三、曝光 …………………………………………… (237)
七十四、单双号 ………………………………………… (240)
七十五、洗钱 …………………………………………… (243)
七十六、障碍 …………………………………………… (246)
七十七、破产 …………………………………………… (251)
七十八、行走 …………………………………………… (254)
七十九、问题 …………………………………………… (258)
八十、危机 ……………………………………………… (262)
八十一、承包 …………………………………………… (265)
八十二、海啸 …………………………………………… (268)
八十三、两岸 …………………………………………… (272)
八十四、下水 …………………………………………… (275)
八十五、封口 …………………………………………… (279)

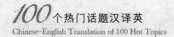

八十六、宽松 …………………………………………… (282)
八十七、包袱 …………………………………………… (286)
八十八、突破 …………………………………………… (289)
八十九、山寨 …………………………………………… (293)
九十、跳水 ……………………………………………… (296)
九十一、慈善 …………………………………………… (299)
九十二、护航 …………………………………………… (304)
九十三、团圆 …………………………………………… (307)
九十四、折腾 …………………………………………… (310)
九十五、着陆 …………………………………………… (313)
九十六、春雨贵如油 …………………………………… (317)
九十七、抄底 …………………………………………… (320)
九十八、代言 …………………………………………… (323)
九十九、申报 …………………………………………… (326)
一〇〇、民生 …………………………………………… (329)
汉语关键词索引 ………………………………………… (332)
英语关键词索引 ………………………………………… (341)

# 一、发帖子

### 汉语关键词
帖子、请帖、名帖、发帖子、看帖子、查帖子、回帖子、跟帖子

### 英语关键词
invitation, invitation card, name card, open a new topic, post a new topic, view a topic, read a thread, reply to a topic

### 句　子
你可以在这个论坛上用英语发帖子。

### 误　译
You may send out invitation cards in English at this forum.

### 正　译
1) You may open a new topic in English at this forum.
2) You can post a new topic in English on this forum.

### 解　释
"帖子"原指"请帖"，即邀请客人的通知。英语可以译为 invitation card 或 invitation。名帖是旧时文人用来交友或访友的名片，英语可以译为 name card。例如：

1. 为庆祝儿子周岁生日，他发帖子给亲戚朋友。
   To celebrate the anniversary of his son's birthday, he sent invitation cards to his relatives and friends.

2. 他广散帖子，为过世的父亲举办丧事。
   In order to hold a funeral ceremony for his deceased father, he sent out a lot of invitations.

3. 在集会上，他散发名帖，广交新朋。
   At the gathering, he handed out his name cards and made a lot of new acquaintances.

# 100个热门话题汉译英
## Chinese-English Translation of 100 Hot Topics

"发帖子"现已成为网络语言,专指在网络论坛上就一个主题发表意见,以期引起讨论。英语可以用 to open a new topic, to post a new topic, to contribute a post on the web 表示。例如:

4. 如果你不登录,你是不能发帖子的。
    1) You cannot open a new topic unless (you are) logged in.
    2) You cannot post a new topic unless (you are) logged in.

5. 这个大学生在互联网上发帖子,反映校园周围秩序混乱。
    The college student opened a new topic at the Internet and made it known that the campus surroundings were in disorder.

6. 她在这个论坛和许多别的论坛上广散帖子,呼吁全社会关注弱势群体的利益。
    She posted a new topic on this forum and many others, calling on the whole society to show concern for the benefits of the social vulnerable groups.

7. 为了泄愤,他在学校 BBS 上散发帖子辱骂他的一个同班同学。
    To give vent to his resentment, he posted a new topic on the school bulletin board to abuse one of his classmates.

8. 他上网发帖子告诉别人他对这个问题的想法。
    He contributed a post on the web to tell others about his ideas on this issue.

"看帖子"或"查帖子"是查看就一个主题帖发表的各种看法。英语可以译为 to view a topic 或 to read a thread。例如:

9. 如果你想在本 BBS 上看已有的帖子,你不需要注册。
    If you want to view current topics on this bulletin board, you don't have to make a registration.

10. 当我试图看就这个主题帖跟的新帖子时,整个一页刚装载一半就结束了,不让我看其余的帖子。
    When I tried to view the topic for new replies, it finished loading halfway through the page, not allowing me to see the rest.

11. 今天早上我在一个大学论坛看了关于如何学习英语的一连串对话的帖子。

This morning I read a thread about how to learn English at a university forum.

"回帖子"或"跟帖子"指回应已有的主题帖,发表自己的看法,表示赞同、支持或反对。英语可以译为 to reply to a topic 等。例如:

12. 我教我父亲如何发帖子和回帖子。

I taught my father how to post a new topic and reply to a topic.

13. 如果你想发帖子或回帖子,你需要注册。

If you wish to post a new topic or reply to an existing topic, you are required to make a registration.

14. 我对他的帖子给了回帖。

I made a reply in response to his posting.

15. 我对已有的一个主题帖给了新的回帖。

I added a new response to an existing topic.

16. 在本论坛,你既可以发帖子,也可以回帖子。

At this forum, you can either open a new topic or send a comment to a topic.

17. 你可以在帖子下面的"评论"部分回帖子。

You can post your response in the "Comment" section below the post.

# 二、清除小广告

● 汉语关键词

小广告、张贴、散发、清除、乱涂、乱写

● 英语关键词

small ad, illegal ad, illegal ad poster, put up, stick, paste, glue, distribute, hand out, remove, get rid of, scribble

## 100个热门话题汉译英
### Chinese-English Translation of 100 Hot Topics

● **句　子**

市政府已经采取积极措施清除小广告。

● **误　译**

1) The municipal government has taken active measures to remove small ads.

2) The municipal government has adopted active measures to remove small ads.

● **正　译**

1) The municipal government has taken active measures to remove illegal ads.

2) The municipal government has adopted active measures to remove illegal ads.

● **解　释**

小广告分为合法的与非法的。清除的是非法小广告。而 small ad 是中性词，没有"非法"的意思。例如：

1. 小广告是登在地方或全国性报纸上而且有时候登在布告栏的短小广告。

    Small ads are short advertisements that are found in local and national newspapers, and sometimes on a notice board.

2. 我需要在报纸上登小广告来宣传我的企业。

    I need to place a small ad in the newspaper to advertise my business.

3. 他想通过在报纸上登小广告来寻找住房。

    He wished to look for housing by placing a small ad in the newspaper.

4. 我曾经同一天在两个不同的报纸上登同一个小广告。

    I once ran the same small ad in two different newspapers on the same day.

"非法小广告"可以译为 illegal ad 或 illegal ad poster。例如：

5. 居民都厌恶被称为"城市牛皮癣"的非法小广告。

The residents all hate the illegal ads that are known as "city psoriasis".

"张贴小广告"可以译为 to put up an illegal ad, to stick an illegal ad, to paste an illegal ad 或 to glue an illegal ad。例如：

6. 在我市，那些张贴小广告的造假者要受到自动连续停机的惩罚。
   In our city, those forgers who put up illegal ad posters are subject to automatic and continuous blocking phone message.
7. 有些贴广告的人常常往人行道和电线杆子上张贴传播虚假信息的小广告。
   Some ad gluers often stick illegal ad posters spreading false information on the pavements and on the telephone poles.
8. 当我回到家时，我发现房门上和墙上贴着小广告。
   When I came back home, I spotted illegal ads pasted on the front door and the wall of my house.
9. 这个制假者雇了几个小男孩在公共设施上张贴小广告。
   The forger hired a few young boys to glue illegal ads on public facilities.

"张贴小广告的行动"可以译为 illegal postering 或 commercial postering。例如：

10. 在本市，乱贴小广告可罚一万元。
    In this city, a person can be fined 10,000 yuan for illegal postering.
11. 在这个地区，张贴商业小广告的行动十分猖獗。
    Commercial postering is rampant in this area.

"散发小广告"可以译为 to distribute illegal ad cards 或 to hand out illegal ad cards。例如：

12. 我看见一个年青人走在马路中间向汽车司机散发小广告。
    I saw a young man walking in the middle of the road to distribute illegal ad cards to car drivers.
13. 那些组织年轻人在大街上散发小广告的人应该受到最严厉的惩罚。
    Those who organize young people to hand out illegal ad cards on the

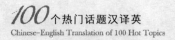

street deserve the most severe punishment.

"清除小广告"可以译为 to remove the illegal ads 或 to get rid of the illegal ads。例如：

14. 来自附近一所大学的志愿者正在设法从这个步行过街桥上清除小广告。
The volunteers from a nearby university were trying to remove illegal ads from the pedestrian overpass.

15. 人们已想出许多办法清除街头小广告。
People have thought of many ways to get rid of the illegal ads in the street.

"乱涂"或"乱写"可以译为 to scribble（动词）或 scribble（名词）。例如：

16. 不要在墙上乱涂！
1) Do not scribble on the wall!
2) No scribble on the wall is permitted.
3) No scribbling is allowed on the wall!
4) No scribbling on the wall!

17. 我发现墙上有乱写的手机号码。
I detected scribbles of mobile phone numbers on the wall.

# 三、出 专 辑

● 汉语关键词
专辑、出专辑

● 英语关键词
special issue, album, publish an album, launch an album, release an album, issue an album

● **句　子**

这个歌星的最新专辑受到他的"粉丝"们的热烈欢迎。

● **误　译**

The pop singer's latest special issue is warmly welcomed by his fans.

● **正　译**

The pop singer's latest album is warmly welcomed by his fans.

● **解　释**

special issue 指的是杂志的专刊。"专辑"的第一个意思是就某一内容或某一文体编成和出版的专刊或专集，载体是纸质出版物，仅与视觉有关。英语可以译为 special issue 或 special collection。例如：

1. 我从报摊上捡起一本这种杂志的最新专刊。

   I picked up a copy of the latest special issue of the magazine from the news stall.

2. 这位学者为出版社编辑了一个莎士比亚研究专辑。

   The scholar edited a special issue on Shakespearean study for the publishing house.

3. 他正在读一本纪念这位民族英雄的专辑。

   He is reading a special issue in commemoration of this national hero.

4. 这本威廉·戈尔丁专辑有助于读者了解这位诺贝尔文学奖获得者。

   The special issue of William Golding serves to help the readers understand this Nobel Prize Laureate in Literature.

5. 我从一个朋友那里借到了一本爱情诗歌专辑。

   I borrowed a special collection of love poems from one of my friends.

"专辑"的第二个意思是唱片公司录制的音乐专辑。英语可以译为 album，指 a collection of pieces of music that have been recorded on one record, CD, VCD or cassette，即录制在唱片、CD、VCD 或盒式磁带上的音乐专辑，载体是音像产品，与听觉和视觉相关。例如：

音乐专辑 music album

唱片专辑 record album

· 7 ·

翻唱歌曲专辑 album of cover songs
制作专辑 to make an album, to produce an album
录制专辑 to record an album
出专辑 to publish an album, to launch an album, to release an album, to issue an album
推销专辑 to promote an album
发行专辑 to distribute an album
又如:

6. 这位影星已经出了五张翻唱歌曲专辑了。
   The film star has already published five albums of cover songs.
7. 这家唱片公司决定为这个新歌手制作和推出一张专辑。
   The record company has decided to make and launch an album for the new singer.
8. 这个乐队计划下个月出一个新的专辑。
   The band planned to issue a new album next month.
9. 歌手们得依靠有资金的公司,因为他们自己制作和发行专辑太昂贵了。
   Singers have to depend on companies with capital because it is too expensive for them to produce and distribute an album themselves.
10. 这两位歌手正在为他们下一个新专辑录制新歌曲。
    The two singers are recording new songs for their next album.
11. 由于推销和发行一个新专辑成本太高,这个歌手被迫通过私自销售的办法发行他的新专辑。
    As it cost so much to promote and distribute an album, the singer was forced to distribute his new album through bootlegs.

"专辑"的第三个意思是在网络上传播的个人多媒体频道。英语可以译为 album,载体是网络,与听觉和视觉相关。例如:
视频专辑 video album
相片专辑 photo album
概念专辑 conceptual album

主题性专辑 thematic album
人气高的专辑 popular album
人气最高专辑 most popular album
推荐专辑 recommended album
创建专辑 to create an album
设计专辑 to design an album
又如:

12. 他在一个网站创建了一个新专辑。
    He created a new album at a website.
13. 我设计了一个关于感情和情感的主题性专辑。
    I designed a thematic album about feelings and emotions.
14. 她出了一个关于友谊的概念专辑。
    She released a conceptual album about friendship.
15. 你可以创建一个专辑帮助组织你的相片,使它们比较容易被找到,而且用你想用的任何体系来分类。
    You can create an album to help organize your photos, make them easier to find, and sort them in any order you wish.
16. 在你的网站创建相片专辑如同点击鼠标一样容易。
    Creating photo albums on your website is as easy as clicking a mouse.
17. 你可以向网络发布专辑供任何人看。
    You can publish an album to the web for viewing by anyone.
18. 他常常用 google 搜索音乐专辑。
    He often searches for music albums by google.

# 四、发 烧 友

● 汉语关键词
　　发烧、发烧友
● 英语关键词
　　have a fever, run a fever, be infatuated with, be obsessed with,

enthusiast, zealot, -fancier, -phile, -manic

● 句　子

这个孩子发高烧说胡话。

● 误　译

The child had a high fever and talked nonsense.

● 正　译

1) The child had a high fever and became delirious.
2) The child became delirious with high fever.

● 解　释

to talk nonsense 的意思是"胡说八道"。"发高烧说胡话"是在神志不清时语无伦次地说话,英语可以译为 to be delirious。它的意思是 to be in an excited state and not able to speak clearly because of fever。例如:

1. 这个孩子发高烧时说胡话,讲了一些奇怪的事情。

   During the fever, the child became delirious and said some strange things.

"发烧"的第一个意思是"超过正常体温"。英语可以译为 to have a fever, to run a fever, to have a temperature, to run a temperature。例如:

发高烧 to have a high fever, to run a high fever

发低烧 to have/run a low fever, to have/run a slight fever, to have/run a slight temperature

又如:

2. 他发烧病倒了。

   He was down with fever.

3. 如果你发烧,你应该卧床休息。

   1) If you have got a temperature, you should stay in bed.
   2) If you are running a temperature, you should stay in bed.

"发烧"的第二个意思是"狂热爱好或非常迷恋音乐或某些高科技产品"。英语可以译为 to be infatuated with, to be obsessed with。例如:

4. 这个学生对网络发烧。

   This student is infatuated with the Web.

5. 这个青年人对汽车发烧。

   The young man was obsessed with cars.

6. 作为一个技术行家,他对数码相机发烧。

   As a technological geek, he was obsessed with digital cameras.

"发烧友"指狂热爱好或非常迷恋音乐或某些高科技产品的人。英语可以译为 enthusiast, zealot, -fancier, -phile 或 -manic。例如:

汽车发烧友 car enthusiast, car zealot, car-fancier, carphile

音乐发烧友 music enthusiast, music zealot, music-fancier, musicphile, musicmanic

音响发烧友 audio enthusiast, audio zealot, audio-fancier, audiophile, audiomanic

网络发烧友 web enthusiast, web zealot, web-fancier, webphile

又如:

7. 这个汽车发烧友怀着激情驾车。

   The car enthusiast drives with passion.

8. 约翰是个进口车发烧友,他喜欢德国汽车。

   John is an import-car zealot and he likes German cars.

9. 这些汽车发烧友最近组织了一个俱乐部。

   These car-fanciers have recently organized a club.

10. 音乐发烧友可以在这个音乐论坛谈论与音乐有关的任何事情和所有事情。

    Music enthusiasts can talk about anything and everything to do with music at the music forum.

11. 她是个激情的音乐发烧友。

    She's a passionate music zealot.

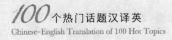

12. 大多数古典音乐发烧友喜欢莫扎特的作品。
    Most classic music-fanciers are keen on Mozart.
13. 这些音乐发烧友欣赏这个乐队微妙的音乐特质。
    These musicphiles appreciate the band for their subtle musical qualities.
14. 这个音乐发烧友爱听来自全世界的新歌曲。
    This musicmanic loves to hear new songs from around the world.
15. 这个音响发烧友陈列室介绍高质量的音响发烧产品。
    The audio enthusiast showroom introduces superior audiophile products.
16. 作为音响发烧友,他热衷于美妙的音乐、美妙的录音,和在家中复制音乐作品的良好设备。
    As an audio zealot, he is devoted to fine music, fine recordings, and fine equipment for reproducing music in the home.
17. 作为音响发烧友,他具有在录音棚里工作的经历。
    As an audio fancier, he has the experience of working in a recording studio.
18. 音响发烧设备使音响发烧友能够在录制和播放音乐作品时达到高保真。
    Audiophile equipment enables audiophiles to achieve high fidelity in the recording and playback of music.
19. 这个音响发烧友在这个网站上发了一个帖子。
    The audiomanic posted a new topic at the website.
20. 我更愿意把自己描述成一个网络发烧友。
    I prefer to describe myself as a web enthusiast.
21. 我当网络发烧友大约有7年了。
    I've been a web zealot for about 7 years.
22. 早期的博客是从网络发烧友开始的。
    Early blogs were set out from web-fanciers.

# 五、追星族

● **汉语关键词**

追星、追星族、粉丝

● **英语关键词**

pursue a star, chase a star, follow around a star, adore a star, idolize a star, star pursuer, star chaser, star fan, star-struck fan, groupie

● **句　子**

这些年青人喜欢追星。

● **误　译**

These youngsters are keen on running after a star.

● **正　译**

These youngsters are keen on pursuing a star.

● **解　释**

to run after sb 有两个意思。一是 to run to try to catch sb，即"追逐"或"追赶"。二是 to try to have a romantic relationship with sb，即"追求"。例如：

1. 这个警察正在追赶一个小偷。

The policeman was running after a thief.

2. 这个男人总爱追求年轻女子。

The man is always running after young women.

"追星"的意思是"极度崇拜、迷恋明星"。英语可以译为 to pursue a star, to chase a star, to follow around a star, to adore a star, to idolize a star 等。例如：

3. 这个追星族从年青时起就一直追一个影星。

The obsessed fan has pursued a movie star since he was young.

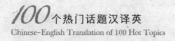

4. 她去好莱坞追星。

   She went off to chase a star in Hollywood.

5. 这个学生花了太多时间狂热追星。结果他耽误了学习。

   The student has spent too much time following a star around. As a result, he has neglected his studies.

6. 当你追星时,你可能变得疯狂。

   You can be crazy when you adore a star.

7. 数以千计的追星族可以追一个明星,但是到头来他还是一个凡人。

   Thousands of star fans may idolize a star, but at the end of the day this person is still a human being.

"追星族"就是"极度崇拜、迷恋明星的人"。英语可以译为 star pursuer, star chaser, star fan, star-struck fan, groupie。例如:

8. 她是一个疯狂的追星族。

   She is a crazy star pursuer.

9. 这个追星族冲向一个影星,说"您能给我签名吗?"

   The star chaser rushed up to a film star and said, "Can I have your autograph?"

10. 我这辈子一直是个追星族。李小龙、成龙和别的动作影星曾是我的偶像。

    I have been a star chaser all my life. Bruce Lee, Jackie Chan and other action movie stars were my idols.

11. 追星族奉明星为偶像。

    Star fans worship a star as their idol.

12. 不管你是不是一个追星族,你需要对你自己现实一些。

    Regardless of whether or not you are a star fan, you need to be real with yourself.

13. 这个追星族已经等了几个小时来看她最喜爱的影星。

    The star-struck fan has waited for hours to see her favourite movie star.

14. 你简直不能想象数以千计的追星族杂乱地拥在一起,为的是看一眼他们的偶像。
You just can't imagine thousands of groupies huddled together in total disorder so as to have a look at their idol.

fan 的意思是 a person who admires sb/sth or enjoys watching or listening to sb/sth very much,如果迷恋的是事物,相当于汉语的"……迷"。例如:
影迷 film fan, movie fan
足球迷 football fan

如果迷恋的是明星,像 star fan 或 star-struck fan,则相当于汉语的"追星族"。近年来,有人将 fans 音译为"粉丝"。"追星族"还可以用 big fan, enthusiastic fan, keen fan, devoted fan, obsessed fan 等词表示。例如:

15. 这位妇女一直是迈克尔·杰克逊的追星族。
This woman has always been a big fan of Michael Jackson.

16. 一个过分热情的追星族跳上舞台,试图唱歌。
An overly enthusiastic fan jumped on stage and tried to sing.

17. 我哥哥是曼联队的狂热球迷。
My brother is a keen fan of Manchester United.

18. 这个女孩是麦当娜的忠实"粉丝"。
The girl is a devoted fan of Madonna.

19. 这个痴迷的追星族声称他在过去的三年里一直盯梢这个影星。
The obsessed fan claimed that he had been stalking the film star over a period of three years.

groupie 还可以指"追星女郎"。例如:

20. 有那么多的追星女郎,到处追逐她们最喜爱的歌手。
There are so many groupies who follow their favourite singers everywhere.

"追星"还有一个意思是"追逐星体",多见于科幻片或科幻小说。英语

可以译为 to chase a star。追逐星体的"追星者"可以译为 star chaser。例如：

21. 在这部科幻小说里，这些科学家在宇宙空间探险，追逐星体。
    In this science fiction, these scientists go on an adventure through space and chase a star.
22. 我追逐一颗星星，结果却找到了太阳。我追逐月亮，结果却发现黑夜已经过去。
    I chased a star but found the sun instead. I chased the moon but found the night had fled.
23. 宇航员作为追星者在宇宙空间飞行，而不是作为站在地球上的观星者。
    The astronaut travels through space as a star chaser, but not as a stargazer standing on earth.
24. 正因为星星从最早的时候就一直指引人们，你也可以变成一个追星者，探寻星座。
    Just as the stars have guided people since the earliest times, you can also become a star chaser, seeking out constellations.

"追星"是崇拜明星偶像，尤其是青少年崇拜明星偶像的现象。"青少年追星"可以译为 adolescent idol worship。例如：

25. 青少年追星是人类在发展中自然的事情，尤其是在现代。
    Adolescent idol worship is a natural thing for human development, particularly in modern times.
26. 如果青少年追星的焦点放在一种魅力型的偶像崇拜，就容易产生负面影响；而如果焦点放在一种成就型的偶像崇拜，就容易产生正面影响。
    Adolescent idol worship tends to have negative impact if it focuses on a glamorous mode of idol worship but a positive impact if it focuses on an achievement mode of idol worship.

# 六、空巢老人

### 汉语关键词
空巢、空巢家庭、空巢者、空巢老人、空巢综合症

### 英语关键词
empty nest, empty nest family, empty nester, empty nest elderly, empty nest syndrome

### 句 子
当这个年青人长大离家后,他的父母留守"空巢"。

### 误 译
When the young man grew up and left home, his parents were left in an empty nest.

### 正 译
When the young man grew up and left home, his parents were left with an empty nest.

### 解 释
to leave sb in a place 的含义为 to go away from a place without taking sb, 即"忘记带走或有意不带走某人而离开某个地方", 与"留守"的意思不符。to leave A with B 的含义为 to allow A to remain in the care of B, 即"把 A 托付给 B 照看", 符合"留下……看家"的意思。例如:
1. 她去度假时把儿子留给她的母亲照看。
   She left her son with her mother while she went on holiday.
2. 我给他的秘书留下口信。
   I left a message with his secretary.

"空巢"原指小鸟长大后飞走离开大鸟,而鸟巢只留下大鸟。英语译为 empty nest。"留守空巢"可以译为 to be left with an empty nest。例如:
3. 小鸟长大飞走以后,母鸟留守空巢。
   After the baby birds were grown and gone, the mother bird was left

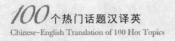

with an empty nest.

"空巢"的比喻意义指子女长大成人后,只有父母单独生活的社会现象。英语译为 empty nest,即 the home of a parent whose children have grown up and left。例如:

4. 空巢不一定就是悲伤的家。
   An empty nest doesn't have to be a sad home.
5. 现在这些父母都单独住在他们的空巢里,没有儿女在一起。
   Now these parents are living alone without children in their empty nest.
6. 当孩子们上大学后,许多父母留守空巢。
   When children go off to college, many parents are left with an empty nest.
7. 当孩子们搬出去住而你们留守空巢时,你们做什么?
   What do you do when the kids move out and you're left with an empty nest?
8. 空巢使得母亲们和父亲们以不同的方式重新评价他们的生活。
   An empty nest causes mothers and fathers to reevaluate their lives in different ways.
9. 所有的父母也许有朝一日都不得不面对空巢的寂寞。
   All parents may one day have to confront the silence of an empty nest.
10. 如果你现在面临空巢的危机,我鼓励你满怀希望迎接挑战。
    If you are currently facing the crisis of an empty nest, I encourage you to meet the challenge with hope.

"空巢家庭"指子女长大成人后,只有父母单独生活的家庭。英语可以译为 empty nest family。例如:

11. 一个空巢家庭可能想要搬到一个小点的房子,以降低开支。
    An empty nest family may want to move to a smaller house to reduce expenses.

"空巢者"可以译为 empty nester,即 a parent whose children have grown up and left home。例如:
12. 我是一个空巢者,但决不是孤独的。
    I am an empty nester but definitely not lonely.

"空巢老人"可以译为 empty nest elderly 或 empty nest elderly parent。例如:
13. 大多数空巢老人感到孤独和抑郁。
    Most of the empty nest elderly feel lonely and depressed.
14. 他们给空巢老人提供家庭服务。
    They provide a home service for the empty nest elderly.
15. 互联网帮助空巢老年家长与他们的成年子女分开居住时保持紧密的互动。
    The Internet helps the empty nest elderly parents to maintain close interactions with their adult children when they are living apart.

empty nest syndrome 指的是 a set of conditions that show a parent whose children have grown up and left home have a particular disease or medical problem,汉语可以译为"空巢综合症"。例如:
17. 这对老年夫妇患了空巢综合症。
    The old couple is in the grips of an empty nest syndrome.
18. 空巢综合症是父母在一个或多个子女离家后感到的一种抑郁和孤独的普遍感情。
    Empty nest syndrome is a general feeling of depression and loneliness that parents feel when one or more of their children leave home.
19. 由于他们的子女已经长大成人,而且离家开始过新生活,他们感到因空巢而产生的忧郁。
    The parents are feeling the empty nest blues since their children have all become adults and left home to start their own new life.

# 七、啃老族

● **汉语关键词**

啃老族

● **英语关键词**

NEET, NEET group, boomerang child, boomerang kid, adult dependent child

● **句　子**

这个啃老族已经30岁，但是仍然靠他的父母生活。

● **误　译**

This NEET is already 30 years old but still lives on his parents.

● **正　译**

This NEET is already 30 years old but still lives off his parents.

● **解　释**

严格地说，to live on 后面要跟 sth, 不跟 sb, 意思是"靠什么活着"。to live off 后面可以跟 sb 或 sth, 意思分别是"靠什么人养活"和"靠什么活着"。从现有常用的英语词典来看，还没有 to live on sb 的搭配。但是，从搜索 google 的结果来看，会偶然发现国外网站有 to live on sb 的说法。也许 to live on sb 会慢慢被接受。例如：

1. 他们靠吃面包和奶酪活着。

   They live on a diet of bread and cheese.

2. 这个失业工人靠失业救济金为生。

   1) This unemployed worker lives on unemployment benefit.

   2) This unemployed worker lives off unemployment benefit.

"啃老族"指既没有上学、也没有就业、或接受职业技能培训，而必须依靠父母养活的青年人。英国英语中，NEET 指啃老族的一员，NEET group 指啃老族群体。NEET 是 Not currently engaged in Education, Employment or Training 或 Not in Education, Employment or Training 的缩略语。美国英语称之为 boomerang child 或 boomerang kid。boomerang 原指澳大利亚土著居民的飞去来镖。例如:

3. 调查显示:我国目前有大约七成的失业青年靠父母养活,因而成为啃老族。

   An investigation indicates that about 70% of the unemployed young people in our country now live off their parents, thus becoming Neets.

4. 大多数啃老族在小时候养成依赖父母的习惯,缺乏独立应对社会的自信和能力。

   As most of the Neets have formed a habit of depending on their parents since they were young, they lack the self-confidence and the ability to cope with the society independently.

5. 许多啃老族不愿意应对来自现实的压力,因而选择靠父母养活。

   Many Neets are reluctant to cope with the pressure from the reality, thus choosing to live off their parents.

6. 一些青年人在择业失败后,成为啃老族。

   Some young people became Neets after they failed to find a job.

7. 这个大学毕业生由于对未来抱有幻想,无法确定自己的方向,变成了啃老族。

   As this university graduate had illusions about his future and couldn't determine his own direction, he became a Neet.

8. 多数啃老族只是呆在家里看看电视、打打游戏,或者做些家务劳动。

   Most of the Neets just stay at home, watching TV, playing electronic games, or doing some housework.

9. 这些啃老族具有工作能力,但是仍靠他们的父母生活。

   These Neets have working abilities but still live off their parents.

10. 实际上,有些啃老族想尽早走出家门,开始工作。

    Actually, some Neets want to leave home and start to work as soon as possible.

11. 越来越多的日本青年加入到既不上学也不工作的啃老族。

    In Japan, more and more young people have joined in the NEET group

who neither go to college nor go to work.
12. 这个啃老族在大学毕业之后,回到家中与父母住在一起。
The boomerang child returned home to live with his parents after graduating from the university.
13. 啃老族现象已成为全国性的社会问题。
The boomerang kid phenomenon has become a social problem on a nationwide scale.

将 adult dependent child 译为"啃老族"是不妥的。它的意思是"有心理缺陷或生理缺陷的需抚养的成年子女",比"啃老族"的含义宽泛。例如:
14. 一个需抚养的成年子女是因为心理缺陷或生理缺陷而不能自理的人。
An adult dependent child is one who is incapable of self-care because of a mental or physical disability.
15. 这个需抚养的成年子女具有永久性的生理缺陷。
The adult dependent child has a permanent physical impairment.

# 八、炒　　股

## 汉语关键词
炒股、炒股者、股民、基金、炒基金

## 英语关键词
invest in stock market, make stock investment, make investments in stock market, trade stocks, buy and sell stocks, pick stocks, stock trader, stock investor, stock picker, mutual fund, stock fund, invest in mutual fund, enter stock fund market

## 句　子
如果你炒垃圾股,你会输掉裤子。

● 误 译

You'd lose your trousers/pants if you invest in junk stocks.

● 正 译

You'd lose your shirt if you invest in junk stocks.

● 解 释

"输掉裤子"是个比喻,就是"输个精光"。英国英语的 to lose one's trousers 和美国英语的 to lose one's pants 的字面意思是"掉裤子"。但是在与赌博相关的语境里,这两个短语才有"输个精光"的比喻意义。美国英语 to lose one's shirt 的意思不是"掉衬衣",而是 to lose everything one owns,相当于"输个精光"。例如:

1. 你最好系紧腰带,而不要掉裤子。
   It is better to tighten your belt than to lose your trousers.
2. 你在战场上掉了裤子,会发生什么情况?
   What happens when you lose your trousers on the battlefield?
3. 如果你的腰带松了,你会掉裤子。
   If your belt is loose, you might lose your pants.
4. 在赌场里,你可能输个精光,也可能赢得盆满钵丰。
   In the gambling house, you can either lose your trousers or make loads of money.
5. 一个赌徒可能在牌桌上输个精光。
   A gambler may lose his pants at the card table.
6. 如果你不想输个精光,你就得下个好点的赌注。
   If you don't want to lose your pants, you have to make smarter bets.
7. 他在一笔糟糕的生意里输了个精光。
   He lost his shirt in a bad business deal.
8. 喝啤酒上瘾,你会肚子大得提不上裤子,也会把钱花光一文不剩。
   Addicted to beer, you will lose your pants and shirt.

"炒股"就是投资股票市场,从事买卖股票活动。英语可以译为 to invest in stock market, to make stock investment, to make investments in

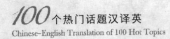

stock market, to trade stocks, to buy and sell stocks, to pick stocks。注意 to pick stocks 有 to select stocks 的意思,即"选择股票"。例如:

9. 因为我依然相信传统的储蓄,所以我不炒股。

    I do not invest in stock market as I still believe in the traditional savings.

10. 当你炒股时,你必须设法使收益最大化,使风险最小化。

    When you invest in stock market, you must try to maximize your returns and minimize your risks.

11. 调查表明:有些大学生用借来的钱当资本炒股。

    An investigation indicates that some university students invested in stock market with the money they had borrowed as capital.

12. 如果你炒你不了解的股,你会输个精光。

    If you invest something you don't know about, you can lose your shirt.

13. 中国现在正处于一个千百万人炒股的热潮中。

    China is now in an upsurge where tens of millions of people are enthusiastic about making stock investment.

14. 我想炒股,但是没有任何经验,也不知道如何开始。

    I want to make investments in stock market but I don't have any experience and don't know how to start.

15. 自控能力不强的人不宜炒股。

    It is inapprpriate for those who are not good at self-control to make investments in stock market.

16. 最近,股市吸引了越来越多炒股的人。

    Recently, the stock market has drawn more and more people who trade stocks.

17. 不要鼓励孩子拿压岁钱去炒股。

    Children are not encouraged to buy stocks with the lucky money given to them as a lunar New Year's gift.

18. 如果你买了坏股票,你会输个精光。

    If you buy a bad stock, you can lose your shirt.

19. 最好在你心态平和而宁静时炒股。

    It is much better to pick stocks when you have some peace and quiet.

20. 你应该设法炒好的股票,卖掉坏的股票。
   You should try to pick good stocks and sell bad ones.
21. 读了一本书就冒险进入市场炒股,如同读了一本书就挑战一位武术高手。
   Venturing into the market to pick stocks after reading a book is like challenging a martial arts expert after reading a book.
22. 作为一个炒股高手,他善于炒赚钱的股票。
   As an artful stock picker, he is good at selecting stocks that make money.

   "炒股者"是投资股票市场,从事买卖股票活动的人,即"股民"。英语可以译为 stock trader, stock investor, stock picker。例如:

23. 一些新股民看到别人在股市上挣了大钱,也来炒股。
   Having seen that other people had made big money in stock market, some novice stock traders also bought and sold stocks.
24. 炒股者须牢记:投资的收益越高,风险越高。
   A stock trader must bear in mind that the higher the returns from an investment are, the higher the risk is.
25. 许多股民想通过炒股挣点钱。
   Many stock investors wish to make some money through trading stocks.
26. 因为股市充满风险,股民炒股须谨慎。
   As the stock market is full of risks, the investors must be cautious in trading stocks.
27. 这个炒股者通过买蓝筹股获得巨大收益。
   The stock picker scored big returns through buying blue-chip stocks.

   "基金"可以译为 mutual fund 或 stock fund。"炒基金"可以译为 to invest in mutual fund, to enter stock fund market。例如:

28. 如果你想知道如何炒基金,你可以阅读我们的建议,这会给你提供更多的成功的机遇。
If you want to know how to invest in stock fund, you can read our tips, which offers you more chances to success.

29. 老年人在初次炒基金时应该慢慢来。
Seniors should go slow in first entering stock fund market.

## 九、理　　财

### 汉语关键词
理财、理财计划、理财师、理财顾问

### 英语关键词
financial planning, make financial planning, financial plan, financial planner, financial adviser, financial advisor

### 句　子
这位理财师正在为他的客户精心准备一份理财计划。

### 误　译
The financial planner is carefully preparing a financial planning for his client.

### 正　译
The financial planner is carefully preparing a financial plan for his client.

### 解　释
planning 指抽象的"规划"活动，前面不能加冠词 a。而 plan 指具体的"计划"，前面可以加冠词 a。

"理财"是对个人和家庭财产的合理管理和规划。其名词译为 financial planning；动词译为 to make financial planning。例如：

1. 理财现在是我们社会的一个热门话题。
Financial planning is now a hot topic in our society.

2. 在我国,越来越多的人关注理财。
   In our country, more and more people show concern for financial planning.
3. 理财的目的就是管好和用好你的钱财,使之发挥最大的效用。
   The purpose of financial planning is to manage your money well and make good use of it, thus bringing it into the fullest play.
4. 许多人发现难以摆脱下列理念:如果他们不富有,他们就不需要做任何理财。
   Many people find it difficult to shake off the notion that if they're not wealthy, they don't need to do any financial planning.
5. 不管你的经济地位如何,你可以因拥有一个客观的理财计划而受益。
   Regardless of your financial status, you can benefit from having an objective financial plan.
6. 理财的核心是使你的投资收益最大化和风险最小化。
   The core of financial planning is to maximize the returns from your investments and minimize the risks you take.
7. 虽然没有对付理财工作的简易办法,但是使理财简易却是可能的。
   There is no easy way of tackling the job of financial planning but it is possible to make financial planning easy.
8. 你可以利用理财工具来帮助你选择你的投资方式。
   You can utilize financial planning tools to help you select your investment choices.
9. 理财师可以全面观察你的财务状况,做出适合你的理财建议。
   The financial planner can take a general view of your financial situation and make financial planning recommendations that are right for you.
10. 在许多国家,理财方案在大学里被更加广泛采用。
    In many countries, financial planning programmes are becoming more widely available in universities.
11. 这家公司专门经营精细的理财。
    This firm specializes in sophisticated financial planning.

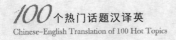

12. 本公司为您提供一对一的理财服务。
    Our company offers you one-to-one financial planning services.

financial plan 对个人来说,就是"理财计划";对企业来说,就是"财务计划";对政府部门来说,就是"财政计划"。例如:

13. 这位理财顾问帮助我建立了一个关于退休金、按揭贷款和家庭预算的理财计划。
    The financial advisor helped me to create a financial plan for my retirement, mortgage and home budget.
14. 这个公司的首席执行官已经起草了一份财务计划,并准备了详细的初步预算。
    The CEO of the company has drafted a financial plan and prepared a detailed preliminary budget.
15. 地方政府已经批准了这个新的年度财政计划。
    The local government has given approval to the new annual financial plan.

"理财师"译为 financial planner。"理财顾问"译为 financial adviser, financial advisor。例如:

16. 理财师帮助个人和企业组织他们的财务事项。
    Financial planners help individuals and businesses organize their financial affairs.
17. 理财师给你提供关于投资、保险、税务和按揭贷款方面的建议。
    Financial planners give you advice regarding investments, insurance, taxes and mortgages.
18. 选择一个好的理财师可能是你为你自己和你的家庭做出的最重要的决定之一。
    Choosing a good financial planner may be one of the most important decisions you make for yourself and your family.

19. 这位理财师在帮助我们达到财务目标方面起重要作用。
    This financial planner plays an important role in helping us achieve our financial goals.
20. 他是一位在积累财富方面具有先进知识的理财顾问。
    He is a financial advisor with advanced knowledge in wealth accumulation.
21. 你的理财顾问将是处理你的全部私密财务事项的人。
    Your financial advisor will be the person who will handle all your confidential financial matters.

# 十、选　秀

● 汉语关键词

选秀、选秀节目、选美、选美比赛、海选、网络海选

● 英语关键词

talent search, talent-search show, talent show, beauty contest, beauty pageant, election through direct voting, first audition, initial audition, extensive audition, large-scale audition, massive audition, Internet audition

● 句　子

在这次选美比赛中,她从一组女性中被选为最美者。

● 误　译

In the beauty contest, she was elected as the most beautiful from a group of women.

● 正　译

1) In the beauty contest, she was selected as the most beautiful from a group of women.

2) In the beauty contest, she was chosen as the most beautiful from a group of women.

# 100个热门话题汉译英
Chinese-English Translation of 100 Hot Topics

### ● 解　释

　　to select 与 to elect 有一个字母之差。to select 的意思是 to choose sb, usually carefully from a group of people, 即"选择",像通过比赛挑选。to elect 的意思是 to choose sb to do a particular job by voting for them, 即"选举",是"通过投票的选择"。

　　"选秀"的第一个意思是"通过比赛选拔才艺优秀者的活动"。英语可以译为 talent search。例如：
1. 这次选秀是以地方性和地区性比赛为开始的。
   The talent search began with local and regional competitions.
2. 他姐姐在一次选秀比赛中作为冠军脱颖而出,成为明星。
   His sister became a star when she emerged as the champion in a talent search contest.
3. 选秀是市场吸引公众兴趣的产物。
   A talent search is an outcome of the market to attract public interest.
4. 许多人不喜欢商业化很浓的选秀。
   Many people dislike the heavily commercialized talent search.
5. 参加太多选秀活动会影响你的学业。
   To participate in too many talent search activities will affect your studies.

　　"选秀节目"译为 talent-search show 或 talent show。例如：
6. 这位著名演员受邀主持这个选秀节目。
   The famous actor got the offer to host the talent-search show.
7. 许多年青人喜欢看这个电视台播放的选秀节目。
   Many young people enjoy watching the talent show aired by this TV station.

　　"NBA 选秀活动"是 draft in NBA。例如：
8. 有些人把这叫做 NBA 选秀活动历史上最糟糕的一次。
   Some people called this the weakest draft in NBA history.

　　"选秀"的第二个意思是"通过比赛选拔最秀丽的美女"即"选美"或"选

美比赛"。英语可以译为 beauty contest 或 beauty pageant。例如:
9. 在这次选美比赛中,评判了这些年轻女性的美丽、个人素质和技能。
   In the beauty pageant, these young women's beauty, personal qualities and skills were judged.
10. 在这次国际选美比赛中,参赛者展示了女性的美丽和智慧。
    In this international beauty pageant, the participants displayed the beauty and wisdom of the female.

"海选"的第一个的意思是"一种不提名候选人的直接选举"。英语可以译为 election through direct voting。例如:
11. 海选是中国农民在村民自治中创造的一种选举方式。
    Election through direct voting is a means of election created by Chinese farmers in villager autonomy.

"海选"的第二个的意思是"不设门槛,人人有机会,谁都可以参加的选拔"。英语的 first audition 和 initial audition,对个人来说具有"初试"或"初次上镜"的意思;对于选秀活动来说,具有"海选"的意思。例如:
12. 在这个年青人初试时,我就真的喜欢他,评委们也都喜欢他。
    I really liked this young man at his initial audition and so did the judges.
13. 我非常同意他一开始就应该被选上,因为他的初试非常好。
    I do agree that he should have been picked in the beginning because his initial audition was good.
14. 你的初试不应该超过5分钟。
    Your initial audition should not take more than 5 minutes.
15. 这个演员在海选中过关,获得在比赛中晋升的机会。
    1) The actor passed the first audition and got a chance of advancing in the contest.
    2) The actor survived the first audition and got a chance of advancing in the contest.

如果指从大量普通报名者中通过初试筛选,"海选"还可以译为 extensive

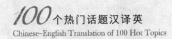

audition, large-scale audition 或 massive audition。例如：

16. 这个业余歌手过了海选关。
    The amateur singer went through an extensive audition process.
17. 这样一次海选花了整整一年的时间。
    Such a large-scale audition took a whole year.
18. 这位导演在伦敦举行的海选中从200个年轻女孩中选上她作为女主角。
    The director picked her as the chief actress over 200 young girls in a large-scale audition held in London.
19. 我鼓足勇气，参加了在北京举行的海选。
    I gathered up courage and attended the first massive audition in Beijing.

"网络海选"译为 Internet audition。例如：

20. 我哥哥通过网络海选成为一名歌手。
    My brother became a singer through an Internet audition.
21. 公众为他们喜欢的歌手投票，而这些网络海选获胜者中间至少有一人将亮相表演。
    The public cast votes for the singers they like and at least one of these Internet audition people will get on the show.
22. 这是一个公开的网络海选论坛，其目的是发现艺术新人。
    This is an open Internet audition forum which is aimed at discovering new artists.

# 十一、作　秀

● 汉语关键词

作秀、谈话秀、脱口秀、工程

● 英语关键词

show, do a show, make a show, put on a show, give a show, stage a show, talk show, chat show, pose, engineering, project

### 句 子

这个所谓的"形象工程",只不过是在作秀。

### 误 译

The so-called image engineering is merely a pose.

### 正 译

The so-called image project is merely a pose.

### 解 释

"工程"的第一个意思指"需用大型复杂设备进行的建设项目",英语译为 engineering。"工程"的第二个意思指"需要投入大量人力和物力,并需要各方通力合作的工作",英语译为 project。"形象工程"是第二个意思。例如:

1. 他的专业是土木工程。
   He is specialized in civil engineering.
2. 大约百分之八十的希望工程小学和希望工程资助的学生都在中国欠发达的中西部地区。
   About 80 percent of the Hope Project primary schools and students aided by the project are in China's middle and western regions, which are less developed.

"秀"音译自英语 show。"作秀"的第一个意思是"表演"或"演出"。英语可以译为 to do a show, to make a show, to put on a show, to give a show, to stage a show。例如:

3. 一大群明星将在这场义演中争相作秀。
   A bunch of stars will get together to do a show in the charity performance.
4. 这个男演员将要给一大群孩子作秀。
   The actor is going to make a show for a large group of children.
5. 这些职业摔跤手常常在摔跤场作秀。
   These professional wrestlers often put on a show on the wrestling ring.

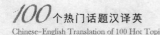
100个热门话题汉译英
Chinese-English Translation of 100 Hot Topics

6. 童星们依次登台作秀。
   The child stars stepped onto the stage in turn to give a show.
7. 为了作秀,这位魔术师从衣袋拿出纸牌,开始玩牌。
   To stage a show, the magician took cards from his pocket and began to play them.

"谈话秀"或"脱口秀",就是"谈话节目",译自 talk show(美国英语)和 chat show(英国英语)。相关的词汇还有:
   电视谈话秀 television talk show, television chat show
   广播谈话秀 radio talk show, radio chat show
   谈话秀主持人 talk show host, chat show host
   谈话秀嘉宾 talk show guest, chat show guest
   例如:
8. 谈话秀是电视或广播节目,一组人聚在一起讨论谈话秀主持人提出的各种各样的话题。
   A talk show is a television or radio programme where a group of people come together to discuss various topics put forth by a talk show host.
9. 我相信在我国将会产生由机器人主持的电视谈话节目。
   I believe there will be television chat shows hosted by robots in our country.

"作秀"的第二个意思是"为竞选或销售而进行宣传和展示"。英语可以译为 to make a show。例如:
10. 一些政客认为这是作秀的好机会。
    Some politicians think it is a good chance to make a show.
11. 这些候选人在竞选活动中使出各自招数作秀。
    These candidates used their own tricks to make a show in the election campaign.
12. 这位推销员只是正在通过展示他的新产品来作秀。
    The salesman was simply making a show by displaying his new products.

"作秀"的第三个意思是"弄虚作假,装样子骗人,或故作姿态,炫耀卖弄,有意显示"。英语可以译为 to be a pose, to make a show。例如:

13. 他向我道歉,那只是作秀。

   He made an apology for me—it's just a pose.

14. 这种关心的表现只是作秀。

   This show of concern is just a pose.

15. 他总是谈论他对哲学的浓厚兴趣——那只是作秀。

   He is always talking about his deep interest in philosophy—it's just a pose.

16. 他的辞职只是在作秀,用来获取名声。

   His resignation is only a pose through which to gain fame.

17. 现在我意识到那种唱高调、强有力的谈话只不过是作秀。

   Now I realize all that kind of high and mighty talk is nothing but a pose.

18. 他的建议只不过是作秀,最终目的是欺骗人民。

   His suggestion is nothing but a pose with the ultimate aim of deceiving the people.

19. 这位妇女通过在其他人面前大哭大闹来作秀。

   This lady made a show by crying in front of other people.

# 十二、换　　客

## 汉语关键词

换客、以物易物、网上以物易物、网上交易中心

## 英语关键词

trade A for B, barter A for B, exchange A for B, swap A for B, online barter, online bartering, online exchange, online swap, online barterer, online swapper, website barterer, online exchanger

# 100个热门话题汉译英
## Chinese-English Translation of 100 Hot Topics

### ● 句 子

在以物易物经济的条件下,一个人能用一把斧头换五只羊。

### ● 误 译

Under barter economy, a person could exchange an axe with five sheep.

### ● 正 译

Under barter economy, a person could exchange an axe for five sheep.

### ● 解 释

"以物易物"是用自己不需要的物品换回自己需要的物品。英语可以用 to trade A for B, to barter A for B, to exchange A for B 和 to swap A for B 等表示。这里要用介词 for 表示以物易物,不可以用 with。for 后面跟 sth, 即"换来的物品";而 with 后面跟 sb, 即"与之进行交换的人"。例如:

1. 他用他的吉普车向一个邻居换了一辆小面包车。
   He traded his jeep to his neighbour for a minivan.
2. 她决定用她的手机换一个数码相机。
   She decided to trade her mobile phone for a digital camera.
3. 一个名叫凯尔·麦克唐纳的加拿大人创造了用一根曲别针换一座二层楼房的奇迹。
   A Canadian named Kyle MacDonald performed a miracle of bartering a paper clip for a two-storey house.
4. 当地人用小麦和棉花换农业机械。
   The local people bartered wheat and cotton for farm machinery.
5. 这个小男孩用他的钢笔跟他妹妹换糖吃。
   The little boy exchanged his pen with his sister for candy.
6. 他想用他在郊区的一套三居室公寓换一套市中心的两居室公寓。
   He wants to exchange his three-room apartment in the suburbs for a two-room apartment in downtown.
7. 我将我的礼品卡换成现金。
   I exchanged my gift card for cash.

8. 他用一辆崭新的自行车换了一辆二手摩托车。

   He swapped a brand new bicycle for a second-hand motorbike.

9. 这个学生用他的足球衫换了一副太阳镜。

   The student swapped his football vest for a pair of sunglasses.

10. 我用我的红围巾跟她换了一条蓝围巾。

    1) I swapped my red scarf with her for a blue one.

    2) I swapped her my red scarf for a blue one.

"网上以物易物"指"通过网络交换物品"。英语可以译为 online barter, online bartering, online exchange, online swap。例如：

11. 他通过网上以物易物结识了许多朋友。

    He made a lot of friends through online barter.

12. 在中国，年青人之间网上以物易物已经成为一种新的潮流。

    Online bartering has become a new trend among young people in China.

13. 网上以物易物，一种拥有许多支持者但是很少有成功者的理念，正作为一种电子商务模式兴起。

    Online bartering, an idea with many proponents but few successes, is emerging as an e-commerce model.

14. 这种网上以物易物的服务为居民提供了一种快捷、简单而免费的出售不需要的家庭物品的方式。

    The service of online exchange offers residents a quick, simple and free means of selling unwanted household goods.

15. 他一直尝试开办一个新的网上以物易物市场，用户可以与其他用户交换书籍、音乐唱片、电影录象带或电子游戏。

    He has been trying out a new online swap market where users can trade books, music, movies, or video games with other users.

"换客"指"通过网络交换物品的人"。英语可以译为 online barterer, online swapper, website barterer。例如：

16. 换客就是用自己的物品或服务与别人进行交换的人。
    An online barterer is a person who exchanges his goods or services with other people.
17. 许多换客是匿名进行交换和交易的。
    Many online barterers swap and trade anonymously.
18. 他用一个小玩具向一个换客换了两张音乐会票。
    He traded a small toy to an online swapper for two concert tickets.
19. 作为一个换客,他正在网络上寻找商务机会。
    As a website barterer, he is seeking business opportunities on line.

注意 online exchanger 的意思不是"换客",而是"网上交易中心"。
例如:
20. 这个网上交易中心对消费者和经营商都是开放的。
    This online exchanger is open to both consumers and merchants.
21. 我们怀着极大的荣幸向您宣布:最便宜的电子网上交易中心现在开张了。
    We have the great pleasure to announce you that the cheapest e-currency online exchanger is now launched.

# 十三、打 工 族

## 汉语关键词
打工、打工族、打工仔、打工妹、农民工、临时工

## 英语关键词
do manual work, do unskilled work, do odd jobs, do casual work, do temporary work, work temporary jobs, do part-time work, work part-time jobs, be employed, be hired, rural migrant worker, manual worker, manual labourer, odd-jobber, odd-job man, odd-job boy, odd-job girl, casual worker, casual labourer, temporary worker, part-time worker,

employed worker, hired labourer

## ● 句　子
作为打工族,他经常变换职业,用双手劳动。

## ● 误　译
As a manual labourer, he often exchanged jobs, working with his hands.

## ● 正　译
As a manual labourer, he often changed jobs, working with his hands.

## ● 解　释
to exchange 的意思是"交换"。to change 的意思才是"变换"。例如:

1. 他决定用他在邮局当邮递员的工作与一个职员的工作相交换,这样他就能够在夜间上班,而在白天上课。
He decided to exchange his job as a letter carrier at the Post Office for that of a clerk so he could work at night and thus attend classes during the day.

2. 他准备好与你交换工作了。
He is ready to exchange his job with yours.

3. 他的妻子对他施加了很大压力,让他变换职业。
His wife exerted a lot of pressure on him to change his job.

"打工"的第一个意思指"农民进城务工",英语可以译为 to go to work in a city。相应的"打工族"就是"农民工"或"民工"。英语可以译为 rural migrant worker。例如:

4. 每年,许多农民离开家乡到沿海城市打工。
Every year, a lot of farmers leave their hometowns and go to work in the coastal cities.

5. 春节前,数以百万计的农民工乘火车回乡与亲人团聚。
Before the Spring Festival, millions of rural migrant workers go back to their hometowns by train to get together with their relatives.

# 100个热门话题汉译英
## Chinese-English Translation of 100 Hot Topics

"打工"的第二个意思指"从事体力劳动,多半是非熟练工种、没有技术的、低报酬的,或又脏又累的活儿"。英语可以译为 to do manual work, to do unskilled work。靠双手劳动的"打工族"相当于"体力劳动者",可以译为 manual worker, manual labourer。例如:

6. 暑假里,这个大学生在一个建筑工地打工,以体验什么是艰苦。
   During the summer vacation, the college student did manual work on a construction site for the purpose of knowing what hardship was.

7. 来自山区的大多数男子没有技能,只能在餐馆或其他公共场所打工。
   Most of the men from the mountainous area have no skills and can only do manual labour in restaurants and other public places.

8. 由于他们几乎没有或完全没有受过正式教育,他们只能打工来谋生。
   As they have little or no formal education, they can only do unskilled work to make a living.

9. 他来北京以后,在一家工厂打工。
   After he came to Beijing, he became a manual labourer in a factory.

"打工"的第三个意思指"做杂活、零活"。英语可以译为 to do odd jobs。在这个意义上,"打工族"就是"打零工的人",可以译为 odd-jobber 或 odd-job man。"打工仔"可以译为 odd-job boy;"打工妹"可以译为 odd-job girl。例如:

10. 这对父母相信他们的孩子已经够岁数,可以离开家门打工了。
    The parents believe that their children are old enough to do odd jobs outside the home.

11. 在我上大学的日子里,我打工来维持我的生计。
    During my college years, I did odd jobs to earn my living.

12. 他花了一个夏天的时间在学校图书馆打工。
    He spent a summer working as an odd-jobber at the school library.

13. 她在这个地区打工多年以后,接受了替一位老年妇人当管家的工作。
After many years as an odd-jobber in the area, she accepted work as a housekeeper for an elderly woman.

14. 作为打工族,约翰在房屋修缮和维护的所有领域具有多年工作经验。
As an odd-job man, John has many years of working experience across all areas of property repair and maintenance.

15. 我在 14 岁时,成为一个高级饭店的打工仔。
At the age of 14 years, I became an odd-job boy in a high-class hotel.

16. 成为乞丐或打工妹,都是我从来没有想要当的。
Becoming a beggar, or an odd-job girl, is something I've never wanted to be.

"打工"的第四个意思指"做非正式的、不固定的、临时性的工作"。英语可以译为 to do casual work, to do temporary work, to work temporary jobs。在这个意义上,"打工族"就是"临时工",可以译为 casual worker, casual labourer, temporary worker。例如:

17. 他最近得到了能在美国打工的签证。
He has recently obtained a visa to do casual work in the United States.

18. 10 年前,他从北京一家公司辞职去深圳打工。
Ten years ago, he resigned from a company in Beijing and went to Shenzhen to do temporary work.

19. 许多人不得不打工以勉强维持生计。
Many people have to work temporary jobs to make ends meet.

20. 技术水平较低的工人有时打工挣点外快。
Workers with a lower level of skills sometimes work temporary jobs to pick up extra cash.

21. 临时工偶尔被人雇佣,没有连续的合同。
A casual worker is employed occasionally, with no continuing contract.

22. 临时工可以在美国停留的最高年限是 3 年。
The maximum period for which a temporary worker may be admitted to

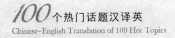

the United States is three years.

"打工"的第五个意思指"半时工作",特指"学生半工半读"。英语可以译为 to do part-time work, to work part-time jobs。在这个意义上,"打工族"可以译为 part-time worker。例如:

23. 放学以后,这个大学生在附近的一家快餐店打工。
    After school, the college student did part-time work at a nearby fast-food restaurant.
24. 这个来自贫困家庭的大学生在一家餐馆打工来挣自己的学费。
    The college student from a poverty-stricken family served as a part-time worker at a restaurant to earn his own tuition fee.

"打工"的第六个意思指"受雇于人"。英语可以译为 to be employed, to be hired。在这个意义上,"打工族"就是"被雇佣的工人"。英语可以译为 employed worker, hired labourer。例如:

25. 他为本村的一位农场主打工。
    He was employed by a farm owner in this village.
26. 几位新面孔的青年男女为这个电视台打工,主持这个节目的编制。
    A few fresh-faced young men and women were hired by the television station to host the show's programming.
27. 这个打工族需要提高技能而上夜校学习。
    The employed worker, who is in need of skills, goes to study at a night school.
28. 由于他穷,就像绝大多数打工族一样,他依靠工资购买他赖以生存的食物。
    As he is poor, like the majority of hired labourers, he depends on the wages to buy food by which to live.

综上所述,"打工"和"打工族"如何译成英语,要视具体语境而定,不可千篇一律译成一种形式。

## 十四、泡 沫

● 汉语关键词

泡沫、股市泡沫、房地产泡沫、互联网泡沫、经济泡沫、泡沫经济

● 英语关键词

bubble, foam, stock market bubble, real estate bubble, Internet bubble, economic bubble, bubble economy, foamy economy

● 句 子

这篇论文讨论我们从泡沫经济破灭中吸取的教训。

● 误 译

This thesis deals with the lessons drawn from the breakout of foamy economy.

● 正 译

This thesis deals with the lessons drawn from the vanishing of foamy economy.

● 解 释

to break out 的意思是"突然爆发",指一个过程的开始。而"破灭"指一个过程的结束。表示泡沫经济(bubble economy)破灭,可以用 to end, to vanish, to burst, to evaporate, to collapse 等词。

1972 年我陪同美国经济学家、诺贝尔经济学奖获得者里昂蒂夫(Wassily Leontief,1905—1999)等人在上海参观。里昂蒂夫是俄裔经济学家,1937 年任南京国民政府经济顾问,曾到过上海。他说当时住在 Bubbling Well Road 附近的一家旅馆,想旧地重游。我第一次到上海,对这个城市一无所知。这座 Bubbling Well(冒泡的井)在哪里?我正在一筹莫展之时,专为我们开车的司机师傅替我解了围。他说 Bubbling Well Road 就是"静安寺路",恐怕 30 年代的老房子都拆了,Bubbling Well 也早就填上了。他开车带我们到 Bubbling Well Road 的旧址转了一圈。这算是圆了里昂蒂夫的梦。我很佩服那位上海司机师傅,他不但对老上海了如指掌,而且英语

# 100个热门话题汉译英
Chinese-English Translation of 100 Hot Topics

非常好。现在恐怕很难找到这样的"上海通"了。

"泡沫"的第一个意思是"聚在一起的许多小泡"。英语可以译为 bubble, foam。例如:

1. 泡沫只有在爆裂之时才会消失。
   Bubble disappears only when it bursts.
2. 这个孩子喜欢用麦秆吸管往水里吹泡泡。
   The child likes to blow bubbles into water through a straw.
3. 这些孩子常常吹肥皂泡而使自己开心。
   The kids often amuse themselves by blowing bubbles with the soap solution.
4. 据说香槟酒的泡沫能更快地使你喝醉。
   It is said that champagne bubbles get you drunk more quickly.
5. 这杯啤酒上面有厚厚一层泡沫。
   The glass of beer has a good head of foam.
6. 这个灭火器充满了化学泡沫。
   The fire extinguisher is filled with chemical foam.

"泡沫"的第二个意思是比喻"某一事物所存在的表面上繁荣兴旺,而实际上虚浮不实的成分"。英语可以译为 bubble。例如:

股市泡沫 stock market bubble
房地产泡沫/楼市泡沫 real estate bubble
互联网泡沫/网络泡沫 Internet bubble

又如:

7. 泡沫可以分为理性泡沫和非理性泡沫。
   Bubble can be divided into rational bubble and irrational bubble.
8. 股市泡沫正在形成,投资者应该防范风险。
   As a stock market bubble is taking shape, the investors should take precautions against the risks.
9. 我国股民最近经历了股市泡沫。
   The stock investors in our country have recently experienced a stock market bubble.

10. 房地产泡沫一旦突然破灭,将对我们的经济和社会产生难以估计的损害。

    Once there appears a sudden burst of the real estate bubble, it will make an inestimable damage to our economy and society.

11. 2000年3月,互联网泡沫突然爆裂。

    In March of 2000, the Internet bubble suddenly burst.

"经济泡沫"译为 economic bubble。而"泡沫经济"译为 bubble economy 或 foamy economy。例如:

12. 房地产泡沫是本地或全球房地产市场周期性发生的一种经济泡沫。

    A real estate bubble is a type of economic bubble that occurs periodically in local or global real estate markets.

13. 泡沫经济通常以虚假繁荣开始,以危机爆发告终。

    Bubble economy usually starts with false prosperity and ends in a breakout of crises.

14. 日本经历了长达10年之久的称作"泡沫经济"的经济过热,它在1991年12月突然停止了。

    Japan experienced a decade-long economic overheat called a 'bubble economy', which suddenly ended in December 1991.

15. 幸运的是,上世纪90年代的泡沫经济没有像20年代的泡沫经济那样接着发生了大萧条。

    Luckily, the bubble economy of the 1990's wasn't followed by a depression like the one in 1920.

16. 许多研究日本经济的学者反思了关于日本泡沫经济如何崩溃的历史。

    Many scholars who studied Japanese economy reflected upon the history about how Japanese foamy economy had collapsed.

17. 为什么在上世纪90年代初日本的泡沫经济蒸发了?

    Why did Japanese foamy economy evaporate in early 1990's?

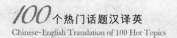

# 十五、作　　弊

### 汉语关键词
作弊、考试作弊、考试作弊者、代考者、枪手、游戏作弊、网络游戏作弊

### 英语关键词
cheat, cheating, cheating in exam, exam cheat, fake examinee, proxy examinee, substitute examinee, substitute testee, exam imposter, video game cheating, game cheating, online game cheating

### 句　子
任何学生一经发现作弊,将被取消考试资格。

### 误　译
Any student is caught cheating will be disqualified from the examination.

### 正　译
1) Any student who is caught cheating will be disqualified from the examination.

2) Any student caught cheating will be disqualified from the examination.

### 解　释
误译句子里出现两个主要动词 is caught 和 will be disqualified,这在英语里是不可以的。

"作弊"的意思是在考试、游戏或比赛中用欺骗手段做不合规则或违法乱纪的事。英语动词可以用 to cheat 表示。例如:
1. 他玩纸牌时总爱作弊。
   He always cheats at cards.
2. 这个学生因考试作弊而受到惩罚。
   The student was punished for cheating in an examination.
3. 你应该服从纪律,遵守规则,因此不准在游戏中作弊。
   As you should obey the disciplines and follow the rules, you are not

allowed to cheat in the game.
4. 由于在比赛中作弊,他被取消了参赛资格。
   As he cheated in the competition, he was disqualified from the competition.

"作弊"的意思,英语名词可以用 cheating 表示。例如:
5. 你在考试中不准看答案,那是作弊。
   You're not allowed to look at the answers in an examination—that's cheating.
6. 政府有关部门已经采取有效措施制止高考作弊。
   The concerning departments of the government have taken effective measures to prevent cheating in national entrance examination.

"考试作弊"可以译为 cheating in exam。例如:
7. 一名大学生有必要知道考试作弊是一种可耻的行为。
   It is necessary for a college student to know that cheating in exam is a shameful conduct.
8. 考试作弊是一种违法的事,它就等同于剽窃。
   Cheating in exam is an offence and it is equated with plagiarism.
9. 近年来,各种各样的高科技装置被用于考试作弊。
   In recent years, various high-tech devices have been used for cheating in exam.
10. 校方将严肃处理这些考试作弊的个案。
    The university authorities will seriously handle the cases of cheating in exam.

"考试作弊者"可以译为 exam cheat(英国英语)或 exam cheater(美国英语)。例如:
11. 这个考试作弊者在从坐在旁边的另一个学生那里抄答案时被当场抓住。
    The exam cheat was caught red-handed when he was copying answers from another student sitting next to him.

12. 监考人员指控这个学生是考试作弊者。
    The invigilator accused the student of being an exam cheater.

"代考者"或"枪手"可以译为 fake examinee, proxy examinee, substitute examinee, substitute testee, 或 exam imposter。例如：

13. 这个"枪手"充当另外一个人的替身出现在考场。
    The fake examinee appeared as a proxy candidate for another person in the examination.
14. 这个"枪手"代表一个名叫约翰·史密斯的学生出现在考场。
    The proxy examinee appeared in the examination on behalf of a student named John Smith.
15. 这个学生雇了一名"枪手"替他参加考试。
    The student hired a substitute examinee to take the test for him.
16. 这个学生未能找到一个代考者，于是他就拒绝参加考试。
    The student failed to find a substitute testee, so he refused to take the test.
17. 这个"枪手"代替了另一个不太聪明但是急于通过考试的学生。
    The exam imposter took the place of another student who was not so clever but desperate to pass the examination.
18. 这个年青人装作参考者,被监考人员当场抓住。
    The young man, posing as an examinee, was caught red-handed by the invigilator.

"游戏作弊"是指在多人游戏、网络游戏中利用修改游戏或者其他不正当手段来达到超出对手成绩目的的行为。英语可以译为 video game cheating 或 game cheating。"网络游戏作弊"可以译为 online game cheating。例如：

19. 许多人认为游戏作弊违背游戏规则，也是可耻行为。
    Many people hold that video game cheating, which is against the game rules, is also a shameful conduct.
20. 有几个人支持游戏作弊,认为它只不过是一种游戏策略。
    A few people are in favour of game cheating, believing that it is nothing

but a game strategy.

21. 不久以前，我写了一篇名叫《如何在网络游戏中作弊》的文章。
Not long ago, I wrote an article called "How to Cheat at Online Games".

# 十六、桑拿天

### 汉语关键词
桑拿天、桑拿日、桑拿浴、洗桑拿浴、桑拿浴室

### 英语关键词
sauna weather, sauna day, sauna bath, sauna, have a sauna bath, have a sauna, take a sauna bath, take a sauna

### 句 子
昨天我市遭遇"桑拿天"。

### 误 译
Yesterday our city encountered sauna day.

### 正 译
Yesterday our city encountered sauna weather.

### 解 释
"桑拿天"就是"桑拿天气"，应译为 sauna weather。而 sauna day 与天气无关，它指的是芬兰人传统的洗桑拿浴的"桑拿日"。例如：

1. 星期六是芬兰传统的"桑拿日"。
Saturday is a traditional sauna day in Finland.
2. 如今，哪一天都可以洗桑拿浴，但是传统的"桑拿日"仍然是星期六。
Today, sauna may be taken on any day, but traditional sauna day is still Saturday.

"桑拿浴"是起源于芬兰的一种利用蒸汽排汗的沐浴方式。其英语是 sauna bath 或 sauna。"洗桑拿浴"可以用 to have a sauna bath, to have a

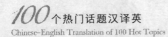

sauna, to take a sauna bath, to take a sauna 表示。"桑拿浴室"和"桑拿房"用 sauna 表示。例如：

3. 桑拿浴是芬兰人民族认同的重要部分，有机会的人通常至少一周洗一次桑拿浴。

 The sauna is an important part of the national identity of the Finnish people and those who have the opportunity usually take a sauna at least once a week.

4. 桑拿浴不仅可以洗净你的皮肤，还可以镇静你的神经，增强你的体魄。

 A sauna bath not only cleanses your skin but also calms the nerves and fortifies your body.

5. 桑拿浴使皮肤上的汗毛孔张开，帮助从人体和血液中排毒。

 Sauna bath opens the pores on skin and helps to remove toxins from within the body and blood.

6. 吃得过饱的两小时内不要洗桑拿浴，如果你喝了酒、咳嗽或感冒，也不要洗桑拿浴。

 Do not have a sauna bath within 2 hours of a heavy meal, or if you are under the influence of alcohol or suffering from a cough or cold.

7. 洗桑拿浴标志着安息日的开始。

 Having a sauna marked the beginning of the day of rest.

8. 人人都可以洗温和的桑拿浴。

 Everyone can take a mild sauna bath.

9. 如果你喝了酒，建议你不要洗桑拿浴。

 It is not recommended to take a sauna if you are under the influence of alcohol.

10. 可以向任何人建议洗桑拿浴。

 Taking a sauna bath can be recommended for anyone.

11. 我住在一个带游泳池和桑拿浴室的旅馆。

 I stayed at a hotel with a swimming pool and sauna.

"桑拿天"指又闷又热,令人浑身汗水外浸的天气。英语可以译为 sauna weather。例如:

12. 从气象学上讲,"桑拿天"是高温和高湿天气的俗称。
    Meteorologically, sauna weather is a common way of saying the weather with high temperature and high humidity.

13. 北京的八月有当地人所谓的"桑拿天"。
    Beijing's August has what locals call sauna weather.

14. 今年,北京的"桑拿天"比往常来得早。
    This year, sauna weather arrived in Beijing earlier than usual.

15. 这个不平常的"桑拿天"已经持续了几乎两周。
    This unusual sauna weather has lasted for almost two weeks.

16. 全省将有阵雨,"桑拿天"将逐渐减弱。
    There will be showers in the whole province, and the sauna weather will be weakening.

17. 我市因连续七日"桑拿天",轻微污染已经影响到人体健康了。
    Because of the sauna weather, which has lasted for seven successive days in our city, slight pollution has affected people's health.

18. "桑拿天"正使人们变得比平常更加懒洋洋了。
    The sauna weather is making people even lazier than usual.

19. 不要让夏季的"桑拿天"将你整垮。
    Don't let the summer sauna weather get you down.

20. 教师们在"桑拿天"里不得不穿着西服坐在外面同毕业生照相。
    The teachers had to sit outside in a suit to have a picture taken with the graduates in the sauna weather.

21. 在上周的"桑拿天"之后,我的脑子正开始恢复功能。
    My brain is starting to regain function after the last week of sauna weather.

22. 最近北京的"桑拿天"已经让城市居民加大马力使用空调和其他降温装置,这使得电力消耗剧增。
    The recent sauna weather in Beijing has seen city residents use

air-conditioners and other cooling devices at full blast, jacking up electricity consumption.

# 十七、中　　暑

### 汉语关键词
中暑、热疾病、热射病、日射病、热虚脱

### 英语关键词
heat illness, heat-related illness, heatstroke, suffer from heatstroke, sunstroke, collapse from sunstroke, suffer from a collapse from sunstroke, heat exhaustion, heat prostration

### 句　子
这位老人在炎热的大晴天中暑了。

### 误　译
This old man suffered from summer heat on a hot sunny day.

### 正　译
This old man suffered from heatstroke on a hot sunny day.

### 解　释
to suffer from summer heat 的意思是"遭受夏天炎热之苦",不是指得了病。例如:
1. 这些工人因大型厂房里空调不灵而正遭受夏天炎热之苦。
The workers are suffering from summer heat because of the impracticality of air conditioning in large plant buildings.
2. 住在这些空调设备差的公寓里的房客容易遭受夏天炎热之苦。
The tenants living in these badly air-conditioned flats are prone to suffer from summer heat.

"中暑"是人们在炎热夏季因高温、日晒或不通风而得的病的俗称,症状为头痛、眩晕、耳鸣、痉挛、虚脱、昏睡、血压下降等。如果泛指"热疾病",英语用 heat illness 或 heat-related illness 表示。因为高温中暑,即"热射病",英语用 heatstroke 表示。因为阳光直接照晒而中暑,即"日射病",英语用 sunstroke 表示。例如:

3. 热疾病可以表现为脱水、热痉挛、热虚脱或中暑。
   Heat illness can be in the form of dehydration, heat cramps, heat exhaustion or heatstroke.
4. 我们怎样能够预防热疾病?我们得了热虚脱或中暑后应该做什么?
   How can we prevent heat illness? What should we do after having heat exhaustion or heatstroke?
5. 中暑和脱水是两种非常普通的热疾病,如果不进行治疗有可能危及患者的生命。
   Heatstroke and dehydration are two very common heat-related diseases that can be life-threatening if the patient is left untreated.
6. 中暑是暴露在过热的情况下发生的一种疾病。
   Heatstroke is a condition that occurs after exposure to excessive heat.
7. 持续暴露于高温会引起中暑。
   Prolonged exposure to very high temperatures may cause heatstroke.
8. 中暑是一种威胁生命的疾病,它需要立即治疗。
   Heatstroke is a life-threatening condition that requires immediate medical attention.
9. 两名青少年在山上徒步旅行时中暑,不得不用直升飞机送往医院。
   Two teenagers suffered from heatstroke when hiking on the hill and had to be taken to hospitals by helicopters.
10. 我的一个朋友差一点死于中暑。
    A friend of mine nearly died from heatstroke.
11. 留在停好的汽车里无人看管的孩子,有中暑,甚至死亡的极大风险。
    Children who are left unattended in parked cars are at greatest risk for heatstroke, and possibly death.

12. 如果在炎热天里不能保持凉爽,所有的动物都会中暑。
    All animals can suffer from heatstroke on hot days if they can't keep cool.
13. 中暑是一种威胁生命的疾病,患病时因为暴露于高温,身体调节体温的系统会失灵。
    Sunstroke is a life-threatening condition in which the body's heat-regulating system fails, due to exposure to high temperatures.
14. 中暑由太阳暴晒引起,特征为体温升高、痉挛和昏迷。
    Sunstroke is caused by exposure to the sun and characterized by a rise in temperature, convulsions, and coma.
15. 由于夏季极度炎热的天气,户外工作的人们随时都会中暑。
    Due to the extremely hot summer weather, outdoor workers would suffer from sunstroke at any time.
16. 在这样的大热天里,筑路工人容易中暑。
    On such a hot day, road builders are liable to collapse from sunstroke.
17. 他在一个大热天里慢跑,结果中暑了。
    He took up jogging on a hot day and suffered a collapse from sunstroke.

"轻度中暑",即"热虚脱",英语用 heat exhaustion 或 heat prostration 表示。例如:

18. 热虚脱的普通症状包括疲倦、眩晕、恶心、呕吐、头痛、心跳加速和血压降低。
    Common symptoms of heat exhaustion include fatigue, lightheadedness, nausea, vomiting, headache, rapid heartbeat and lowered blood pressure.
19. 当人们在一个炎热而湿闷的地方工作,他们的体液因出汗而流失,从而引起身体过热时,常常会出现热虚脱。
    Heat exhaustion often occurs when people work in a hot, humid place and their body fluids are lost through sweating, causing the body to overheat.
20. 在大多数情况下,跑步者由于脱水而中暑或热虚脱。
    In most cases, runners suffer from heatstroke and heat exhaustion due

to poor hydration.
21. 热虚脱的症状有神志不清、肌肉痉挛、常常还有恶心或呕吐。
Heat prostration is characterized by mental confusion, muscle cramps, and often nausea or vomiting.
22. 热虚脱如果治疗不及时,能够使你的宠物永久性脑损伤、患血液病并最终死亡。
Heat prostration, when not treated in time, can cause your pet permanent brain injury, blood disorders, and eventually death.

# 十八、义 工

### 汉语关键词
义务、义工、志愿者

### 英语关键词
obligation, duty, compulsory, voluntary, voluntary work, volunteer work, voluntary worker, volunteer worker, volunteer

### 句 子
我国义务兵服役期限为2年。

### 误 译
In our country, a voluntary soldier must serve in the army for two years.

### 正 译
In our country, a compulsory serviceman must serve in the army for two years.

### 解 释
有人认为既然 voluntary labour 是"义务劳动",那么以此推理,voluntary soldier 就应该是"义务兵"。其实不然,voluntary soldier 是"志愿兵"。compulsory serviceman 才是"义务兵"。

作为形容词,"义务的"的第一个意思是"按照法律必须做的",即"强制性的"。英语可以译为 compulsory,即 required by law。例如:
1. 我国于1955年7月始实行义务兵役制。
   Compulsory military service was first introduced in our country in July 1955.
2. 义务教育是根据法律儿童必须接受而政府必须提供的教育。
   Compulsory education is education which children are required by law to receive and governments to provide.
3. 我国已实行9年义务教育制。
   Our country has instituted a system of nine-year compulsory education.

但是注意 compulsory 的原义是"强制的"。compulsory labour 的意思是"强制劳动",而不是"义务劳动"。例如:
4. 不得要求任何人进行强迫或强制劳动。
   No one shall be required to perform forced or compulsory labour.

作为形容词,"义务的"的第二个意思是"自愿参加而无报酬的"。"义务劳动"可以译为 voluntary labour 或 volunteer labour。例如:
5. 国家鼓励公民参加义务劳动。
   The state encourages citizens to take part in voluntary labour.
6. 下星期我们将要下乡参加义务劳动。
   Next week, we are going to the countryside to participate in volunteer labour.

但是,"义务演出"或"义演"不可以译为 voluntary performance。这是因为 performance 与艺术或娱乐相关时,意思为"演出"。与工作情况相关时,意思为"业绩"、"绩效",或"表现"。voluntary performance 不是"义务演出",而是"自发性绩效",是与商业有关的专门名词。比如,Customer Voluntary Performance,简称CVP,译为"顾客自发性绩效",指顾客提供无条件的贡献来支持企业在传送服务品质之行为。"义务演出"可以译为 free performance, benefit performance 或 charity performance。例如:

7. 昨天,艺人们为本社区老人举行了义务演出。
   1) Yesterday, the actors gave a free performance to the elderly people in this community.
   2) Yesterday, the actors gave a benefit performance to the elderly people in this community.
   3) Yesterday, the actors gave a charity performance to the elderly people in this community.

作为名词,"义务"的第一个意思是"法律上应尽的责任",与"权利(right)"相对而言。英语可以译为 obligation, duty。例如:
8. 作为公民,我们有义务维护社会治安。
   1) As citizens, we have the obligation to maintain public order.
   2) As citizens, we have the duty to maintain public order.
9. 纳税是公民义务。
   1) Paying taxes is the obligation of a citizen.
   2) Paying taxes is the duty of a citizen.
10. 你必须履行公民权利与义务。
    1) You must fulfill the rights and obligations of a citizen.
    2) You must fulfill the rights and duties of a citizen.

作为名词,"义务"的第二个意思是"道德上应尽的责任"。英语同样译为 obligation, duty。例如:
11. 我们从道德上讲有义务保护环境。
    We have a moral obligation to protect the environment.
12. 我觉得有义务帮助学习困难的同学。
    I feel under some obligation to help those fellow-students of mine who have difficulties in their study.
13. 我觉得没有义务告诉他实情。
    I didn't feel under any obligation to tell him the truth.
14. 你没有非买什么东西不可的义务。
    You are under no obligation to buy anything.

15. 我觉得有义务提供一个简单的解释。
    I feel duty-bound to offer a simple explanation.
16. 我觉得有义务帮助他学习。
    I feel duty-bound to help him with his study.

"义工"指"自愿参加的无报酬公益性工作",即"义务工作"。英语可以译为 voluntary work, volunteer work。例如:

17. 周末,他常常到附近社区做义工。
    At weekends, he often goes to the nearby community to do voluntary work.
18. 我定期在本地医院做些义工。
    I regularly do some voluntary work at the local hospital.
19. 义工能帮助你建立与社区的联系。
    Voluntary work can help you establish connections with the community.
20. 义工是你在帮助你的社区的同时取得工作经验的一种方式。
    Volunteer work is a way of getting work experience while helping out your community.

"义工"还可以指"自愿参加无报酬公益性工作的人"。英语可以译为 voluntary worker, volunteer worker, volunteer。例如:

21. 如果你符合这些条件,你可以从海外申请来到我国当义工。
    You can apply to come to our country as a voluntary worker from overseas if you meet these conditions.
22. 在业余时间,他在一个敬老院当义工。
    In his spare time, he serves as a volunteer worker at a home for the aged.
23. 她为一家慈善机构当义工。
    She works as a volunteer for a charity.

"志愿者"指"自愿为社会公益活动、大型赛事或会议等服务而不要报酬的人",与"义工"意思相当。英语可以译为 volunteer。例如:

24. 我想当2008年北京奥运会志愿者。
    I want to be a volunteer for the 2008 Beijing Olympic Games.
25. 成为一名奥林匹克志愿者,需经许多训练。
    To become an Olympic volunteer takes a lot of training.

# 十九、八　　卦

### ● 汉语关键词
八卦、娱乐八卦、八卦新闻、八卦杂志、狗仔队

### ● 英语关键词
Eight Trigrams, Eight Hexagrams, gossip, be gossipy, be fond of gossip, entertainment gossip, gossip news, gossipy news, gossip magazine, gossipy magazine, paparazzo, paparazzi

### ● 句　子
相传伏羲创造八卦。

### ● 误　译
Fuxi was said to invent the Eight Trigrams.

### ● 正　译
1) Fuxi was said to have invented the Eight Trigrams.
2) The Eight Trigrams were said to have been invented by Fuxi.

### ● 解　释
在这句话里,"相传"发生在后,用过去时;"创造"发生在先,要用不定式的完成体形式。例如:

1. 据说他爷爷活到了100岁。
   His grandfather was said to have lived to the age of 100.
2. 据说他已得到奖学金。
   He was said to have been granted a scholarship.

# 100个热门话题汉译英
## Chinese-English Translation of 100 Hot Topics

"八卦"是中国古代的基本哲学概念,反映了古人对现实世界的朴素认识。英语可以译为 the Eight Trigrams 或 the Eight Hexagrams。例如:

3. "八卦"是中国古代创造的一套有象征意义的符号。
   1) The Eight Trigrams are a set of symbolic signs created in ancient China.
   2) The Eight Hexagrams are a set of symbolic signs created in ancient China.
4. "八卦"的理论在《易经》里有详细的论述。
   1) The theory of the Eight Trigrams is expounded in detail in the Book of Changes.
   2) The theory of the Eight Hexagrams is expounded in detail in the Book of Changes.

粤语中,"八卦"的意思是"闲言碎语"或"流言蜚语"。英语可以译为 gossip。例如:

5. 不要相信你从这位博客那里听来的八卦。
   Don't believe the gossip you hear from the blogger.
6. 所有关于这个演员的风流韵事都只不过是些无聊的八卦。
   All this talk about the actor's love affairs is just idle gossip.

"八卦"还可以指喜欢探听和谈论流言蜚语或闲言碎语。英语译为 to be gossipy 或 to be fond of gossip。例如:

7. 他这个人很八卦。
   1) He is very gossipy.
   2) He is very fond of gossip.
8. 娱乐圈的一些名人很八卦。
   1) Some celebrities in the circle of entertainment are very gossipy.
   2) Some celebrities in the circle of entertainment are very fond of gossip.
9. 他是一个非常八卦的人——他最喜欢的事就是传播谣言和惹点乱子了!
   He is a very gossipy person—there is nothing he likes better than passing on a rumour and stirring up some trouble!

"娱乐八卦"指娱乐界的花边新闻和绯闻等娱乐消息,也指其他领域里名人的隐私性消息和绯闻。英语可以译为 entertainment gossip 或 gossip。例如:

10. 本网站报道的不仅有最新的名人八卦,还有所有普通的娱乐八卦。
This website covers not only the latest celebrity gossip but also all the general entertainment gossip.

11. 这个名人八卦博客会给你带来关于著名明星的最新娱乐八卦、传闻、丑闻、狗仔队照片和新闻。
This celebrity gossip blog brings you the latest gossip, rumours, scandals, paparazzi photos and news about famous celebrities.

"八卦新闻"是娱乐新闻和狗仔队为了吸引读者,到处挖掘明星的隐私广而告之的新闻。英语可以译为 gossip news 或 gossipy news。例如:

12. 你可以在这个网站上找到最新的名人八卦新闻。
You can find the latest celebrity gossip news at this website.

13. 这个电影明星希望报界在八卦新闻上把他忘掉。
The film star hopes the press would ignore him on gossipy news.

14. 很奇怪,没有任何关于这个歌星离婚的八卦新闻。
It is strange that there's not any gossipy news about the divorce of the pop star.

15. 真实新闻变得没有那么有趣了,因为它不像充满美女变秃的妙趣横生的故事之类八卦新闻那样有轰动效应。
Real news became less interesting, because it was not as "sensational" as the gossipy news filled with juicy stories of a beautiful girl gone bald.

"八卦杂志"可以译为 gossip magazine 或 gossipy magazine。例如:

16. 他们开办了一个在线名人八卦杂志。
They launched an online celebrity gossip magazine.

17. 从这本八卦杂志,读者可以得到最新的名人八卦、星座、健康、美容和怀孕的信息。
From this gossip magazine, the readers can get the latest celebrity gossip, horoscopes, health, beauty and pregnancy information.

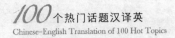

18. 我认为你对这些八卦杂志能相信的唯一事情就是封面上的价格。
    I think that the only thing you can believe in the gossip magazines is the cover price.
19. 这个名人八卦杂志的最近一期周刊引起了来自这个歌星的"粉丝"们的一场暴风雨般的抗议。
    The latest issue of the weekly celebrity gossip magazine has caused a storm of protest from the fans of the pop star.
20. 当她休息时,哪怕是只有5分钟,她也会沉醉在她心爱的八卦杂志里。
    When she takes a break, even if it's just for five minutes, she would indulge in her favourite gossipy magazine.

"狗仔队"是偷拍名人私生活的摄影记者。英语可以译为 paparazzo(单数),paparazzi(复数)。例如:
21. 作为一名狗仔队记者,他追踪名人以拍摄他们的有趣的照片来卖给杂志或报纸。
    As a paparazzo, he follows famous people around in order to get interesting photographs of them to sell to a magazine or a newspaper.
22. 据报导这个电影明星设法摆脱了狗仔队。
    The film star was reportedly to have managed to evade the paparazzi.
23. 他们喊出了对狗仔队和无聊小报的愤怒之情。
    They voiced their outrage at the paparazzi and the tabloid press.

# 二十、短　　信

> **汉语关键词**
> 短信、发短信、彩信
>
> **英语关键词**
> short message, text message, send a short message, multimedia message

● 句　子

他发了一些短信为他最喜欢的参赛选手投票。

● 误　译

He delivered a few short messages to vote for his favourite contestants.

● 正　译

He sent a few short messages to vote for his favourite contestants.

● 解　释

　　to send 和 to deliver 都有 to have sth taken to a place 的意思，即"将对象物送至某个地方"。但是用法不同。to deliver 表示职业人员将对象物送到接收者手中，而且常常是定期递送。to send 表示当事人通过邮寄传送对象物或通过电讯传送信息。例如：
1. 邮递员每天挨家挨户送信和报纸。
　　Every day the postman delivers letters and newspapers from house to house.
2. 每天早晨6点钟，送牛奶的将玻璃瓶装牛奶送到我家门阶上。
　　A milkman delivers milk in glass bottles to my doorstep at six every morning.
3. 是你们送货，还是得我来商店取货？
　　Will you deliver, or do I have to come to the shop to collect the goods?
4. 我通过航空将信寄给了我在美国的朋友。
　　I sent the letter by airmail to my friend in the United States.
5. 一旦你下了定单，我们会通过电子邮件发出信息确认费用，通常是在6小时以内。
　　Once you place an order, we send a message by email confirming the fee, usually within six hours.

　　"短信"的第一个意思是"篇幅短的信件"，是用笔或打字机写的。英语可以译为 short letter。例如：
6. 我给我父母写了一封短信表示问候。
　　I wrote a short letter to my parents to express my greetings.

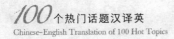

7. 他正在读他在美国的笔友写来的一封短信。
   He is reading a short letter from his pen pal in the United States.
8. 我收到一封短信,没有多少细节。
   I received a short letter, with not much detail.
9. 到达澳大利亚以后,他从悉尼给我寄了一封短信报了个平安。
   After he arrived in Australia, he sent me a short letter from Sydney to say he was OK.

"短信"的第二个意思是"短信息",是用手机通过移动通信网发出,在对方手机显示屏上显示的简短文字。例如:

短信 short message
文字信息 text message, text messaging
文字信息收发 text messaging
收发文字信息 to send and receive text messaging
短信服务 short-message service, SMS service, SMS
发短信 to send a short message, to text message

又如:

10. 他用手机给我发了一个短信。
    He sent me a short message by mobile phone.
11. 我国使用短信的手机用户逐年增多。
    There has been an increasing number of mobile phone users who send short messages year by year in our country.
12. 中国现在有4亿多手机用户使用短信服务收发文字信息。
    In China there are more than 400 million cell phone users who send and receive text messaging through short-message service.
13. 有没有免费发短信的方法?
    Is there a way to send text messages for free?
14. 短信服务(SMS)是用于通过数字蜂窝式网络系统发送和接收文字短信的一种协议。
    Short-message service (or SMS, for short) is a protocol for sending and receiving text messaging over digital cellular networks.

15. 利用短信服务收发文字信息业务正在我国迅速增长。
    SMS text messaging is fast growing in our country.
16. 我哥哥刚发了短信。
    My brother has just text messaged.

"彩信"是"集彩色图像和声音、文字为一体的多媒体信息业务",又称"多媒体短信"。英语可以译为 multimedia message。"多媒体信息服务"可以译为 multimedia messaging service (MMS)。例如:

17. 你可以给一个电话号码或一个电子邮件地址发彩信。
    You can send a multimedia message to a phone number or an e-mail address.
18. 一个发信者可以同时将彩信发给许多接收者。
    A sender may send a multimedia message to numerous recipients at once.
19. 请告诉我怎样在我的手机上写彩信和发彩信。
    Please tell me how I can write and send a multimedia message on my mobile phone.
20. 多媒体信息服务 (MMS) 是为电话信息系统设立的一种标准,它允许发送包含多媒体对象(图像、声频、视频和丰富多彩的文本)的信息。
    Multimedia Messaging Service (MMS) is a standard for telephony messaging systems that allows sending messages that include multimedia objects (images, audio, video, and rich text).

# 廿一、忽  悠

### 汉语关键词
忽悠、忽悠一下

### 英语关键词
sway, flicker, jerk sb around, hoodwink, bamboozle, suddenly, all of

a sudden, before we realized it

● 句　子

各种各样的忽悠手段是防不胜防的。

● 误　译

Various deceptive means are hardly preventive.

● 正　译

Various deceptive means are hardly preventable.

● 解　释

preventive 的意思是"预防性的",具有主动含义,只能用作定语,不用作表语。preventable 的意思是"可以防止的",具有被动含义。"防不胜防的"是"几乎不能防止的"意思,应该译为 hardly preventable。例如:

1. 我们必须采取预防性行动来保护我们的环境。

   We must take preventive actions to protect our environment.

2. 世界上欺诈的和奸诈的交易是防不胜防的。

   Tricky and treacherous dealings in the world are hardly preventable.

"忽悠"的第一个意思指"人体或物体的晃动"。英语可以译为 to sway 或 to flicker。例如:

3. 走钢丝的杂技演员在具有一定高度的细钢丝绳上忽悠个不停。

   The tightrope walker continuously swayed on the thin wire at a great height.

4. 一面大旗在旗杆上被微风吹得直忽悠。

   1) A huge flag swayed on the pole in the gentle breeze.

   2) A huge flag fluttered on the pole in the gentle breeze.

5. 光秃的旗杆在狂风中忽悠过来,忽悠过去。

   1) The bare flagpole swayed to and fro in the strong winds.

   2) The bare flagpole swayed to and fro under the hard gusts.

6. 长长的扁担在他肩上直忽悠。

   The long carrying-pole swayed on his shoulder.

7. 油灯忽悠忽悠的,一会儿亮,一会儿灭。
   The oil-lamp flickered on and off.
8. 夜色中,江面上渔船的灯火忽悠忽悠的。
   In the darkness of the night, lights flickered on the fishing boats on the river.
9. 我看见一个影子在树后忽悠忽悠地晃动。
   I saw a shadow flickering behind the tree.

"忽悠"的第二个意思原为东北方言,相当于"愚弄"、"糊弄"或"捉弄",具有诙谐、生动的意味。英语最好不译为 to deceive 或 to cheat 这样普通的动词,而译为 to jerk sb around, to hoodwink, to bamboozle 等俚语说法,更能表达出"忽悠"的细微含义。"被忽悠"可以相应地译为 to be jerked around, to be hoodwinked, to be bamboozled。例如:

10. 别忽悠我!我不会上当。
    Don't jerk me around! I won't be taken in.
11. 虚假电视广告在忽悠消费者。
    False commercials are jerking the consumers around.
12. 许多顾客被这个大公司忽悠了。
    Many customers were jerked around by the big company.
13. 骗子忽悠这个老太太,让她买了条一文不值的项链。
    The swindler hoodwinked the old lady into buying a worthless necklace.
14. 他以能忽悠,让人相信各式各样的胡言乱语而臭名远扬。
    He is notorious for hoodwinking people into believing all kinds of nonsense.
15. 记者揭露了这个医药大亨是如何忽悠消费者的。
    The news reporter revealed how the pharmaceutical giant had hoodwinked the consumers.
16. 这个股民被忽悠买了垃圾股。
    The investor was hoodwinked into buying junk stocks.
17. 这本书表明媒体是如何忽悠受众的。
    The book shows how the media has bamboozled the audience.

# 100个热门话题汉译英
## Chinese-English Translation of 100 Hot Topics

18. 在一篇博客里,这位记者说布什总统忽悠了美国人民,让他们卷入伊拉克战争。
    In a blog, the news reporter stated that President Bush had bamboozled the American people into the Iraqi War.
19. 我被忽悠签了这个不合理的合同。
    I was bamboozled into signing the irrational contract.

"忽悠一下"作为副词短语的第一个意思是"忽然晃动的结果"。英语可以译为 suddenly, all of a sudden。例如:

20. 我感到两腿一软,忽悠一下就跌倒在地上。
    My legs felt like jelly, and I suddenly fell off on the ground.
21. 鱼儿在水面上忽悠一下就不见了。
    Suddenly, the fish disappeared from the surface of the water.
22. 她的心忽悠一下提到嗓子眼儿上了。
    All of a sudden, she had her heart in her mouth.
23. 汽车忽悠一下就掉进河里去了。
    All of a sudden, the car fell off into the river.

"忽悠一下"作为副词短语的第二个意思是"不知不觉地",与"时间过得快"有关。英语可以译为 before we realized it。例如:

24. 暑假忽悠一下就过去了。
    1) Summer vacation passed quickly before we realized it.
    2) Summer vacation passed swiftly before we realized it.
25. 天忽悠一下就冷了。
    It turned cold before we realized it.
26. 天忽悠一下就黑了。
    It got dark before we realized it.
27. 夜幕忽悠一下就降临了。
    Evening came before we realized it.

# 廿二、漫 游

● 汉语关键词

漫游、手机漫游、漫游费

● 英语关键词

ramble, roam, wander, roaming call, roaming, roaming fee, roaming charge, cost of roaming

● 句 子

这个旅游者在北京大街上漫游。

● 误 译

The tourist rumbled in the streets of Beijing.

● 正 译

The tourist rambled in the streets of Beijing.

● 解 释

　　to rumble 和 to ramble 只有一个字母之差,可是意思大不相同。to rumble 的意思是 to move slowly and heavily, making a rumbling sound,即"笨重的车辆轰隆地缓慢行进"。to ramble 的意思是 to walk for pleasure, especially in the countryside,即"(尤指人在乡间)漫游"。ramble 也可以当名词用。例如:

1. 偶尔几辆牛车轰隆轰隆走过大街。

    Occasionally a few ox-carts rumbled the street.

2. 我看见坦克轰隆轰隆驶过大街。

    I saw tanks rumbling through the street.

3. 我们在树林中漫游。

    1) We rambled through the woods.

    2) We went for a ramble through the woods.

    3) We were on a ramble through the woods.

"漫游"的第一个意思指"人随意游览"。英语除了 to ramble 以外,还可以译为 to roam, to wander。例如:

4. 这个年青作家漫游世界找寻灵感。

   The young writer roamed the world in search of inspiration.

5. 你可以同你的家人漫游乡村。

   1) You can roam the countryside with your family.

   2) You can ramble in the countryside with your family.

   3) You can go for a ramble in the countryside with your family.

6. 这些失业的成年人在大街上无目标地漫游。

   These unemployed adults roamed the street aimlessly.

7. 昨夜当我在大街上漫游时,我抬头看天空,看见一颗非常明亮的星星。

   Last night when I wandered in the street, I looked up to the sky and saw a very bright star.

8. 我不喜欢单独在树林中漫游。

   I don't like to wander in the woods alone.

9. 我们有些自由时间在雨中漫游。

   We had some free time to wander in the rain.

"漫游"的第二个意思指"鱼随意在水中游动,或动物随意在地面走动"。英语可以译为 to roam。例如:

10. 几头鲸在海洋中漫游。

    A few whales were roaming in the ocean.

11. 鲑鱼在靠近沿岸的大海里漫游。

    The salmons roam in the sea near the coasts.

12. 你可以观看鹿、狗、鸭子和鸡在田野漫游。

    You can watch the deer, dogs, ducks and chickens roam across the fields.

13. 大象通常被允许在这个印度城市漫游。

    The elephant is usually allowed to roam in this Indian city.

"漫游"的第三个意思指手机离开注册的服务区到另一个区域后,通过网络进行通信联络的功能。英语可以译为 roaming call 或 roaming。例如:

14. 有时候我利用手机漫游,但是贵得吓死人。
    Sometimes I made a roaming call but it was outrageously expensive.
15. 你可以在你去旅行的国家内利用手机漫游。
    You can make roaming calls from your mobile within the country you are travelling to.
16. 这位技术专家争论说,漫游实际上给运营商几乎没有造成额外成本。
    The technology expert argues that roaming calls actually incur almost no extra cost for operators.
17. 每年大约一亿五千万欧盟手机用户在他们的国家以外利用漫游打电话。
    Some 150 million mobile phone customers in the EU use roaming to make calls outside their home nation every year.

"(手机)漫游费"可以译为 roaming fee, roaming charge, cost of roaming。"漫游费价格"可以译为 roaming price。例如:

18. 这个移动通讯运营公司有计划调整漫游费。
    The mobile operator has plans to regulate roaming fees.
19. 高昂的漫游费已经引起中国消费者的抱怨。
    High roaming fees have drawn complaints from Chinese consumers.
20. 这位官员说中国不会立刻取消漫游费。
    The official says that China will not eliminate roaming fees immediately.
21. 一些欧盟议会议员已经支持新计划降低在国外打手机的漫游费。
    Some Euro-MPs have backed new plans to cut roaming charges for mobile phone calls made abroad.
22. 一些移动通讯运营商声称要降低漫游费。
    Some mobile operators claim to be cutting the cost of roaming.
23. 这位专家认为中国只能逐步降低漫游费价格。
    This expert holds that China can only cut the roaming price step by step.

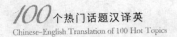

# 廿三、倒 计 时

### 汉语关键词
倒计时、倒数读秒、计时、计时收费、计时工资

### 英语关键词
countdown, count down, count the time, count by time, charge by the hour, time-rate wage, tell the time

### 句子
北京2008年奥运会倒计时一周年已经开始。

### 误译
The one-year countdown for the 2008 Beijing Olympic Games has begun.

### 正译
The one-year countdown to the 2008 Beijing Olympic Games has begun.

### 解释
countdown 后面要跟 to sth,表示离某件大事发生的时刻还有多少时间,而不能用 for sth。

"倒计时"的第一个意思是"倒数读秒",表示的是一个较短的时段,像从10数到0。英语可以译为 countdown。例如:
1. 卫星发射倒计时开始。
   The countdown to the launching of the satellite began.
2. 他教给我如何制作从10到0的倒数读秒器。
   He taught me how to make a countdown timer from 10 to 0.

"倒计时"的第二个意思是"从未来的某件大事预计发生的时刻往现在推算还剩多少时间",是一个较长的时段。英语同样译为 countdown。例如:
3. 2007年8月8日在天安门广场举行了庆祝北京2008年奥运会倒计时一周年盛大活动。

On August 8, 2007, a grand gala was held on the Tian'anmen Square celebrating the one-year countdown to the 2008 Beijing Olympic Games.

4. 倒计时钟显示离北京2008年奥运会开幕还有360天。

The countdown clock shows there are 360 days left until the opening of the 2008 Beijing Olympic Games.

5. 工程已进入倒计时阶段。

The countdown to the completion of the project has started.

6. 那些请柬一送出,婚礼倒计时就开始了。

The countdown to the wedding begins as soon as those invitations are sent.

7. 倒计时钟显示离目标日期还剩多少天、小时、分钟和秒。

A countdown clock shows how many days, hours, minutes and seconds are left to the target date.

8. 倒计时日历是标明从现在到未来的重要事件还有多少时间的一种方法。

A countdown calendar is one way to mark time from the present to an important event in the future.

9. 她在厨房里有个倒计时器。

She has a countdown timer in the kitchen.

10. 你可以建立一个免费的倒计时网页,它会准确显示离生日、结婚、学期结束日、婴儿出生、晚会等一类重大事件还剩多少时间。

You can create a free countdown page that shows exactly how much time is left until a big event, like a birthday, wedding, last day of school, baby birth, party, etc.

"倒计时"的第三个意思是作为动词,表示"倒着计算时间"。英语可以译为 to count down,即 to record the time passing until an important event happens。例如:

11. 我们正在倒计时看离假日还有几天。

We're counting down our holiday.

12. 她已经在对她的结婚日倒计时了。
    She is already counting down to her wedding day.

to count down 还有"倒着数"的意思,例如:

13. 我要你从20倒着数到0。
    I want you to count down from twenty to zero.
14. 我要你从20倒着数到0,每次减2。
    I want you to count down from twenty to zero by twos.

"计时"的第一个意思是"计算时间"。英语可以译为 to count the time。例如:

15. 当你准备好了的时候,你就可以开始计时。
    You may begin to count the time when you are ready.
16. 你一按钮,这两块表将同时开始计时。
    Press the button and the two watches will start to count the time simultaneously.
17. 你怎么能以秒计算时间?
    How can you count the time in seconds?

"计时"的第二个意思是"按照时间计算"。英语可以译为 to count by time。例如:

18. 当这个停车场从顾客那里收停车费时,他们是计时的。
    When the car park charges the parking fee from a customer, they count by time.

"计时收费"的意思是"按照小时收费"可以译为 to charge by the hour。例如:

19. 在这个城市,租汽车是计时收费的。
    In this city the car rentals charge by the hour.

"计时工资"是"按照劳动时间多少和技术熟练程度来计算的工资"。

英语可以译为 time-rate wage。例如：
20. 这个工厂实行计时工资制，而不是计件工资制。
In this factory, they implement the system of time-rate wage instead of the system of piece-rate wage.

"计时"的第三个意思是"显示时间"或"报时"。英语可以译为 to tell the time。例如：
21. 日晷是古代中国用来计时的装置。
Sundial was a device used to tell the time in ancient China.

# 廿四、房　　奴

● 汉语关键词

房奴、按揭

● 英语关键词

mortgage slave, mortgage

● 句　子

这么高的房价已使我沦为房奴。

● 误　译

Such high housing prices have rendered me a house slave.

● 正　译

Such high housing prices have rendered me a mortgage slave.

● 解　释

不可将 house slave 译成"房奴"。house slave 与 field slave 形成对比，指当年美国从事家务劳动的黑奴，即"家奴"；而 field slave 是从事农耕劳动的黑奴，即"田奴"。例如：
1. 乔治的祖母是从事家务劳动的黑奴，祖父是从事农耕劳动的黑奴。
George's grandmother was a house slave and his grandfather was a field

slave.
2. 家奴通常生活得比田奴好。他们通常吃得好一点，而且有时候能得到主人家扔掉的旧衣服。
House slaves usually lived better than field slaves. They usually had better food and were sometimes given the family's cast-off clothing.
3. 简是个家奴，她被主人强迫嫁给另一个黑奴。
Jane was a house slave who was forced by her master to marry another slave.

"房奴"的意思是"按揭购房者"。英语可以译为 mortgage slave。例如：
4. 房奴被采用来描述那些按揭还款超过月薪一半的人。
Mortgage slave is adopted to describe those people whose mortgage payment is more than half of their monthly salary.
5. 你肯定会得到那所好房子，但是你将不得不变成一个房奴来养房子。
Sure, you can have that nice house, but you're going to have to become a mortgage slave to keep it.
6. 约翰是个心力交瘁的房奴，挣扎着在压力大的职业、不愉快的婚姻和四个小孩的需求之间争取平衡。
John is a stressed mortgage slave, struggling to balance a high-pressure career, an unhappy marriage and the demands of four small children.
7. 当房奴并没有真正使我充满热情。
Being a mortgage slave doesn't really fill me with enthusiasm.
8. 他已使自己从一个房奴变为一个房地产投资商。
He has transformed himself from a mortgage slave into a property investor.
9. 我有点处于房奴的状态。
I'm somewhat in the mortgage-slave situation.

西方人除了买房和买车，还买游艇或帆船。mortgage-slave 的本义是"按揭购买者"，除了"房奴"，也可以指"车奴"或"船奴"。例如：

10. 他把自己描述为他的公寓的房奴和他的汽车的车奴。

    He described himself as a mortgage slave to his apartment and car.

11. 我想你只是一个买帆船给你的邻居们留下好印象的船奴。

    I think you are just a mortgage slave buying boats to impress your neighbours.

"按揭"是一种购房或购物的贷款方式,以所购房屋或物品为抵押向银行贷款,然后分期偿还。英语可以译为 mortgage。例如:

12. 我以我的新居得到了一笔固定利率的按揭贷款。

    I've got a fixed-rate mortgage on my new home.

13. 他正千方百计设法不让他的按揭还款上涨。

    1) He is trying hard not to let his mortgage payment go up.

    2) He is trying hard not to let his mortgage repayment go up.

14. 这个买主以他现有的财产来按揭贷款。

    The buyer raised a mortgage on his existing property.

15. 你可以从他那里得到如何申请按揭贷款的建议。

    You can get tips from him on how to apply for a mortgage.

16. 我们是应该付现金,还是取得按揭贷款来买第二套居所?

    Should we pay cash or take out a mortgage to buy a second home?

17. 他已从他有帐户的银行取得按揭贷款。

    1) He has taken out a mortgage from the bank he has his current account with.

    2) He has started to have a mortgage from the bank he has his current account with.

18. 她还没有还清用于购买房屋的全部按揭贷款。

    1) She hasn't paid off all the mortgage for the house she's bought.

    2) She hasn't paid back all the mortgage loan for the house she's bought.

19. 如果你在三个交易日以内通知你的债权人,你有权取消这个抵押交易。

1) You have the right to cancel the mortgage transaction if you notify your lender within three business days.
2) You have the right to rescind the mortgage transaction if you notify your lender within three business days.

## 廿五、写　真

### 汉语关键词
写真、人体写真、写真集

### 英语关键词
portray sb, paint a portrait, draw a portrait, sketch a picture, take a photo of sb, take a picture of sb, portrait, photo of a person, nude photography, true description, true-to-life depiction, true-to-life portrayal

### 句　子
这本书是一位"海归"在国外留学时的生活写真。

### 误　译
This book is a returnee's daily life photo taken when he was studying abroad.

### 正　译
This book is the true description of a returnee's life in the days when he was studying abroad.

### 解　释
"生活写真"有两层意思。一是"日常生活照片"，英语可以译为 daily life photo。二是"对生活的真实描述"，英语可以译为 true description of life。例如：
1. 我喜欢这张在家乡的生活写真。
   I love this daily life photo in my hometown.
2. 这本书是一艘战舰上的生活写真。

This book is the true description of life aboard a battleship.

注意下面这个句子有歧义,有两种不同的理解:
3. 这是一个演员的生活写真。
   1) This is a daily life photo of an actor. (这是一个演员的日常生活照片)
   2) This is the true description of an actor's life. (这是对一个演员的生活的真实描述)

"写真"的第一个意思是"画人物肖像或拍摄人像"。英语可以译为 to portray sb, to paint a portrait, to draw a portrait, to sketch a picture, to take a photo of sb, to take a picture of sb。例如:
4. 美术学校的学生们请一位老人做模特儿以练习写真。
   The students of the art school asked an old man to pose as a model, so that they could practise sketching.
5. 这位画家擅长写真。
   The painter is strong in portraying a person.
6. 这个画家画了一张他的年轻新娘的写真像。
   The artist painted a portrait of his young bride.
7. 她画了一张她想象的人物的写真像。
   She drew a portrait of the figure she imagined.
8. 这个学习美术的学生正在画这个模特儿的写真像。
   The art student was sketching a picture of the model.
9. 她在卧室里自拍了一张写真像。
   She took a photo of herself in her bedroom.
10. 这个摄影师拍了一张大卫·贝克汉姆的写真像。
    The photographer took a picture of David Beckham.

"写真"的第二个意思是"画像或拍摄的人像"。英语可以译为 portrait, photo of a person。例如:

# 100个热门话题汉译英
Chinese-English Translation of 100 Hot Topics

11. 这位女士拍写真是为了展示和记录自己的美。
    This lady had her photos taken to demonstrate and record her own beauty.
12. 这个女演员决定为一家杂志拍写真。
    This actress decided to have her photos taken for a magazine.

"人体写真",或称"人体艺术写真",就是"人体艺术摄影"。英语可以译为 nude photography, nude photo, nude portrait, nude picture。例如:

13. 这个评论者认为人体写真追求的是自然和真实。
    The critic holds that nude photography is intended to pursue naturalness and truthfulness.
14. 这个年青女子把拍人体写真当作一种时尚。
    The young woman regards nude photography as a fashion.
15. 拍人体写真已逐渐成为一些女性的一种时尚消费。
    Nude photography has gradually become a kind of fashionable consumption for some females.
16. 近年来这个摄影师因为给女性拍人体写真而名声大噪。
    In recent years, this photographer has made a big name for his taking nude pictures of females.
17. 这个电影明星为拍一张人体写真而摆姿势。
    The film star posed for a nude portrait.
18. 这个中年妇女后悔年轻时没有拍人体写真。
    The middle-aged lady regrets that she failed to have her nude photos taken when she was young.

"写真集"的意思,就是"人像集",英语可以译为 portrait album 或 photo album。"人体写真集"就是"人体艺术摄影集",英语可以译为 nude photo album。例如:

19. 这些影迷追逐他们偶像们的写真集。

· 80 ·

These film fans chased after the portrait albums of their idols.
20. 这个电影明星最近推出了她的人体写真集。
    This film star has recently released her nude photo album.

"写真"的第三个意思是"对事物的真实描述"。英语可以译为 true description, true-to-life depiction, true-to-life portrayal。例如:
21. 这位评论家指出这部游记是中国人民生活的写真。
    The critic points out that this travel note is a true description of the life of the Chinese people.
22. 这本书是股民心态的写真。
    This book is a true description of the stock investors' mentality.
23. 这部小说是当今社会代沟的写真。
    The novel is a true-to-life depiction of the generation gap in the present-day society.
24. 这部电影展现的是这位古代罗马国王的写真。
    The film presents a true-to-life portrayal of the ancient Roman king.
25. 我们不要把生活写真与艺术虚构混淆起来。
    We mustn't confuse the true description of life with artistic fiction.

# 廿六、遗　　产

● **汉语关键词**

　　遗产

● **英语关键词**

　　heritage, inheritance, legacy

● **句　子**

　　他从父亲那里得到一份遗产。

### 误 译

He received a heritage from his father.

### 正 译

1) He got a legacy from his father.
2) He received an inheritance from his father.

### 解 释

heritage 只能表示"历史留下的遗产",不能表示"死者留下的遗产"。

"遗产"的第一个意思是"死者留下的财产,包括动产、不动产和债权"。英语可以译为 inheritance, legacy。例如:

遗产继承人 inheritor, legatee
遗产继承法 inheritance law
遗产税 estate tax, inheritance tax, succession duty
遗产纠纷 legacy dispute
留下遗产 to leave a legacy
继承遗产 to inherit a legacy
接受遗产 to take one's inheritance/ legacy, to take possession of one's inheritance/ legacy, to come into one's inheritance/ legacy
得到遗产 to get a legacy, to receive a legacy

又如:

1. 他父亲给他留下一万美元的遗产。
   His father left him a legacy of $10,000.
2. 这个男孩很可能从父母那里继承一笔遗产。
   The boy will probably inherit a legacy from his parents.
3. 他已接受父亲的遗产。
   1) He has taken his father's inheritance/ legacy.
   2) He has taken possession of his father's inheritance/ legacy.
   3) He has come into his father's inheritance/ legacy.
4. 他们每人得到一万美元的遗产。
   They each received a legacy of $10,000.

"遗产"的第二个意思是,指"历史上遗留下来的物质和精神财富"。英语可以译为 heritage, inheritance, legacy。例如:

文化遗产 cultural heritage, cultural legacy, cultural inheritance
历史遗产 historical heritage, historical legacy, historical inheritance
文学遗产 literary heritage, literary legacy, literary inheritance
艺术遗产 artistic heritage, artistic legacy, artistic inheritance
自然遗产 natural heritage, natural legacy, natural inheritance
民族遗产 national heritage, national legacy, national inheritance
物质遗产 tangible heritage, tangible legacy, tangible inheritance
非物质遗产 intangible heritage, intangible legacy, intangible inheritance
口头遗产 oral heritage, oral legacy, oral inheritance
文化遗产保护 preservation of cultural heritage, protection of cultural heritage
保护文化遗产 to preserve cultural heritage, to protect cultural heritage

又如:

5. 中国以其古代文明和丰富的文化遗产而驰名于天下。
   China is famous all over the world for her ancient civilization and rich cultural heritage.

6. 这座博物馆保存了我们生活的城市的历史遗产。
   The museum preserves the historical heritage of the city we live in.

7. 由塞万提斯无与伦比的天才创造使之不朽的堂·吉诃德和桑丘·潘札两个人物,构成了西班牙人民的优秀文学遗产的一部分。
   The figures of Don Quixote and Sancho Panza, immortalized by the incomparable genius of Cervantes, constitute part of a splendid literary heritage to the Spanish people.

8. 目前在这个博物馆陈列的一个美术展览赞颂了达芬奇的艺术遗产。
   An art exhibit currently on display in this museum celebrates the artistic legacy of Leonardo da Vinci.

9. 像故宫、颐和园与长城等建筑物是我们的民族遗产的一部分。
   Such buildings as the Imperial Palace, the Summer Palace and the Great

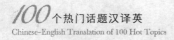

Wall are part of our national heritage.

10. 长城已被列入联合国教科文组织的《世界文化遗产名录》。

The Great Wall has been included in UNESCO's World Cultural Heritage List.

11. 保护文化遗产就是保护人类文明，就是保护人类生存的环境。

The protection of cultural heritage means the protection of human civilization, and also the protection of the environment for the survival of humankind.

12. 过热的旅游业正在危害我们的文化遗产。

The overheated tourism is doing harm to our cultural heritage.

13. 我们不能抛弃反映历史和体现传统的文化遗产。

We can't cast away the cultural heritage that is a reflection of our history and an embodiment of our tradition.

14. 非物质文化遗产是文化遗产的重要组成部分。

Intangible cultural heritage is an important component part of cultural heritage.

15. 非物质文化遗产世代相传。

Intangible cultural heritage has been passed down from generation to generation.

16. 中国拥有丰富的非物质文化遗产。

China has rich intangible cultural heritage.

17. 非物质文化遗产包括口头传统、民俗、礼仪、节日庆典、传统表演艺术和传统手工艺技能。

Intangible cultural heritage includes oral tradition, folklore, ceremonial rituals, festival rituals, traditional performing arts, and traditional craftsmanship.

18. 非物质文化遗产是中国历史的见证。

Intangible cultural heritage is a witness to the history of China.

19. 非物质文化遗产是中华文化的重要载体。

Intangible cultural heritage is an important vehicle of Chinese culture.

20. 他记录下他遇到的当地人民讲述的故事,以保存他们丰富的口头遗产。

He recorded stories told by the local people he met to preserve their rich oral legacy.

# 廿七、继　　承

### 汉语关键词

继承、继任、接班、继任者、接班人、继承王位、继承传统

### 英语关键词

inherit, succeed, successor, succeed to the throne, succeed to the crown, carry on, carry forward, advance, carry on sb's unfinished work, continue the work left by sb

### 句　子

他继承父亲担任公司总裁。

### 误　译

He inherited his father as president of the company.

### 正　译

1) He succeeded his father as president of the company.
2) He succeeded his father to become president of the company.
3) He became the successor of his father as president of the company.
4) He became the successor to his father as president of the company.

### 解　释

to inherit sth 和 to succeed to sth 所继承的是前人的遗产;to succeed sb as sth 所继承的是前人的职位。

"继承"的第一个意思是"依法承受死者的遗产"。英语可以译为 to inherit, to succeed to。例如:

# 100个热门话题汉译英
## Chinese-English Translation of 100 Hot Topics

继承父母遗产 to inherit one's parents' inheritance
继承财产 to inherit the property
继承权 right of inheritance
王位继承权 right of succession
继承法 inheritance law, law of succession
继承税 inheritance tax
继承人/传人 inheritor, successor, heir

又如：

1. 他从父亲那里继承了一份家产。
   He inherited an estate from his father.
2. 她从母亲那里继承了一笔财富。
   She inherited a fortune from her mother.
3. 在这个地方，长子继承父亲财产。
   In this place, the eldest son succeeds to his father's estate.
4. 主人已经通过准备一份遗嘱来决定由谁继承财产。
   The owner has decided who will inherit the property by preparing a will.
5. 他无缘无故被剥夺了继承权。
   He was deprived of the right of inheritance for no reason at all.
6. 王位继承权永远属于在位君主的长子，然后属于长孙。
   The right of succession always belongs to the eldest son of the reigning sovereign, and then to the eldest son of the eldest son.
7. 大多数国家都有一部关于死者在遗嘱中包括的遗赠的继承法。
   Most countries have an inheritance law regarding the bequests that a deceased person includes in a will.
8. 继承法涉及一个人死后财产分配的问题。
   The law of succession concerns the distribution of a person's property on his death.
9. 我们是一个伟大文化传统的继承人。
   We are the inheritors of a great cultural tradition.

"继承"的第二个意思是"接替王位"或"接替职位"。英语可以译为 to succeed sb as sth，其意思是 to come next after sb and take their place or

position, 即"继任"或"接班"。successor 是"继任者"或"接班人"。"继承王位"译为 to succeed to the throne 或 to succeed to the crown。例如：
10. 伊丽莎白于1952年继承王位。
    1) Elizabeth succeeded to the throne in 1952.
    2) Elizabeth succeeded to the crown in 1952.
11. 布朗接替布莱尔担任工党领袖。
    1) Brown succeeded Blair as the leader of the Labour Party.
    2) Brown succeeded Blair to become the leader of the Labour Party.
    3) Brown became the successor of Blair as the leader of the Labour Party.
    4) Brown became the successor to Blair as the leader of the Labour Party.

"继承"的第三个意思是"接受前人的知识、文化、传统或作风"。英语可以译为 to carry on, to carry forward, to advance, to inherit。例如：

继承传统 to carry on the tradition, to carry forward the tradition, to advance the tradition, to inherit the tradition

继承文化遗产 to inherit cultural heritage

又如：

12. 这位作家尽力继承鲁迅开启的传统。
    1) The writer did his best to carry on the tradition started by Lu Xun.
    2) The writer did his best to carry forward the tradition launched by Lu Xun.
13. 这个地区的人民正在继承那种保持、改良和明智使用与开发他们的土地和水资源的传统。
    The people in this area are carrying forward the tradition of conservation, improvement, and wise use and development of their land and water resources.
14. 他作为音乐教师的主要目标是继承中国民间音乐的传统。
    His main goal as a music teacher was to advance the tradition of Chinese folk music.
15. 应该教育儿童如何尊重并继承人类文化遗产。
    Children should be taught how to respect and inherit cultural heritage

of the humankind.
16. 这个地区的妇女继承了纺纱与织布的传统。
The women in this region have inherited the tradition of spinning and weaving.

"继承"的第四个意思是"继续做前人未完成的事业"。英语可以译为 to carry on sb's unfinished work, to continue the work left by sb。例如：
继承父业 to inherit one's father's profession
继承领导权 to take over the mantle of leadership
又如：
17. 这个农民的儿子不想再继承父业，而想进城市居住和工作。
The farmer's son didn't want to inherit his father's profession any more, but wanted to go to live and work in the city.
18. 他正努力继承他父亲未完成的事业。
He is trying to carry on his father's unfinished work.
19. 这个青年人将以最大的努力来继承他父亲留下的事业。
The young man will continue the work left by his father with the utmost effort.
20. 尽管这位将军战死在沙场，但他的儿子继承了他的领导权。
Although the general was killed in battle, his sons took over the mantle of leadership.

# 廿八、人　　质

● 汉语关键词

人质、抵押品、绑架、绑票、绑架者、绑匪、拘押、拘留、赎金、释放人质、撕票

● 英语关键词

hostage, capture, kidnap, abduct, captor, kidnapper, abductor, hostage-taker, hold sb, hold sb prisoner, take sb hostage, ransom, free the hostage, release the hostage, kill the hostage

### 句 子

这次人质危机最终解决了。

### 误 译

The hostage crisis was finally addressed.

### 正 译

1) The hostage crisis was finally solved.
2) The hostage crisis was finally resolved.

### 解 释

to address 的意思是 to think about a problem or a situation and decide how you are going to deal with it，即"设法解决"、"准备解决"或"着手解决"，而不是"实际上已经解决"的意思。例如：

1. 这篇文章解释了如何客观地设法解决这个危机。

   The article explains how the crisis was addressed in an objective manner.

2. 几个国际组织批评了准备解决这个危机的方式。

   Several international organizations have criticized the way the crisis was addressed.

"人质"是被拘留的人，用来要挟对方满足政治或经济要求。英语可以译为 hostage。例如：

3. 这些军人已准备好搜索和营救人质。

   The army men are ready to search and rescue the hostage.

4. 他设法使人质获释。

   He secured the release of the hostages.

5. 昨日，韩国官员与塔利班就21名人质的命运开始直接会谈。

   Yesterday South Korean officials and the Taliban started direct talks on the fate of 21 hostages.

# 100个热门话题汉译英
Chinese-English Translation of 100 Hot Topics

hostage 还可以指物,即"抵押品"。例如:
6. 这家公司把汽车当做抵押品。
   The company took the cars as hostage.

"绑架"是为了政治目的或为了获得赎金而劫持人质。"绑票"是为了获得赎金而劫持人质。英语可以译为 to capture, to kidnap, to abduct。例如:
7. 放学回家时,这个小男孩被一个绑架者绑票了。
   The young boy was captured by a kidnapper when he was going back home after school.
8. 他为了得到一大笔赎金而威胁要绑架一个商人的儿子。
   He threatened to kidnap the son of a businessman for a big ransom.
9. 几名枪手从巴格达的一家餐馆绑架了一名外国记者。
   A few gunmen abducted a foreign journalist from a restaurant in Baghdad.

"绑架者"或"绑匪",英语可以译为 captor, kidnapper, abductor, hostage-taker。例如:
10. 这个绑架者把飞行员当做人质。
    The captor kept the pilot as a hostage.
11. 国际社会敦促绑架者释放人质。
    The international community urged the captors to release the hostage.
12. 绑架者肯定早就计划好了这次犯罪行动的方方面面以防被抓。
    The kidnapper must have planned every aspect of the crime before anybody could catch him.
13. 这个失踪女孩的父亲昨天对绑架者发布了一个特别呼吁,请求立即释放人质,结束这个家庭的噩梦。
    The father of the missing girl yesterday issued an extraordinary plea to her abductor to release the hostage immediately and end the family's nightmare.
14. 警方在机场逮捕了这名绑架者。
    The police arrested the hostage-taker at the airport.

"拘押"、"拘留"。英语可以译为 to hold sb, to hold sb prisoner, to

take sb hostage。例如:
15. 人质是被绑架者拘留的人。
    A hostage is a person held by a captor.
16. 这个女孩在10岁时被绑架,后来在一个偏远的山村被拘押了8年。
    The girl was kidnapped at the age of ten and held prisoner for eight years in a remote mountainous village.
17. 他第一次作为电视记者被派往国外时被当作人质遭到拘留。
    He was taken hostage while on his first foreign assignment as a television journalist.

"赎金"是赎回人质或抵押品所用的钱。英语可以译为 ransom。例如:
18. 这些绑架了一名德国记者的绑匪要求一百万美元赎金。
    The kidnappers of a German journalist demanded a million-dollar ransom.
19. 被索马里海盗扣押的一艘丹麦货轮的船员在船主付了一笔赎金后获释。
    The crew of a Danish cargo ship held by Somali pirates were freed after its owners paid a ransom.

"释放人质"的意思是"不再拘留人质,使其获得自由"。英语可以译为 to free the hostage, to release the hostage。例如:
20. 两名人质有望在今后数日内获释。
    It is hopeful that two hostages will be freed in the next few days.
21. 当警官们无法说服绑匪释放人质时,一名警官开枪打死了绑匪。
    When the police officers couldn't persuade the kidnapper to release the hostage, an officer shot and killed him.

"撕票"是"绑匪杀死人质"的意思。英语可以译为 to kill the hostage。例如:
22. 这个恐怖主义分子威胁要撕票,而人质很严肃地对待这种威胁。
    The terrorist threatened to kill the hostage, and the hostage took the threat seriously.

# 廿九、主 持

### 汉语关键词

主持、主持会议、主持小组讨论会、主持宴会、主持电视访谈节目、主持典礼、主持婚礼、主持日常工作、主持公道、主持公正、主持正义、住持、方丈

### 英语关键词

preside over, chair, host, act as host, preside over a meeting, chair a meeting, preside over a group discussion, chair a group discussion, host a dinner party, act as host at a banquet, host a television programme, host a television show, preside over a ceremony, preside over a wedding ceremony, perform a wedding ceremony, do a wedding ceremony, take charge of, be in charge of, take care of, be responsible for, direct, take charge of day-to-day work, be in charge of day-today work, take care of day-to-day work, take care of the routines, stand for fair play, uphold justice, maintain justice, do justice, maintain righteousness, abbot

### 句 子

董事长正在主持一个会议。

### 误 译

The chairman of the board of directors is taking charge of a meeting.

### 正 译

The chairman of the board of directors is presiding over a meeting.

### 解 释

to take charge of 是"负责管理"的意思。to take charge of a meeting 是"负责管理会议具体事务"的意思。董事长一般是不会亲自管理具体事务的。to preside over 是"负责掌握"的意思。to preside over a meeting 是"充当会议主席,掌握、引导和协调会议进程"的意思。例如:

1. 管理会议事务的人必须保证大楼的门在离开时锁好。

The person in charge of the meeting must be sure that the building door

is locked upon leaving.
2. 管理会议事务的人负责打扫房间,包括桌子、椅子、地板和柜台。
The person in charge of the meeting is responsible for cleaning up the room, including tables, chairs, floors, and counters.

"主持"的第一个意思是"负责掌握"。英语可以译为 to preside over, to chair, to host, to act as host。例如:

主持会议 to preside over a meeting, to chair a meeting

主持小组讨论会 to preside over a group discussion, to chair a group discussion

主持宴会 to host a dinner party, to act as host at a banquet

主持电视节目 to host a television programme, to host a television show

主持典礼 to preside over a ceremony

主持婚礼 to preside over a wedding ceremony, to perform a wedding ceremony, to do a wedding ceremony

又如:

3. 当总裁不在时,一位副总裁可以主持会议。
In the absence of the President, a vice-president may preside over a meeting.

4. 他正在学习如何为他的公司有效地主持会议。
He is learning how to chair a meeting effectively for his business.

5. 在一个温暖的夏夜,她在教室里主持一个小组讨论会。
On a warm summer evening, she presided over a group discussion in the classroom.

6. 他将主持一个小组讨论会,集中研究我们社区事物的现状。
He will chair a group discussion focusing on the present state of affairs in our community.

7. 这位影星正在主持一个慈善宴会。
The film star is hosting a charitable dinner party.

8. 总理主持了招待来自35个国家的外交部长和其他代表的宴会。

# 100个热门话题汉译英
Chinese-English Translation of 100 Hot Topics

The Premier acted as host at a banquet for foreign ministers and other representatives of 35 nations.

9. 她为儿童主持一个电视节目。

   She hosts a television programme for children.

10. 上周我应邀主持了一个电视节目。

    Last week I was invited to host a television show.

11. 他主持一个受欢迎的周末电视访谈节目。

    He hosts a popular weekend television talk show.

12. 市长将主持一个仪式悼念这位在火灾中救了五名儿童的警察。

    The mayor will preside over a ceremony to pay tribute to the policeman who saved five children in a fire.

13. 在教堂里,牧师为这对年轻人主持了婚礼。

    1) In the church, the priest presided over a wedding ceremony for the young couple.

    2) In the church, the priest performed a wedding ceremony for the young couple.

    3) In the church, the priest did a wedding ceremony for the young couple.

"主持"的第二个意思是"负责处理具体事务"或"负责管理具体事务"。英语可以译为 to take charge of, to be in charge of, to take care of, to be responsible for, to direct。例如:

主持日常工作 to take charge of day-to-day work, to be in charge of day-to-day work, to take care of day-to-day work, to take care of the routines 又如:

14. 副总裁的职责是当总裁不在时主持公司的事务。

    The duty of the vice-president is to take charge of the affairs of this company in the absence of the president.

15. 秘书长主持修改方案的工作。

    The executive secretary is in charge of revising the plan.

16. 根据今天计划安排,我将主持这段时间工作。

    According to the order of the programme today, I will be responsible

for this session.
17. 当总裁不在时,副总裁将承担主持公司日常工作的责任。
When President is away, Vice-President will assume the responsibility of taking care of the company's routines.
18. 这位副总经理主持和管理这个合资公司的日常工作。
The Deputy General Manager directs and manages the day-to-day work of the joint venture.

"主持"的第三个意思是"主张"或"维护"。英语可以译为 to uphold, to champion, to stand for。例如:
主持公道 to stand for fair play
主持公正 to uphold justice, to maintain justice, to do justice
主持正义 to maintain righteousness
又如:
19. 如果你们继续支持侵略者,你们怎么能说你们是主持公道的?
If you carry on backing the invaders, how can you say you stand for fair play?
20. 中国政府将一如既往地支持联合国主持公正、维护和平和促进全球繁荣的行动。
The Chinese government will as always support the UN efforts to uphold justice, maintain peace and promote global prosperity.
21. 法官与陪审员在法庭上应该主持公正。
The judge and the jurors should maintain justice in the court.
22. 本法庭将代表受害者负责主持公正。
This court will see to it on behalf of the victim that justice should be done.
23. 我们必须主持正义,反对邪恶的行径。
We must maintain righteousness and oppose sinful acts.

"主持"的第四个意思是"负责掌管寺院的人",即"住持"或"方丈"。英语可以译为 abbot。例如:

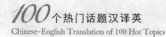

24. 昨天我拜访了这座寺院的主持。
Yesterday I paid a visit to the abbot of the temple.

# 三十、主 持 人

● 汉语关键词

主持人、典礼主持人、婚庆主持人、节目主持人、广播主持人、电视主持人、音乐节目主持人、项目主持人

● 英语关键词

master of ceremonies, emcee, compere, microphone jockey, professional master of wedding ceremonies, professional presider of wedding ceremonies, person in charge of a programme, programme compere, host, hostess, anchorperson, anchor, anchorman, anchorwoman, television host, TV anchor, TV anchorperson, disc jockey, person in charge of a project

● 句 子

他在一家婚庆公司当婚庆主持人。

● 误 译

He serves as an anchorperson at a wedding ceremony company.

● 正 译

1) He serves as a professional master of wedding ceremonies at a wedding ceremony company.

2) He serves as a professional presider of wedding ceremonies at a wedding ceremony company.

● 解 释

anchorperson 的意思是 person who presents a radio or television programme and introduces reports by other people, 即"广播/电视主持人"。西方婚礼,传统是在教堂举行,由牧师主持。不在教堂举行婚礼时,大都由亲友主持。"婚庆主持人"叫做 master of wedding ceremonies。近年来,我

国出现专业的婚庆公司,专门操办婚礼。同时出现职业的婚庆主持人,专门主持婚礼,即 professional master of wedding ceremonies。英语中有 professional presider 一词,专指"职业的会议主持人"。我们不妨套用,或可将"婚庆主持人"译为 professional presider of wedding ceremonies。与"主持人"相关的词组有:

典礼主持人/娱乐节目主持人/司仪 master of ceremonies, MC, emcee, compere, microphone jockey, MJ

职业的会议主持人 professional presider

婚庆主持人 professional master of wedding ceremonies, professional presider of wedding ceremonies

节目主持人 person in charge of a programme, programme compere

广播/电视主持人 host, anchorperson, anchor

广播/电视男主持人 host, anchorman

广播/电视女主持人 hostess, anchorwoman

电视主持人 television host, TV anchor, TV anchorperson

音乐节目主持人 disc jockey, DJ

项目主持人 person in charge of a project

例如:

1. 该公司为婚礼提供婚庆主持人服务。
   This company offers master of ceremonies services for weddings.
2. 你将会发现他是一个能满足你所有娱乐活动需求的职业主持人。
   You'll find him a professional compere for all your entertainment needs.
3. 我是一名体育新闻作者和一名体育节目主持人。
   I am a sports writer and a sports microphone jockey.
4. 她以她职业的会议主持人的优雅举止著称。
   She is known for her poise as a professional presider.
5. 作为筹款活动的主持人,你不一定需要协调这个社会活动的其他方面。
   As the host of the fund-raising event, you don't necessarily have to coordinate other aspects of the social function.
6. 她以当节目主持人开始职业生涯。

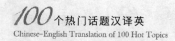

She began her career as a programme compere.

7. 这位新闻主持人未能提及这个事件的重要性。
The news anchorperson failed to mention the significance of the event.

8. 这位女新闻记者正在学习当主持人。
The news reporter was learning to be an anchorwoman.

9. 这位演员在电影中扮演了一个成功电视主持人的角色。
The actor played the role of a successful television anchor in the film.

10. 这位电视主持人正在采访一位科学家。
The television host was interviewing a scientist.

11. 她目前正在担任新闻领域的电视主持人。
She is currently working as a television hostess in the news area.

12. 除了当广播主持人以外,他还花时间当专栏作家和编辑。
In addition to working as a radio host, he spent time working as a columnist and editor.

13. 这位女广播主持人正在做时事新闻报道。
The radio hostess was giving a news report of current events.

14. 我猜想她配得上"第一女主持人"的称号。
I guess she deserves the title of "First Female Anchor".

15. 这位男电视主持人正在报道晚间新闻。
The TV anchorman was reporting evening news.

16. 这个前模特现在已是我市顶尖的女电视主持人。
The former model is now the top TV anchorwoman in our city.

17. 我们为婚礼、公司活动和私人晚会提供音乐节目主持人服务。
We provide disc jockey services for weddings, corporate events and private parties.

18. 这个节目主持人据说夸大了该节目的积极效果。
The person in charge of the programme was said to have exaggerated its positive effects.

19. 我认为一个项目主持人应该献身于他的项目。
I think a person in charge of a project should be dedicated to his project.

20. 项目主持人最好自始至终一直控制着项目。
The person in charge of a project had better remain in control of the project from start to finish.

## 三十一、第 三 者

● 汉语关键词

第三者、第三方、第三党、插足、踏足

● 英语关键词

third party, the other man, the other woman, get involved in, be involved in, get involved in one's marriage, set foot at, set foot in, set foot on

● 句　子

有个第三者插足于他们的婚姻。

● 误　译

There is a third party who has set foot in their marriage.

● 正　译

1) There is a third party who has involved in their marriage.
2) There is a third party involved in their marriage.

● 解　释

to set foot in/on/at 的意思是 to arrive in/on/at，即"到达"或"踏足"。例如：

1. 美国宇航员尼尔·阿姆斯特朗、埃德温·奥尔德林和迈克尔·科林斯是第一批踏足月球的人。
American astronauts Neil Armstrong, Edwin Aldrin and Mike Collins were the first humans to set foot on the Moon.
2. 这位地理学家已经踏足于每个大陆。
The geographer has set foot on every continent.

3. 自从我踏足校园的第一天起,我就努力争取当一名科学家。
   Since the first day I set foot on the campus, I have endeavoured to become a scientist.
4. 我将永远不再踏足这所房子。
   I'll never set foot in this house again.
5. 他拒绝在后半辈子踏足这个城镇。
   He refused to set foot in this town for the rest of his life.
6. 这位探险家是踏足北极的第一人。
   The explorer was the first man to set foot at the North Pole.

"第三者"的第一个意思是"当事双方以外的人或团体",或称"第三方"。英语可以译为 third party。例如:
7. 这位专家认为水污染酿成的损失是由第三者故意或疏忽所造成的。
   This expert holds that the loss from water pollution was caused by a third party intentionally or negligently.
8. 第三者应当承担赔偿责任。
   The third party shall be liable to make compensation.
9. 我们决不会把你的个人信息泄露给第三者的。
   We will not disclose your personal information to third parties.
10. 我问了几个关于强制性第三方保险的问题。
    I asked a few questions about the compulsory third party insurance.

third party 还有"第三党"的意思。例如:
11. 他是一个第三党的领袖,该党走中间路线。
    He is the leader of a third party, which takes the middle road.

"不让第三者知道",就是在两个当事人之间保密,即"只有我们俩知道"。英语可以译为 to keep sth between the two of us 或 to keep sth between you and me。例如:
12. 咱们俩保密,不让第三者知道。

1) Let's keep this between us.
2) Let's just keep it between you and me.

"第三者"的第二个意思是特指"插足他人婚姻,与已婚者有恋情或有暧昧关系的人"。英语的译法很多,要视具体情况而定。常常译为 third party, the other man, the other woman。例如:

13. 充满和谐与温馨的婚姻不会有第三者插足。
    There is no involvement of a third party in the marriage filled up with harmony and warmth.
14. 这对夫妻由于那个女的第三者插足而离婚了。
    The husband and wife were divorced because of the involvement of the other woman.
15. 由第三者插足造成的夫妻感情疏远,是构成离婚率急剧上升的一个重要因素。
    Alienation of affections due to the involvement of the other man or woman, accounts for an important factor for the soaring divorce rate.

"插足"的第一个意思是"介入某种活动"。英语可以译为 to get involved in 或 to be involved in。例如:

16. 许多家长已经意识到插足他们的孩子的学习有多么重要。
    Many parents have realized how important it is to get involved in their children's learning.
17. 这个网站插足视频广告。
    This website is involved in video advertising.
18. 这个协议很可能因第三者插足而告吹。
    This agreement will probably break up because of the involvement of a third party.

"插足"的第二个意思是特指"第三者与已婚夫妇中的一方有暧昧关系"。英语可以译为 to get involved in one's marriage。例如:

19. 她痛恨这个女的第三者插足他们的婚姻。

She hated the other woman for getting involved in their marriage.

20. 她与丈夫刚刚分居五周以后,这个妇女意识到有个女的第三者插足他们的婚姻。

Just about 5 weeks after her separation with her husband, the woman realized that there was a third party involved in their marriage.

# 三十二、拓　　展

- **汉语关键词**

拓展、拓展训练、个人拓展、团队拓展、传播

- **英语关键词**

expand, extend, enlarge, broaden, widen, develop, spread, development, personal development, team development, outward bound

- **句　子**

他正在教新推销员如何拓展推销技能。

- **误　译**

He is teaching new salespersons how to spread their sales skills.

- **正　译**

He is teaching new salespersons how to develop their sales skills.

- **解　释**

在这里,to spread 的意思是 to cause sth to be known to, or used by more people,即"传播"。to spread the skills 的意思是"向别人传播技能",而不是表示"拓展自己的技能"。例如:

1. 我正思考如何在我的工厂里向别人传播这些技能。

   I am thinking about how to spread the skills to others in my factory.

2. 回到你的机构你打算怎样传播你在培训班上学到的技能和想法?

   How do you plan to spread the skills and ideas you have learned during

the workshop back in your institution?

"拓展"的第一个意思是"扩展空间或范围"。英语可以译为 to expand, to extend, to enlarge, to broaden, to widen, to develop。例如:

3. 我们最近已把市场拓展到新的业务领域。

We have recently expanded/extended/enlarged/broadened/widened/developed our market into new business areas.

4. 他负责拓展公司的销售业务。

He is responsible for expanding/extending/enlarging/broadening/ widening/developing the company's sales.

5. 这些年青人想拓展他们的视野。

1) These young people want to expand/extend/enlarge/broaden/widen/develop their horizons.

2) These young people want to expand/extend/enlarge/broaden/widen/develop their field of vision.

6. 两国政府正努力拓展双边的经济合作。

The two governments are striving to expand/extend/enlarge/ broaden/widen/develop their bilateral economic cooperation.

7. 伽利略继续并拓展了哥白尼的工作。

Galileo continued and expanded/extended/enlarged/broadened/widened/developed the work of Copernicus.

8. 在我国,外商投资领域正不断拓展。

In our country, the field for foreign investment is being expanded/extended/enlarged/broadened/widened/developed.

9. 计算机的广泛应用拓展了我们的知识。

The widespread use of computers has expanded/extended/enlarged/broadened/widened/developed our knowledge.

10. 我们将拓展法律服务,并提供有效的法律援助。

We will expand/extend/enlarge/broaden/widen/develop legal services and provide effective legal aid.

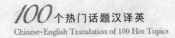

11. 人的想像力可以拓展到超越时空的界限。
    Human imagination may expand/extend/enlarge/broaden/widen/develop beyond the bounds of space and time.
12. 你应该经常读那些能拓展你的思维的书籍。
    You should often read those books that will expand/extend/enlarge/broaden/widen/develop your mind.

"拓展"的第二个意思是"发展能力"。英语可以译为 to expand, to extend, to enlarge, to broaden, to widen, to develop。例如:
13. 我想拓展一些有用的技能。
    I want to expand/extend/enlarge/broaden/widen/develop some useful skills.
14. 这种方法可以帮助拓展我们读写的能力。
    This method can help to expand/extend/enlarge/broaden/widen/develop our ability to read and write.
15. 他希望为学术目的而拓展他的英语能力。
    He wishes to expand/extend/enlarge/broaden/widen/develop his competence in English for academic purposes.
16. 这些年青教师已经过专门培训,以拓展他们在英语教学中的能力。
    These young teachers have been specially trained so as to expand/extend/enlarge/broaden/widen/develop their capability in English teaching.
17. 他们正努力拓展他们创造财富的能力。
    They are trying to expand/extend/enlarge/broaden/widen/develop their capacity to create wealth.

"拓展"作为名词,英语译为 development,可以构成下列词组:
个人拓展 personal development
团队拓展 team development
组织拓展 organization development, organizational development
职业拓展 career development
专业拓展 professional development

领袖才能拓展 leadership development
素质拓展 quality development
潜能拓展 break-bound development
例如：

18. 个人拓展规划将帮助你界定和探索你的目标，并策划各种方法使目标变为现实。
    Personal development planning will help you define and explore your goals and map out ways to turn them into reality.
19. 你们应该建立一个团队拓展的环境，并在这个环境中成功地进行工作。
    You should set up a team development environment and work successfully within it.
20. 组织拓展领域的重点在于提高组织自身与组织中的人们的效率。
    The field of organization development is focused on improving the effectiveness of organizations and the people in those organizations.
21. 职业拓展是所有个人独有的一个毕生的过程。
    Career development is a lifelong process that is unique for every individual.
22. 有效的专业拓展被认为对学校成功与教师满意越来越重要。
    Effective professional development is seen as increasingly vital to school success and teacher satisfaction.
23. 通过领袖才能拓展，你能提高你的领导技能以在工作中取得成功。
    Through leadership development, you can improve your leadership skills to achieve success in your work.
24. 此项研究的重点在于小学教育中的素质拓展。
    This research study focuses on quality development in primary education.

"拓展"的第三个意思是"拓展训练"的简称，指在自然地域，通过模拟探险活动进行的情景式心理训练、人格训练、管理训练。英语可以译为 outward bound，可以用作名词或形容词。例如：

25. 拓展训练通过在新环境中进行挑战性体验活动，帮助人们发现和

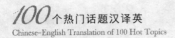

拓展他们照顾自己、他人和周围世界的潜能。
Outward bound helps people discover and develop their potential to care for themselves, others and the world around them by engaging in challenging experiences in new environments.

26. 这个拓展活动计划提供通过户外体验式教育进行的个人拓展。
This outward bound programme provides personal development through outdoor experiential education.

27. 自从这个拓展培训学校毕业以来,汤姆真的已经变成一个非常有责任心的青年人。
Tom has really transformed into quite a responsible young man since his graduation from this outward bound school.

# 三十三、科学发展观

● **汉语关键词**

科学发展观、观、观点、看法、观念、概念、理念

● **英语关键词**

viewpoint, view, concept, conception, outlook, Scientific Outlook on Development

● **句 子**

我们必须深入贯彻落实科学发展观。

● **误 译**

We must thoroughly apply the scientific viewpoint of development.

● **正 译**

We must thoroughly apply the Scientific Outlook on Development.

● **解 释**

"科学发展观"曾有不同译法:the scientific viewpoint of development, the scientific view of development, the scientific concept of development, the scientific conception of development。现在依据17大决议英语文本，改为the Scientific Outlook on Development。"……观"是对事物的认识、看法或态度。根据它是个人的还是普遍的、具体的还是抽象的、主观的还是客观的、针对一个问题还是表示一个思想体系的区别，有5种译法：viewpoint，view，concept，conception和outlook。

  viewpoint 的意思是 a point of view 或 a way of thinking about a subject，即"思考一个话题或问题的方式"，指具体的看法或观点。用来说"科学发展观"这样宏大的思想体系，不合适。例如：
1. 他对这件事将会有自己的看法。
  He will have his own viewpoint on the matter.
2. 我试图从不同的观点来看这个问题。
  I tried to look at the issue from a different viewpoint.
3. 我不是完全赞同你对这部电影的看法。
  I don't exactly share your viewpoint about the film.

  view 的第一个意思是 a personal opinion about sth or an attitude towards sth，即"个人对事物的意见或态度"，带有主观性。例如：
4. 我对素质教育持有不同的意见。
  I hold a different view about quality education.
5. 我们的意见是这样一部法律是必要的。
  It is our view that such a law is necessary.
6. 他对这个问题持乐观/悲观态度。
  He took an optimistic/a pessimistic view of the problem.

  view 的第二个意思是 a way of understanding，thinking about or examining sth，即"理解、思考或审视事物的方式"，带有客观性，可以用来表达"……观"。例如：
7. 这本书对我们周围正在发生的事提供了全面的看法。
  The book offers an overall view of what is happening around us.
8. 你说的每个词句，都表达了你的世界观。

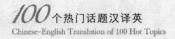

With every word you utter, you state your world view.
9. 一项调查表明:越来越少的美国人对上帝拥有传统看法,而读圣经也变得越来越不普及。
A survey shows that fewer Americans embrace a traditional view of God and Bible reading is becoming less popular.

concept 的第一个意思是 a widely held idea of what sth is or should be, 即"普遍看法"。例如:
10. 我们是在广泛持有的教育观的基础上进行工作的。
We work on the basis of a widely held concept of education.
11. 这是一种新的普遍看法,还是一种对现有普遍看法的补充?
Is this a new general concept or an addition to an existing general concept?

concept 的第二个意思是 a general idea that is connected with sth abstract or a principle that has been generalized from particular instances, 即"与抽象事物联系的想法或由特定事例概括出来的原则",指抽象的"观念"、"概念"或"理念",可以用来表达"……观"。例如:
12. 他倡导人人应该机会均等的观念。
He advocates the concept that everyone should have equality of opportunity.
13. 这个学生熟悉物理学的基本概念。
The student is familiar with the basic concepts of physics.
14. 她掌握不了工程设计中的基本概念。
She can't grasp the fundamental concepts in engineering design.
15. 不幸的是,你们正在讨论的东西远远超出了大多数人的理念。
Unfortunately what you are discussing is far beyond the concept of most people.

conception 的意思是 a general idea about what sth is like, or a general understanding of sth, 即"对事物的普遍想法或理解",指"一般观念"或"一般理解",可以用来表达"……观"。例如:

16. 爱因斯坦的相对论被认为是一种新的宇宙观。
    Einstein's theory of relativity is regarded as a new conception of the universe.
17. 他的人生观已被证明是错误的。
    His conception of life has been proved to be false.
18. 美国人的审美观与我们的有很大的不同。
    The American conception of aesthetics is quite different from that of ours.

outlook 的意思是 the attitude to life and the world of a particular person, group or culture，即"一个特定的人、群体或文化对待人生和世界的态度"，特别指"人生观"或"世界观"，可以用来表达"……观"。例如：
19. 他的经济学知识赋予他务实的人生观。
    His knowledge of economics has given him a practical outlook on life.
20. 这位科学家采取机械唯物主义作为他的世界观。
    The scientist adopted mechanical materialism as his world outlook.
21. 这两位经济学家在经济观方面有极大分歧。
    The two economists differed widely in their economic outlook.

# 三十四、小康社会

## 汉语关键词

小康、小康社会、小康之家

## 英语关键词

moderate prosperity, moderately prosperous, moderately prosperous society, well-off, moderately well-off, fairly well-off, well to do, moderately well-to-do, fairly well-to-do, moderately well-off family, fairly well-to-do family, family of moderate means

## 句 子

我们正在为建设全面小康的社会而奋斗。

# 100个热门话题汉译英
Chinese-English Translation of 100 Hot Topics

● **误 译**

We are striving for the building of an overall well-off society.

● **正 译**

We are striving to build a moderately prosperous society in all respects.

● **解 释**

"小康"过去主要指"可以维持中等水平生活的家庭经济状况",经常用来说明一个家庭,例如"小康人家"、"家道小康"。笔者在20世纪50年代末上大学时,老师教我们将"小康人家"译为 well-off family 或 well-to-do family。将"家道小康"译为 to be well-off 或 to be well-to-do。那时,我国依然贫穷,"小康"就是"富裕"的另一种说法。现在,"小康"更多用来说明一个国家或社会的经济状况。目前,我国正从温饱型向小康型过渡。而"小康"的标准就是达到中等发达国家水平的社会经济状况。"小康"是介于温饱与富裕之间的中间状态。将"小康社会"译为 well-off society 或 well-to-do society 是不妥的。这是因为 well-off 或 well-to-do 的意思是 rich,与 poor 和 badly-off 是反义词,意思是"有钱"或"富裕",比"小康"的经济状况要好多了。还因为 well-off 或 well-to-do 更多地用来形容个人或家庭。例如:

1. 他们有钱,但是生活相当简朴。

   They are well-off, but live quite simply.

2. 在这个城镇,大多数居民比10年前有钱了。

   In this town, most people are better-off than they were ten years ago.

3. 他买得起那些只有富人才买得起的奢侈品。

   He can afford to buy the luxurious goods that only the well-off can afford.

4. 他们很有钱。

   They are very well-to-do.

5. 他生在一个富裕家庭。

   He was born in a well-to-do family.

6. 新加坡在某些方面可以算是一个富裕国家,但是有些人依然非常贫穷。

   Singapore might be a well-to-do country in some ways, but some people

are still very poor.
7. 这些是为富人建造的豪宅。
   These are luxury homes for the well-to-do.

  "富裕社会"的特点是经济繁荣,物质极大丰富。英语可以译为 prosperous society。"小康"的第一个意思指"中等发达国家水平的社会经济状况",英语可以译为 moderately prosperous(形容词)和 moderate prosperity(名词)。"小康社会"译为 moderately prosperous society,较为贴切。例如:

8. 我们的人民渴望一个充满希望的稳定而富裕的社会。
   Our people desire a stable and prosperous society filled with hope.
9. 没有农村的小康,就不会有整个国家的小康。
   Without moderate prosperity in the rural areas, there will be no moderate prosperity for the whole country.
10. 我们正在为奔向建成全面小康社会的目标而稳步前进。
    We are making steady progress toward the goal of building up a moderately prosperous society in all respects.
11. 建成全面小康社会是中国人民在2020年以前要达到的目标。
    Building up a moderately prosperous society in all respects is a goal for the Chinese people to reach by 2020.
12. 当我们达到那个目标时,我国将彻底摆脱贫困,实现小康。
    When we reach that goal, our country will completely shake off poverty and achieve moderate prosperity.

  "小康"的第二个意思是"家庭经济状况可以维持中等水平的生活"。不同国家、不同地区和不同时期的"小康",即"中等水平"是不一样的。所以"小康"是个相对的概念。一般是自己与过去纵向比较,不好与别人横向比较。英语可以译为 moderately/ fairly well-to-do 或 moderately/ fairly well-off。例如:

13. 他出生在一个小康之家。
    1) He was born in a moderately/ fairly well-to-do family.
    2) He was born in a moderately/ fairly well-off family.

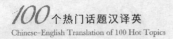

14. 在过去5年里,这里的村民已过上温饱生活。他们现在正努力奔小康。
    1) In the past five years, the villagers here have got adequate food and clothing. And they are now striving to become moderately well-off.
    2) In the past five years, the villagers here have been adequately fed and clad. And they are now striving to become fairly well-to-do.
15. 随着经济的发展和技术的进步,我国达到小康水平的人越来越多。
    With the development of economy and the progress of technology, there are more and more people who have become moderately well-to-do in our country.
16. 在这个欧洲国家,小康家庭占到人口的大多数。
    In this European country, moderately well-off families constitute the majority of the population.

"小康之家"还可以译为 family of moderate means。例如:

17. 他来自一个小康之家。
    He came from a family of moderate means.
18. 他在一个小康之家里长大,而且他通过工作来支持自己读完法律学校。
    He was raised in a family of moderate means, and he worked to support himself through law school.
19. 我们都曾经听说从前几乎每个小康之家都有一架钢琴。
    We've all been told that once upon a time there was a piano in the home of almost every family of moderate means.

# 三十五、飙　　升

> **汉语关键词**
> 狂飙、飙升、飙涨、飙车、飙戏、发飙

● 英语关键词

very strong wind, hurricane, whirlwind, rise rapidly, rise drastically, rise sharply, soar, skyrocket, rocket up, run up sky high, shoot sky high, drive a car at top speed, speed for the thrill of driving fast, speed for the thrill of it, act, play a role, get wild, go crazy, go mad

● 句　子

最近国际市场油价飙升。

● 误　译

Recently oil prices have raised in the international market.

● 正　译

1) Recently oil prices have risen rapidly in the international market.

2) Recently oil prices have increased drastically in the international market.

3) Recently oil prices have increased sharply in the international market.

4) Recently oil prices have soared in the international market.

5) Recently oil prices have skyrocketed in the international market.

● 解　释

to raise 是及物动词，应改为不及物动词 to rise 的过去分词 risen。但是 to rise, to increase 等仅表示一般意义的"上升"，而不能表示"急剧上升"，需要加 rapidly, drastically, sharply 等副词来修饰。

"飙"的本义是"狂风"或"暴风"。"狂飙"可以译为 very strong wind, hurricane, whirlwind。例如：

1. 国际悲歌歌一曲，狂飙为我从天落。

To the stirring strains of the *Internationale*, a wild whirlwind has swooped for me from the sky.

"飙"可以后加动词，构成复合词，表示"像狂风一样"。"飙升"和"飙涨"的意思是"价格或数量急剧上升"。英语可以译为 to soar, to

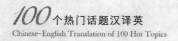

skyrocket, to rocket up, to run up sky high, to shoot sky high, to rise rapidly, to rise drastically, to rise sharply。例如：

2. 自年初以来，翡翠等珠宝的价格一路飙升。
   Since the beginning of the year, the prices of such jewels as halcyon have skyrocketed.
3. 近来，许多城市的住房销量一直飙升。
   Recently, housing sale has been soaring in many cities.
4. 似乎这个城市的房价还要飙升。
   It seems that the real estate prices will skyrocket in this city.
5. 近年来，这个地区的天然气消费量飙升。
   In recent years, the consumption of natural gas has soared in this region.
6. 我从无数的人那里听说他们的电话费飙升。
   I heard from countless people that their telephone bills had run up sky high.
7. 这家石油公司的股票价格一直飙升。
   The stock prices of this oil company have been rocketing up.
8. 在过去的几个月里，沪深指数从4,500点一路飙升。
   Over the last few months, Shanghai Composite Index and Shenzhen Sub-Index have rapidly risen up all the way from 4,500 points.
9. 如果经济衰退，失业率就会飙升。
   If economy goes into recession, unemployment will rise sharply.
10. 最近，我国股价飙涨。
    Recently, stock prices have skyrocketed in our country.
11. 我害怕这个地区的房价会飙涨，造成当地居民经济困难。
    I am afraid that the real estate prices will shoot sky high in this area, causing financial troubles for the local residents.

"飙车"的意思是"寻求刺激而疯狂地开快车"。英语可以译为 to drive a car at top speed, to speed for the thrill of driving fast, to speed for the thrill of it。例如：

12. 在高速公路上飙车是违法的，而且也是非常危险的。
    Driving a car at top speed on the expressway is illegal, and also very

dangerous.
13. 这个年青人醉酒飙车,酿成惨祸。
The young man drove a car at top speed while intoxicated, causing a terrible road accident.
14. 年轻司机更容易为寻求刺激而飙车。
Young drivers are more likely to speed for the thrill of driving fast.
15. 在公路上为寻求刺激而飙车的司机可能对他们周围所有的人造成危险。
Drivers who speed for the thrill of it on highways may endanger everyone around them.
16. 他为寻求刺激而飙车。
He drove his car at high speed for the thrill.

"飙戏"的意思是"演戏"。"飙"可能是说明演员投入的状态。英语可以译为 to act, to play a role。例如:
17. 这个电影明星将在一部新影片中飙戏。
1) This film star will act in a new film.
2) This film star will play a role in a new film.

"发飙"就是"情绪失控"或"发狂"的意思。英语可以译为 to get wild, to go crazy, to go mad。例如:
18. 这些拉拉队员在球场上真的发飙了。
The cheerleaders really got wild on the field.
19. 机器的噪音使我发飙了。
1) The noise of the machine made me go crazy.
2) The noise of the machine drove me crazy.
20. 当他们心爱的球队在世界杯比赛中惨败时,这些足球流氓发飙了。
These football hooligans went mad when their favourite team was defeated in the World Cup.

## 三十六、晒 工 资

### 汉语关键词
晒、晒工资、晒秘密、晒生活、晒成绩单

### 英语关键词
reveal, expose, publicize, disclose, divulge, lay bare, reveal one's salary, reveal one's private secret, lay bare one's private secret, reveal one's real life, reveal one's real-life situation, reveal one's real-life story, reveal one's school report

### 句 子
过去,没有人敢在网上晒工资。

### 误 译
In the past, nobody dared to lay bare his salary on the web.

### 正 译
In the past, nobody dared to divulge his salary on the web.

### 解 释
"晒"原来指"暴露在阳光之下"。现在被网民引申用来指"将隐私的信息通过网络公布于众"。to lay sth bare 的意思是 to show sth that was covered or to make sth known that was secret,具有"揭露秘密"或"暴露秘密"的意思。但是搜索 google,没有见到 to lay bare one's salary 这样的搭配。to lay bare 后面可以跟 secret, feeling, thought 等当宾语用。例如:

1. 他们私生活的各个方面都已爆光了。
   Every aspect of their private lives has been laid bare.
2. 害羞的人们不喜欢暴露他们的感情。
   Shy people don't like to lay bare their feelings.
3. 他把最内心的思想暴露在我面前。
   He laid bare his inmost thoughts before me.
4. 她揭示了她成功的秘密。

She laid bare the secret of her success.

to reveal 和 to expose 的意思是 to make sth known to sb,即"揭露"或"暴露",可以表示"晒"的这个意思。to publicize 的意思是 to make sth known to the public,即"公之于众",也可以表示"晒"的这个意思。to disclose的意思是 to give sb information about sth, especially sth that was previously secret,而 to divulge 的意思是 to give sb information that is supposed to be secret,二者都有"泄露秘密"的意思,也可以表示"晒"。上述5个动词都可以用 salary, wage, income 等当宾语,表示"晒工资"的意思。例如:

5. 近来,有些门户网站设立了供人们晒工资的专门区域。
Recently, some portal websites have set up special sections for people to divulge their salaries.
6. 在这些网站上,几乎各行各业的人都晒了他们的工资。
On these websites, people from almost all walks of life revealed their incomes.
7. 为什么有人在网上匿名晒他们的工资。
Why do people expose their salaries on line anonymously?
8. 这位官员拒绝在网上晒他的工资。
1) This official refused to divulge his salary on the net.
2) This official declined to publicize his salary on the net.
9. 虽然他拒绝晒工资,但是他说他收入颇丰。
Though he declined to disclose his salary, he said he was well paid.

"晒秘密"的意思是"公开个人隐私秘密"。可以译为 to reveal /expose /publicize /disclose /divulge one's private secret,也可以说 to lay bare one's private secret。例如:

10. 一些白领为减轻压力而在网上掀起晒秘密的热潮。
A few white-collared workers have set off an upsurge on line in revealing their private secrets so as to relieve pressure.
11. 现在网上流行晒秘密,其内容大多涉及个人隐私。
Disclosing one's private secret has become popular on the web, which

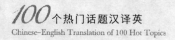

mostly involves a person's privacy.
12. 个人秘密一旦晒出来,就不再是秘密了。
Once laid bare, a person's private secret is no longer secret.

"晒生活"的意思是"公开生活的各种情况"。可以译为 to reveal one's real life, to reveal one's real-life situation, to reveal one's real-life story。例如:
13. 我愿意看本BBS上已有的晒生活的帖子。
I like to view the current topics on this bulletin board, which reveal people's real life.
14. 看了网上一连串晒生活的帖子,我了解到社会的真实状况。
After reading a thread on the web that revealed people's real-life situation, I came to know the genuine conditions of society.
15. 他建议大家都去网上晒生活,无论是烦恼,还是欢乐。
He suggests that everybody should reveal their real-life story on line, no matter whether it is an annoyance or a merriment.

"晒成绩单"的意思是"公开学习成绩"。可以译为 to reveal one's school report。例如:
16. 许多大学生在网上晒成绩单,互相比较分数。
Many university students have revealed their school reports on the net, comparing scores with each other.

# 三十七、拼　　车

● 汉语关键词
拼车、拼车族、拼车伙伴、拼车服务、拼车服务公司、拼车族车道
● 英语关键词
carpool, carpooling, take the carpool, share the ride in a carpool,

carpool partner, carpool buddy, carpooling service, ridematching service, carpool lane

### 句 子

由于燃料价格飙升,拼车吸引了越来越多的上班族。

### 误 译

As fuel prices have risen sharply, riding a car together has attracted more and more commuters.

### 正 译

As fuel prices have risen sharply, carpooling has attracted more and more commuters.

### 解 释

"拼车"的意思是"合伙乘车,并分摊费用"。to ride a car together 仅表示"同乘一辆车",并不包含"分摊费用"的意思。"拼车"的名词译为 carpool, carpooling,动词译为 to take the carpool, to share the ride in a carpool。例如:

1. "拼车"的意思是指两个或两个以上的上班族共同乘坐一部汽车,并且分摊行车费用。

   A carpool means two or more commuters ride together in one car and share driving expenses.

2. 拼车是一种合伙乘车和分摊费用的精明方法。

   Carpooling is a smart way to share your ride and your expenses.

3. 拼车的人越多,就越省钱。

   The more people there are in a carpool, the greater the savings.

4. 这个免费在线拼车数据库向你提供住处和工作离你近的其他感兴趣的上班族的名单。

   The free online carpool database provides you with a list of other interested commuters who live and work close to you.

5. 我们每隔一天拼车去学校。

   We take the carpool to school on every other day.

6. 我宁愿拼车上班，也不坐昂贵的火车。

   I would take the carpool to work, rather than the expensive train.

7. 由于我没有车，而且觉得公交车太慢，地铁太挤，打的太贵，就和一个邻居拼车。

   As I don't have a car, and I think the bus is too slow, the underground is too crowded, and the taxi is too expensive, I share rides in a carpool with one of my neighbours.

8. 我想我们一星期应该拼车或搭乘公交系统至少一两次。

   I think we should take the carpool or the public transportation system at least once or twice a week.

"拼车族"或"拼车伙伴"的意思是"合伙使用汽车的人"。英语可以译为 carpool partner, carpool buddy。例如：

9. 他正在寻找一个拼车伙伴，住处离他家在一两公里以内。

   He is seeking a carpool partner, who lives within one or two kilometres away from his home.

10. 你能帮助减少空气污染的最简便的方法之一，是找一个至少一周一次合伙乘车的拼车伙伴。

    One of the easiest ways you can help to cut down on the air pollution is to find a carpool partner to share the ride with at least one day a week!

11. 这个免费拼车网站能够协助你找寻拼车伙伴。

    This free carpooling website can assist you in the search for carpool partners.

12. 我需要一个拼车伙伴，每天早晨我能跟他乘车上班。

    I need a carpool buddy with whom I can ride to work each morning.

13. 我找到了一个拼车伙伴，他跟我有同样的日程安排，而且住得离我很近。

    I have found a carpool buddy who has the same schedule as I and lives very close to me.

"拼车服务"或"拼车服务公司"可以译为 carpooling service, ridematching service。例如:

14. 拼车服务因协助上班族拼车而受到热烈欢迎。
    Carpooling service is well received for its assistance in matching commuters.
15. 这个拼车服务公司为司机和乘客提供搭乘和驾车服务。
    This carpooling service offers lifts and rides for drivers and passengers.
16. 这个拼车服务公司给你提供在这个地区找到其他对拼车上班感兴趣的人的简便方法。
    This ridematching service provides you with an easy way to find others in this area that are interested in sharing the ride to work in a carpool.

国外有些城市鼓励拼车,为拼车族设立专门的车道,称为 carpool lane (拼车族车道)。例如:

17. 如果你在车里有至少两位乘客,你就可以走拼车族车道。
    If you have at least two passengers in your car, you may take the carpool lane.
18. 如果你能找到跟你乘车的人,你就可以走快得多的拼车族车道。
    If you can find someone to drive with, you can take the carpool lane that is a lot faster.
19. 如果汽车里就只有你一个人,你是不准走拼车族车道的。
    You are not allowed to take the carpool lane if you're the only person in the car.

# 三十八、恶 搞

● 汉语关键词

恶搞、恶搞文化、恶搞者

● 英语关键词

abusive imitation, mischievous distortion, practical joke, hoax, hoaxer, spoofing culture, juggled culture

### 句 子
这位电影导演正在遭受恶搞之苦。

### 误 译
This film director was suffering from evil doing.

### 正 译
This film director was suffering from mischievous distortion.

### 解 释
evil 的意思是"罪恶的",doing 的意思是"做"或"搞"。但是不能将"恶搞"字对字地译为 evil doing。实际上,evil doing 的意思是"罪恶行动",含义比较严重。例如:

1. 他拒绝参与罪恶的行动。
   He refused to participate in evil doing.

"恶搞"就是"恶劣的或恶作剧的搞笑",是当前流行娱乐中以文字,图片或动画为手段模仿、扭曲或篡改的一种搞笑。英语可以译为 abusive imitation, mischievous distortion, practical joke。例如:

2. 恶搞一部经典影片是不得人心的。
   An abusive imitation of a classic film is unpopular.

3. 2006 年,"恶搞"是中国最流行的词汇之一。
   In 2006, mischievous distortion was one of the most popular expressions in China.

4. 意思混淆不清给恶搞提供了许多机会。
   Confusion of meaning offers plenty of opportunity for mischievous distortion.

5. 把这样一位英雄描写成一个坏蛋,只不过是对事实的恶搞。
   Portraying such a hero as a villain is nothing but a mischievous distortion of facts.

6. 这首电视广告歌简直就是对一首古诗的恶搞。
   This jingle is simply a mischievous distortion of an ancient poem.

7. 把这种现象简单地看作"网络恶搞"是不恰当的。

   It is inappropriate to simply regard this phenomenon as a practical joke on the net.

   hoax 的意思是 an attempt to trick an audience into believing that something false is real，即"企图蒙骗观众，使其相信某个假的东西是真的"。hoax 和由 hoax 构成的词组，也可以表示"恶搞"的意思。例如：

   网络恶搞 Internet hoax
   恶搞电影 hoax film, hoax movie
   恶搞电子邮件 hoax email
   恶搞图片 hoax picture
   恶搞照片 hoax photo
   又如：

8. 我们是否能够肯定这张相片是恶搞？

   Can we be certain that this photo is a hoax?

9. 有些人深信华南虎的照片是恶搞。

   Some people believe the photo of a South China tiger is a hoax.

10. 这些恐龙图片已被揭露是恶搞。

    These pictures of dinosaurs have been exposed as hoaxes.

11. 与欺诈、欺骗和诈骗等比较激烈的字眼相比，恶搞是个相当温和的词汇。

    Compared with harsher words like fraud, cheat and swindle, hoax is a rather gentle term.

12. 公鸡下蛋是头号恶搞新闻。

    That the cock laid an egg tops the hoax list.

13. 这个网络恶搞以一名 13 岁女孩自杀而告终，这引起她家人的呼吁，要求得到更好的保护从而不受网络骚扰。

    This Internet hoax ended with the suicide of a 13-year-old girl, which has led to calls from her family for better protections against online harassment.

14. 许多人不喜欢这部恶搞电影，认为它不道德。

    Many people dislike this hoax film, thinking it immoral.

15. 你可以完全不理睬这些恶搞电子邮件。

    You may completely disregard these hoax emails.

16. 这是他创造的恶搞图片。

    This is the hoax picture that he created.

17. 我们需要找三个不同的人来评价这张恶搞图片。

    We need to get three different people to evaluate this hoax picture.

"恶搞文化"是当前流行的玩笑文化。英语可以译为 spoofing culture 或 juggled culture。例如：

18. 恶搞文化最近在中国网络上兴起。

    Spoofing culture has recently emerged on the web in China.

19. 恶搞文化的兴起表现出传媒素养教育的缺失。

    The emergence of spoofing culture shows the lack of quality education on the part of media.

20. 新型的恶搞文化是一种在高科技支助下的玩笑文化。

    New juggled culture is a kind of joking culture supported by high technology.

"恶搞者"可以译为 hoaxer。例如：

21. 恶搞者把自身的愉悦建立在别人的痛苦之上，是很不道德的。

    It is immoral for those hoaxers to base their own happiness on the suffering of other people.

22. 这些恶搞者正试图通过戏说经典作品来颠覆传统文化。

    These hoaxers are trying to subvert traditional culture through altering classic works in a ridiculous way.

# 三十九、违 章

### 汉语关键词
违章、违章作业、违章开车、违章建筑

### 英语关键词
break the regulation, disobey the regulation, violate the regulation, be against regulations, go against regulations, work against regulations, operate against regulations, drive against traffic regulations, unauthorized construction, unauthorized building works, unauthorized building, unauthorized house

### 句 子
你在这里停车是违章的。

### 误 译
You are against the regulation to park your car here.

### 正 译
It is against the regulation for you to park your car here.

### 解 释
这句话的逻辑主语是"你在这里停车",而不是"你"。此外,英语没有 You are against the regulation to do sth 这样的句型。

"违章"就是"违反规章或法规,尤其指违反交通法规"。英语可以译为 to break the regulation, to disobey the regulation, to violate the regulation。例如:

1. 谁也无权违反校规。
   Nobody has the right to break the school regulations.
2. 违章者将受到惩罚。
   Those who broke the regulations would be punished.
3. 公司可以警告、惩罚或甚至开除那些违反规章和纪律的人。
   The corporation may warn, punish or even fire those who disobey the regulation and discipline.

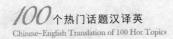

# 100个热门话题汉译英
## Chinese-English Translation of 100 Hot Topics

4. 下雪或其他恶劣的天气状况并不是可以违章的正当理由。

   Snow or other severe weather conditions are not valid reasons to disobey the regulations.

5. 那些违章的人面临严重的罪名。

   Those who disobey the regulations are faced with serious charges.

6. 他因违反交通法规而被罚款。

   He was fined for violating traffic regulations.

   "违章"还可以译为 to be against regulations, to go against regulations。

例如：

7. 超速驾驶是违章的。

   It is against traffic regulations to drive over the speed limit.

8. 司机闯红灯是违章的。

   1) It is against traffic regulations for a driver to go through a red light.

   2) It is against traffic regulations for a driver to drive through a red light.

   3) It is against traffic regulations for a driver to run a red light.

9. 酒醉开车是违章的。

   Driving while intoxicated is against traffic regulations.

10. 乱穿马路是违章的。

    Jaywalking is against traffic regulations.

11. 行人在红灯亮时走过十字路口是违章的。

    It is against traffic regulations for a pedestrian to go through an intersection when the light is red.

12. 作弊违反考场规则。

    Cheating goes against exam room regulations.

13. 直排轮滑者要注意：在马路上轮滑是违章的。

    Inline skaters are to note that it is against traffic regulations to skate on roads.

14. 这个摩托车手不戴头盔驾车，那是违章的。

The motorcyclist drove without a helmet, which was against traffic regulations.

"违章作业"可以译为 to work against regulations, to operate against regulations。例如:
15. 违章作业是危险的。
    Working against regulations is dangerous.
16. 禁止煤矿工人违章作业。
    Coal miners are forbidden to operate against regulations.
17. 乘坐违章作业的车辆旅行是不安全的。
    It is not safe for you to travel by vehicles that operate against regulations.

"违章开车"可以译为 to drive against traffic regulations。例如:
18. 他因违章开车而被罚款。
    He was fined for driving against traffic regulations.

"违章建筑"的第一个意思是指"未经授权或批准而私自搭建的建筑物"。英语可以译为 unauthorized construction, unauthorized building works, unauthorized building, unauthorized house 等。例如:
19. 铁路当局采取了步骤来清除沿铁路主干线的违章建筑。
    The railway authorities took steps to remove the unauthorized constructions along the main rail-line.
20. 地方当局要求这家工厂拆除这些违章建筑。
    The local authorities required the factory to tear down these unauthorized constructions.
21. 违章建筑是应该被拆除的非法建筑物。
    Unauthorized building works are illegal works that should be removed.
22. 违章建筑一定会拆除。
    An unauthorized building is liable for demolition.
23. 这些在公共露天空地上建造的违章房屋将被拆除。
    These unauthorized houses constructed on the public open space will be

demolished.

"违章建筑"的第二个意思是指"无视规章而私自搭建的建筑物"。英语可以译为 house/building that was put up in defiance of regulations。例如：

24. 这些居民已经拆除了在公共绿地上搭建的违章建筑。

These residents have knocked down the houses that were put up in defiance of regulations on the public meadow.

25. 这些违章建筑不受法律保护。

These buildings that were put up in defiance of regulations are not under the protection of law.

# 四十、上　市

● 汉语关键词

上市、上市公司、非上市公司、上市股票

● 英语关键词

appear on the market, be available on the market, come in, go to the market, go public, be listed, public company, listed company, private company, unlisted company, listed share, listed stock

● 句　子

他在一家私营公司工作。

● 误　译

He works in a private company.

● 正　译

He works in a privately-owned company.

● 解　释

汉语的"公"与"私"，英语可以分别用 public 和 private 表示。但是

public company 的意思不是"公有公司",而是"上市公司";private company 的意思不是"私营公司",而是"非上市公司"。汉语的"公有"指"全民所有"或"集体所有"。"公有公司"可以指"国有公司",英语译为 state-owned company,或"国营公司",英语译为 state-run company;还可以指"集体所有公司",英语译为 collectively-owned company。汉语的"私有"与"公有"相对立,指"私人所有"。"私有公司"和"私营公司"都译为 privately-owned company。

　　"上市"的第一个意思是"货物(尤其是应时商品,如新鲜水果和蔬菜、及服装等)开始在市场出售"。英语可以译为 to appear on the market, to be available on the market, to come in。例如:
1. 今天,西瓜开始上市。
　　Today, watermelons have begun to appear on the market.
2. 阳澄湖的大闸蟹刚一上市就受到顾客们的青睐。
　　As soon as the live freshwater crabs from the Yangcheng Lake appeared on the market, they received welcome from the customers.
3. 秋季女装刚刚上市。
　　Ladies' autumn fashions have just appeared on the market.
4. 一种新型小汽车现在上市了。
　　A new type of tiny cars is now available on the market.
5. 这种新型计算机还未上市。
　　This new type of computers is not yet available on the market.
6. 我问他新鲜草莓是否已经上市。
　　I asked him if fresh strawberries had come in.

　　"上市"的第二个意思是"到市场去"。英语可以译为 to go to the market。例如:
7. 每天早晨,我妈妈提着篮子上市去买新鲜蔬菜。
　　Every morning, my mother goes to the market to buy fresh vegetables with a basket in her hand.

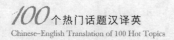

"上市"的第三个意思是"股票、债券和基金等经批准后在证券交易所挂牌交易"。英语可以译为 to go public, to be listed。例如:

8. 这个公司最近在香港上市。
   This company has recently gone public in Hong Kong.
9. 你的公司做好上市的准备了吗?
   Is your company ready to go public?
10. 2000年,我们的公司在纽约证券交易所上市。
    Our company was listed on the New York Stock Exchange in 2000.
11. 在香港注册上市的大陆公司发行的股票被列为红筹股。
    The mainland-funded corporations registered and listed in Hong Kong are referred to as red chips.
12. 中国在新加坡股票市场上市最早的企业可以追溯到1993年。
    The earliest Chinese company listed on Singapore stock market can be dated back to 1993.

"上市公司"的意思是"经有关部门核准公开发行股票并在证券交易所挂牌交易的股份有限公司"。英语可以译为 public company, listed company。例如:

13. 这家芯片制造商是纳斯达克上市公司。
    The chip manufacturer is a listed company on the NASDAQ.
14. 每个上市公司都必须设立一个内部审计职能部门。
    Every listed company must have an internal audit function.

"非上市公司"的意思是"不在证券交易所挂牌交易的公司"。英语可以译为 private company, unlisted company。例如:

15. 通常一家上市公司的股票为许多投资者所拥有,而一家非上市公司的股票为相对少的股东所拥有。
    Usually, the securities of a public company are owned by many investors while the shares of a private company are owned by relatively few shareholders.
16. 这家非上市公司已被一个匿名的投资者接管。

This unlisted company has been taken over by an anonymous investor.

"上市股票"的意思是"可以在证券交易所挂牌交易的股票"。英语可以译为 listed share, listed stock。例如：

17. 这位投资者持有这个电脑公司上市股票的30%。
    The investor owns 30% of the listed shares of this computer company.
18. 在德国，小股民常常通过银行买卖上市股票。
    In Germany, small shareholders often buy and sell listed stocks through banks.

## 四十一、瓶　　颈

### ● 汉语关键词
瓶颈、突破瓶颈

### ● 英语关键词
neck of a bottle, shoulder of a neck, bottleneck, break through the bottleneck, open the bottleneck, break open the bottleneck

### ● 句　子
我们正在努力突破经济发展中的瓶颈。

### ● 误　译
We are trying hard to break the bottleneck in economic development.

### ● 正　译
We are trying hard to break through the bottleneck in economic development.

### ● 解　释
to break 的意思是"打破"，其宾语是具体实物。to break through 的意思是"突破"，其宾语是具有比喻意义的事情。例如：

1. 他打碎了瓶子的颈部。
   He broke the neck of a bottle.

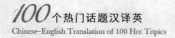

2. 你在外国旅行时怎样突破语言障碍?
   How do you break through the language barrier when you travel in a foreign country?

"瓶颈"的字面意思是指瓶口下面较细的部分。英语可以译为 neck of a bottle。而 shoulder of a neck 指紧靠瓶颈以下部位。例如:

3. 当你打开啤酒瓶时,瓶颈部分会形成一小团白烟。
   A small cloud forms in the neck of a bottle of beer when you open it.
4. 围着瓶颈可以贴上酒瓶标识,这样能够很容易看到与其他酒瓶的区别。
   A bottle identifier may be placed around the neck of a bottle so that the bottle may be readily visually distinguished from other bottles.
5. 沉渣上升到紧靠瓶颈以下部位的时候,就不要倒酒了。
   As soon as the sediment starts creeping up the shoulder of the bottle, stop pouring.
6. 裂纹出现在瓶颈及紧靠瓶颈以下部位。
   The defect occurred in the neck and shoulder of a bottle.
7. 为了避免在瓶颈上进行加工时损坏紧靠瓶颈以下的部位,先使瓶颈以下部位硬化是大有帮助的。
   To avoid destroying the shoulder of a bottle while working on the neck, it is helpful to allow the shoulder to stiffen first.
8. 山谷轮廓呈瓶状,瓶颈朝向东北,而朝南部分变得非常宽阔。
   The valley is bottle-shaped in contour, with the neck of the bottle to the northeast, and it widens very considerably towards the south.

"瓶颈"的引申意思是比喻事情进行中容易发生障碍的关键部分。英语可以译为 bottleneck。例如:

9. 瓶颈是在一个过程中造成全过程减缓速度或停止不前的一个阶段。
   A bottleneck is a stage in a process that causes the entire process to slow down or stop.

10. 电力供应不足已经成为经济发展的一个瓶颈。
    The insufficiency of power supply has become a bottleneck in economic development.
11. 缺乏诚信已成商务活动中的瓶颈。
    Lack of honesty has become a bottleneck in commercial activities.
12. 只有一个人做秘书事务,已造成我们工作中的真正瓶颈。
    Having only one person to do the clerical job has caused a real bottleneck in our work.
13. 交通不便已造成山区经济发展的瓶颈。
    The inconvenience in transportation has created a bottleneck in the economic development in mountainous areas.

"瓶颈"还可以指"道路容易引起交通阻塞的狭窄部分或拥堵现象"。英语可以译为 bottleneck。例如:

14. 高速公路路线的真正瓶颈在高速公路本身。
    The true bottleneck on the expressway route is at the expressway itself.
15. 我不得不坐在车里通过高速公路上的瓶颈,不知道我是否会赶不上9点钟的会议。
    I have to sit through that bottleneck on the expressway, wondering if I'll be late for the 9 o'clock meeting.
16. 关闭高速公路上的一个或一个以上的车道会造成高速公路的瓶颈。
    The closure of one or more lanes of a freeway section causes a bottleneck on the freeway.
17. 他在慢车道里缓慢行驶,于是越来越多的人在高速公路上形成一个大的瓶颈,会造成严重堵车。
    He drove slowly in the slow lane, so more and more people could build a huge bottleneck on the freeway that would cause a major traffic jam.
18. 地方交通部门领导人害怕因为消除了大桥附近的瓶颈,在高速公路上的下一处瓶颈堵车会更加严重。
    Local transportation leaders feared that by eliminating the bottleneck

near the bridge, congestion would worsen at the next bottleneck on the freeway.

19. 由于我开车上下班，我就试图在过了高峰时间以后上路，但是我偶尔也会遭遇高速公路上的瓶颈。
    As I drive to or from work, I try to leave after rush hours, but occasionally I find myself in a traffic bottleneck on the freeway.
20. 谁也不想开车陷在高速公路上的瓶颈里。
    Nobody wants to be stuck in a car bottleneck on the freeway.
21. 每天早晨我开车送孩子上学时，我们都会在高速公路上遭遇瓶颈。
    Every morning when I take my child to school in my car, we would encounter a bottleneck on the freeway.

"突破瓶颈"可以译为 to break through the bottleneck, to open the bottleneck, to break open the bottleneck。例如：

22. 那是能够突破我省高速公路瓶颈的一个想法。
    That's an idea that could break through the bottleneck on the freeways of our province.
23. 我们的目标是突破保护历史遗产和经济发展之间的瓶颈。
    Our aim is to break through the bottleneck between the protection of historic heritage and the development of economy.
24. 他正在思考如何突破英语学习中的瓶颈。
    He is thinking about how to break through the bottleneck in his English learning.
25. 他们正在讨论如何突破我们城市拥堵的空中空间的瓶颈。
    They are discussing how to open the bottleneck of our city's congested airspace.
26. 我们正在使用这个新模型来帮助突破革新的瓶颈。
    We're using this new model to help break open the bottleneck of innovation.

# 四十二、潜 规 则

### 汉语关键词
潜规则、被潜规则

### 英语关键词
hidden rule, latent rule, underlying rule, unspoken rule, casting couch, be forced to share a casting couch with sb

### 句 子
这个女演员自曝曾被某导演潜规则。

### 误 译
The actress exposed that she had been taken in by a certain director through the potential rule.

### 正 译
The actress exposed that she had been forced to share a casting couch with a certain director.

### 解 释
潜规则指在一个圈子里心照不宣、然而大多数成员默许和恪守的不成文的行为规则。它本来是个名词,在这里变成了动词。to be taken in 的意思是 to be deceived,"被欺骗"没有表达出"被潜规则"的含义。娱乐圈的潜规则,指的是"演员为上镜与导演之间进行性交换",带有贬义。potential 是个中性词,指"现在还不是,而将来会变成的",即"潜在的",例如:potential customer(潜在的顾客),potential buyer(潜在的买主),potential problem(潜在的问题),potential threat(潜在的威胁),potential effect(潜在的效果)。而 potential rule 的意思是"现在还不是,而将来可能会变成的规则",将"潜规则"译成 potential rule 是不妥的。美国好莱坞圈内潜规则事件屡见不鲜,英语可以用 casting couch 表示"潜规则";用 to be forced to share a casting couch with sb 表示"被潜规则"。casting 的字面意义是"导演选择演员",couch 则指"试镜室内的躺椅"。casting couch 的比喻意义为

a euphemism for a sociological phenomenon that involves the trading of sexual favours by an aspirant, apprentice, employee, or subordinate to a superior, in return for entry into an occupation, or for other career advancement within an organization,即"为进入圈内或晋升而与上司进行性交换"。例如:

1. 这个年轻女演员利用潜规则进入电影业。
   The young actress used the casting couch to enter the film industry.
2. 实际上,潜规则并不完全是那样起作用的。
   Actually that's not quite how Casting Couch works.
3. 潜规则是神话,还是现实?
   Is the casting couch a myth or a reality?
4. 人们就好莱坞的潜规则已经写了许多文章。
   Much has been written about the casting couch in Hollywood.
5. 潜规则的事在娱乐圈内不再是什么秘密。
   The casting couch is no longer a secret in the entertainment circles.

"潜规则"在一般不带有负面意义情况下,可以译为 hidden rule, latent rule, underlying rule 或 unspoken rule。例如:

6. 各行各业都有潜规则。
   All trades and professions have their own hidden rules.
7. 娱乐圈的潜规则是什么?
   What is the latent rule in the entertainment circles?
8. 如果你想进入演艺界从业,你必须接受和遵循娱乐圈的潜规则。
   If you want to pursue a career in the entertainment industry, you have to accept and follow the latent rule in the entertainment circles.
9. 显然,他没有意识到官场存在潜规则。
   Obviously, he was unaware of the existence of an underlying rule in the officialdom.
10. 这位女市长遭遇了官场潜规则。
    The mayoress encountered the hidden rule in the officialdom.

11. 这位职业经理人现身说法揭露了商场潜规则。
    The professional manager exposed the underlying rule in the commercial circles through his own examples.
12. 谁也不想破除这个在职场久已存在的潜规则。
    Nobody wanted to break this unspoken rule that had long existed in the professional circles.
13. 这些玩家正在试图了解这个游戏的潜规则。
    The players are trying to understand the hidden rule of the game.
14. 关于财富的一个潜规则是人们不谈论钱,但是谈论投资。
    A hidden rule of wealth is that money is not discussed but investments are.
15. 外人不知道的是:在演艺圈内有个潜规则。
    What the outsiders do not know is that there is a hidden rule in the show business.
16. 我认为在牙医中间有个潜规则,就是他们必须让你再次回来看牙,所以他们永远不会把治疗全部恰当地做完。
    I think there is this underlying rule with dentists that they must keep you coming back for more, so they never quite finish the job properly.
17. 他试图挑战和抵御这个潜规则,但是白费力气。
    He tried in vain to challenge and resist the underlying rule.
18. 不管你对此是否理解,它就是潜规则。
    Whether you understand this or not, it is the underlying rule.
19. 在英国这里的潜规则是:开门见山就谈生意是不礼貌的。
    The underlying rule here in England is that it is impolite to start talking business right away.
20. 关于这类事情存在潜规则。
    There is an unspoken rule about this kind of thing.
21. 我问过演艺圈内几十个人是否听说过这个潜规则。
    I asked dozens of people in the entertainment business if they had heard of this unspoken rule.

22. 这个潜规则已被当作常识而实行。
    This unspoken rule has been enforced as a common sense.
23. 常常会遇到这样一个潜规则，就是一个家庭的母亲是呆在家里抚养孩子的家长。
    It has often been an unspoken rule that the mother of a family is the parent to stay at home to raise the children.
24. 在世界的每个部分，在每种文化里，都存在一种社交生活的潜规则。
    In every part of the world and in every culture, there is an unspoken rule of social life.

# 四十三、盘　　点

● 汉语关键词

盘点、盘货、盘存、盘库、盘账

● 英语关键词

stocktaking, make an inventory of, take an inventory of, take inventory, take stock, review, examine, check accounts, examine accounts

● 句　子

年终时，这位博客盘点了今年我国娱乐圈10大新闻。

● 误　译

At the end of the year, the blogger took stock of the ten top news items of the year in China's entertainment circles.

● 正　译

1) At the end of the year, the blogger reviewed the ten top news items of the year in China's entertainment circles.

2) At the end of the year, the blogger examined the ten top news items of the year in China's entertainment circles.

## 解 释

　　to take stock 的字面意思是"盘货";而其引申意思是 to consider a situation carefully so as to take a decision,即"仔细考虑形势以做出决定"。这句话中的"盘点"是"回顾总结"的意思,应译为 to review 或 to examine。例如:

1. 人们需要不时地从繁忙的生活中回过来考量一下他们正在做什么,他们正在向何处去。
   People need to occasionally step back from their busy life to take stock of how they're doing and where they're going.
2. 在做出不可改变的决定之前,你应该先坐下来估量一下形势。
   You should sit back and take stock of the situation before you make an irrevocable decision.

　　"盘点"原义是"清点存货"。英语可以译为 to make an inventory of, to take an inventory of, to take inventory, to take stock 或 stock-taking。to make an inventory of 的意思是 to make a list of all the things in a place 或 to check and count all the things in a place,即"清点";尤其指 to make a list of all the goods in a shop 或 to check and count all the goods in a shop,即"盘货"。例如:

3. 你们应该学会如何盘点你们的个人财产。
   You should learn how to make an inventory of your personal property.
4. 我们应定期盘点库存物资。
   We should make a periodical inventory of the goods in our warehouse.
5. 今日盘点,暂停营业。
   Business is suspended today for stocktaking.
6. 每逢星期一下午,那家商场进行盘点。
   Every Monday afternoon, the department store takes stock.

　　to make/take an inventory of 还有 to make a list of all the people in a place 或 to check and count all the people in a place 的意思,即"清点人数"。

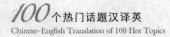

例如:
7. 让我们清点一下到目前为止所有已经捐献的慷慨人士。
   Let's take an inventory of all the generous people that have donated so far.

"盘点"的比喻意义是"逐个重新审视或回顾总结"。英语可以译为 to review, to examine。例如:
8. 今天这家报纸用一整版篇幅盘点了本市今年10大新闻。
   Today, this newspaper devotes a whole page to reviewing the top 10 news items of the year in our city.
9. 这一年里,教育界有不少值得盘点的事件。
   In this year, there are quite a lot of events that are worth examining in the educational circles.
10. 这个杂志在最近一期盘点了当前流行的5种减肥方法。
    In the latest issue of the magazine, they have reviewed the five slimming ways that are fashionable at the moment.

"盘点"的比喻意义也可以用 to make an inventory of 表示。例如:
11. 他盘点了他作为本科生所做的一切事情。
    He made an inventory of everything he had done as an undergraduate.

"盘存"、"盘货"和"盘库"都有"盘点存货"或"清点与核查现有资产的数量和情况"的意思。英语也可以译为 to make an inventory of, to take an inventory of, to take inventory, to take stock 或 stock-taking。例如:
12. 本店月底定期盘存。
    Our store takes inventory regularly at the end of a month.
13. 有些商店每月盘货一次。
    Some stores take their stock once a month.
14. 年终时,我们彻底盘了一次库。
    We made a complete inventory of everything in the warehouse at the end of the year.

"盘账"的意思是"清点与核对账目"。英语可以译为 to check accounts, to examine accounts。例如:

15. 不论怎样,你们必须经常盘账。
    In any case, you have to check accounts often.
16. 这个商店一年盘一次账。
    In this store, they check accounts once a year.
17. 他受权在这个公司盘账。
    He is authorized to examine accounts in this company.

## 四十四、膨　　胀

### 汉语关键词
膨胀、人口膨胀、通货膨胀

### 英语关键词
expand, swell, dilate, population expansion, inflation

### 句　子
物体热胀冷缩。

### 误　译
Objects inflate when heated and contract on cooling.

### 正　译
Objects expand when heated and contract on cooling.

### 解　释
这句话的译者以为既然 inflation 是"通货膨胀",那么反推 to inflate 就有"膨胀"的意思。其实,to inflate 的意思是 to fill with air or gas,即"充气使之胀大",与热胀冷缩无关。例如:

1. 他用气筒将气球充满气。
   He used a tyre pump to inflate the balloon to its full.

# 100个热门话题汉译英
## Chinese-English Translation of 100 Hot Topics

"膨胀"的第一个意思指"物体因温度升高而体积增大或长度增加",是自然现象。英语可以译为 to expand, to swell, to dilate。例如:

2. 金属受热膨胀。
   1) Metals expand when heated.
   2) Metals undergo expansion when heated.
3. 水结冰时体积膨胀。
   Water expands as it freezes.
4. 热使物质膨胀。
   1) Heat causes matter to expand.
   2) Heat is the cause of the expansion of matter.
5. 热使空气膨胀。
   Heat causes air to expand.
6. 发动机汽缸内的气体膨胀。
   The gas in the cylinder of an engine expands.
7. 管道因液体膨胀或收缩而变形。
   The tube is distorted as the liquid expands or contracts.
8. 水银和酒精等大多数液体热胀冷缩。
   Most liquids, such as mercury and alcohol, expand when heated and contract on cooling.
9. 木材潮湿后往往会膨胀。
   Wood often swells when wet.
10. 木头在水里膨胀。
    Wood swells in water.
11. 当血管膨胀时,体温下降。
    When blood vessels dilate, the body temperature is reduced.
12. 发炎时,如果脑血管膨胀,脑中血流可能紊乱,导致脑损伤。
    During inflammation, if brain blood vessels dilate, then blood flow can become maldistributed in the brain, leading to brain damage.
13. 这位眼科专家解释了为什么我们的眼球会膨胀。
    The eye specialist explained why the pupils in our eyes could dilate.

"膨胀"的第二个意思指"某些事物增长或扩大",是社会现象。英语可以译为 to expand 或 expansion。例如:
14. 世界人口正在迅速膨胀。
    The world population is expanding rapidly.
15. 希特勒的征服世界的野心进一步膨胀。
    Hitler's ambition to conquer the world expanded further.
16. 腐朽思想的恶性膨胀导致这名官员的腐败。
    The malignant expansion of decadent thinking gave rise to the corruption of this official.

"人口膨胀"可以译为 population expansion;"通货膨胀"可以译为 (currency) inflation。例如:
17. 人口膨胀已给这个非洲国家的经济产生负面影响。
    Population expansion has made negative effects on the economy of this African country.
18. 在这个亚洲国家,通货膨胀率已经超过了8%。
    In this Asian country, the level of inflation has gone beyond 8%.
19. 这位经济学家把通货膨胀大幅度增长归咎于石油价格的上涨。
    The economist blamed the rise in oil prices for the big increase in inflation.
20. 政府正试图缓和通货膨胀的影响。
    The government is trying to mitigate the effects of inflation.
21. 经济学家们预言明年通货膨胀率将会增长。
    The economists predicted an increase in the rate of inflation next year.
22. 新政府的主要任务是减低通货膨胀的水平。
    The new government's prime task is to reduce the level of inflation.
23. 政府已采取新措施控制通货膨胀。
    The government has adopted new measures to curb inflation.
24. 政府已采取各种措施控制通货膨胀。
    The government has taken various measures to control inflation.

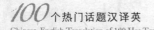

25. 中国政府下决心努力在2008年将通货膨胀率控制在4.8%以下。
    The Chinese government has determined to make an effort to control the inflation rate less than 4.8% in 2008.
26. 这个南美国家政府试图通过削减货币供应来抑制通货膨胀。
    The government of the South American country seeks to stem inflation by cutting money supply.
27. 目前没有证据表明在中国通货膨胀已经失去控制。
    So far, there has been no evidence showing that inflation has got out of control in China.
28. 在这个拉丁美洲国家,通货膨胀已使食物价格飞涨。
    In this Lain American country, inflation has sent food costs soaring.
29. 在这个非洲国家,去年的通货膨胀率是一位数。
    In this African country, inflation was single-digit last year.
30. 我的工资跟不上通货膨胀。
    My salary can't keep up with inflation.

## 四十五、枪　　手

● 汉语关键词

枪手、神枪手、火枪手、射击手、持枪杀手、职业杀手、代考者、捉刀代笔者

● 英语关键词

marksman, expert marksman, sharpshooter, crack shot, musketeer, gunman, hit man, hatchet man, proxy examinee, substitute examinee, substitute testee, ghostwriter

● 句　子

这位总统候选人被一名枪手谋杀。

● 误　译

The presidential candidate was deliberately shot by a gunner.

### 正 译

The presidential candidate was deliberately shot by a gunman.

### 解 释

汉语有"枪"与"炮"之分,而英语都用 gun 表示。我们可以用 big gun 或 large gun 表示"炮"或"大炮"。英语的 gunner 和 gunman 不是一回事。gunner 的意思是 a member of the armed forces who is trained to use large guns,即"炮手"。gunman 的意思是 a man armed with a gun to rob or kill people,即"持枪杀手",与 criminal(罪犯)或 terrorist(恐怖分子)有关。

"枪手"的第一个意思是"射击手"。英语可以译为 marksman,即 a person who is trained to shoot precisely with a certain type of rifle。"神枪手"译为 expert marksman, sharpshooter, crack shot。"火枪手"译为 musketeer。例如:

1. 这个枪手能从远处非常准确地射击。
The marksman can shoot very accurately from a long distance.
2. 这个枪手站在房顶上对着空中开枪。
The marksman standing on the roof of a house fired a gun into the air.
3. 对于一名枪手来说,找到一支好枪并知道如何使用它是不够的。
For a marksman, finding a good gun and knowing how to use it won't be enough.
4. 他是一名神枪手,曾因卓越的步枪射击技术而数次获奖。
He was an expert marksman who had won awards for his excellent rifle skills.
5. 神枪手需要一支轻便、准确而性能可靠的步枪。
A sharpshooter needs a rifle that is light, accurate and reliable.
6. 我估摸一个月的紧张训练将会使他变成一名神枪手。
I figure one month of intense training will turn him into a crack shot.
7. 这部电影是根据法国作家大仲马的小说《三个火枪手》改编的。
The film was adapted from the novel entitled *The Three Musketeers* by the French writer Alexandre Dumas.

# 100 个热门话题汉译英
## Chinese-English Translation of 100 Hot Topics

8. 大家是否知道法国作家大仲马笔下的三个火枪手？
   I wonder whether you all know about the three musketeers portrayed by the French writer Alexandre Dumas.

"枪手"的第二个意思是"持枪杀手"。英语可以译为 gunman。例如：

9. 报纸的大标题为："八人被枪手杀害"。
   "Eight shot dead by gunmen" ran the newspaper headline.

10. 搜查范围已经缩小到枪手可能藏身的几条街。
    The searching has narrowed down to a few streets where the gunman might be hiding.

11. 他拔枪的速度快于任何其他枪手。
    1) He can draw his gun from a holster faster than any other gunman.
    2) He can outdraw any other gunman.

12. 在枪击后的混乱中,枪手逃走了。
    In the midst of the chaos which followed the shooting, the gunman escaped.

13. 三个人被一名精神失常的枪手打死。
    Three people were killed by a deranged gunman.

"枪手"的第三个意思是"受雇替人卖命杀人者",即"职业杀手"。英语可以译为 hit man 或 hatchet man。例如：

14. 这名枪手是名受雇于一个犯罪组织的职业杀手。
    The hit man was hired by a crime syndicate as a professional killer.

15. 这个人因企图雇佣枪手杀死对手而被判处五年徒刑。
    The man was sentenced to serve five years in prison for trying to hire a hatchet man to kill his opponent.

"枪手"的第四个意思是"受雇替人考试者",即"代考者"。英语可以译为 proxy examinee, substitute examinee, substitute testee。例如：

16. 这个网站公开招聘考研枪手提供考试作弊服务。
    The website openly invites applications for proxy examinees in the

entrance examination of postgraduates so as to provide service for exam cheating.

17. 这所大学的布告栏上出现了"寻考研枪手"的广告。
On the notice board of the university there has appeared an advertisement to seek substitute examinees for the entrance examination of postgraduates.

18. 有人张贴广告高薪聘请考研枪手。
Someone has put up an ad to employ a substitute testee for the entrance examination of postgraduates with high pay.

19. 这个学院有一名大学生雇枪手代考四级考试。
A student from this college hired a substitute examinee on his behalf in CET Band 4.

"枪手"的第五个意思是"受雇替人撰写论文或书籍者"或"捉刀代笔者"。英语可以译为 ghostwriter。例如：

20. 她雇了一名枪手替她写论文。
She hired a ghostwriter to write an article on her behalf.

21. 这个出版商正在寻找枪手写一本儿童书籍。
The publisher is looking for a ghostwriter to write a children's book.

"枪手"的第六个意思是"受雇替人写文章攻击和漫骂他人者"。英语可以译为 ghostwriter。例如：

22. 娱乐圈内不时地有枪手炮制影星丑闻。
From time to time, some ghostwriters in the entertainment circles cook up scandals about film stars.

23. 在论坛上有些人时常聘请枪手来污蔑他们的对手或者帮助抬高他们的身价。
In the forum, some people often employ ghostwrites to slander their opponents or help to build up them.

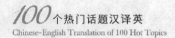

# 四十六、雪　灾

● 汉语关键词

暴雪、暴风雪、大雪、雪灾、冻雨、灾区

● 英语关键词

snowstorm, blizzard, heavy snow, snow disaster, snow havoc, frozen rain, freezing rain, icy rain, sleet, disaster-affected area, disaster-attacked area, disaster-hit area, disaster-plagued area, disaster-stricken area

● 句　子

一些村庄已被这场大雪隔绝。

● 误　译

Several villages have been separated by the heavy snow.

● 正　译

1) Several villages have been isolated by the heavy snow.
2) Several villages have been cut off by the heavy snow.

● 解　释

to separate 的意思是 to divide things into different parts，只表示将事物分成不同部分，没有"隔绝"的含义。

"暴雪"或"暴风雪"可以译为 snowstorm, blizzard。"大雪"可以译为 heavy snow。例如：

1. 最近，这个地区遭受强烈暴风雪袭击。
   1) Recently, this area has been affected by a bad snowstorm.
   2) Recently, this area has been attacked by an intense snowstorm.
   3) Recently, this area has been hit by a severe snowstorm.
   4) Recently, this area has been plagued by a strong snowstorm.
   5) Recently, this area has been stricken by a violent snowstorm.
2. 几千辆汽车在高速公路上被暴雪围困了一个星期。
   1) Thousands of cars got stuck in a bad snowstorm on the expressway

for a week.
2) Thousands of cars were snowed up in a blizzard on the expressway for a week.
3) Thousands of cars were snowed in on the expressway for a week.
4) Thousands of cars were surrounded by heavy snow on the expressway for a week.

3. 全中国人民团结起来援助华中和华南地区遭受严重暴雪袭击的灾民。
All the Chinese people rallied to assist the victims affected by the heavy snowstorms in Central and Southern China.

4. 这场大雪切断了水电供应,使得几百万想回家过年的人们滞留。
The heavy snow cut off power and water supplies and stranded millions of people trying to get home for the Lunar New Year.

"雪灾"可以译为 snow disaster, snow havoc。例如：

5. 只要我们紧密团结,就一定能够克服雪灾造成的困难。
We can surely overcome the difficulties caused by the snow disaster as long as we are closely united.

6. 中国政府面对国家几十年未遇的最严重暴风雪立即采取了有效行动。
The Chinese government took immediate and effective actions in the face of the country's worst snow disaster for decades.

7. 很难估计最近的雪灾所造成的巨大损失。
It is hard to estimate the tremendous damage caused by the recent snow disasters.

8. 在过去的6天里,雪灾迫使3,250个航班被取消。
Snow havoc has forced cancellation of 3,250 flights over the past six days.

9. 最近的雪灾已使我国遭受严重经济损失。
The recent snow havoc has caused heavy economic losses in our country.

"灾区"可以译为 disaster-affected area, disaster-attacked area, disaster-hit area, disaster-plagued area, disaster-stricken area。例如:

10. 这些灾区已从长时间恶劣天气造成的交通和电力供应中断的混乱中恢复过来。
    These disaster-affected areas have recovered from transport and power chaos triggered by a long spell of bad weather.

11. 在这个灾区,当地人民已经停电几个星期了。
    In this disaster-attacked area, the local people have seen its power supply cut for a few weeks.

12. 在这些灾区,人们遭受了持续的大雪、冻雨和寒冷天气的袭击。
    In these disaster-hit areas, the people have suffered from prolonged heavy snow, icy rain and cold weather.

13. 随着中断的交通和电力供应一天天恢复以及人民生活状况一天天改善,华东和华南一些省份的灾区生活正在逐渐恢复正常。
    Life in disaster-plagued areas in some provinces of East and South China is gradually returning to normal, with the disrupted transport and power supply being resumed and the living conditions of the people being improved day by day.

14. 这些灾区的生活必需品的价格一直保持平稳。
    Prices of living necessities in these disaster-stricken areas have remained steady.

"冻雨"可以译为 frozen rain, freezing rain, icy rain, sleet。例如:

15. 冬季的暴风雨可能带来普通的雨、冻雨和雪。
    Winter storms can bring ordinary rain, freezing rain and snow.

16. 雪和冻雨袭击了这个地区。
    A mix of snow and freezing rain has pummeled this area.

17. 华南许多地区仍然有大雪和冻雨。
    Much of South China is still getting heavy snow and sleet.

18. 当下冻雨时,雨雪混合由天空落下。
    When it sleets, a mixture of rain and snow falls from the sky.
19. 在一些地区,大雪、冻雨以及狂风天气使得人们难以驾车。
    In some areas, snow, icy rain and blustery conditions have made it difficult to drive.
20. 许多人不会区分冻雨和冰雹。
    Many people can't make a distinction between frozen rain and hail.

# 四十七、高　　峰

● 汉语关键词

高峰、高峰期、高峰时间、高峰会议、峰会

● 英语关键词

peak, peak period, height, summit, travel peak, traffic peak, summit meeting, summit conference

● 句　子

今天,中国有望出现铁路客流高峰。

● 误　译

China is expected to see a rush hour of railway traffic today.

● 正　译

1) China is expected to see a peak of railway traffic today.
2) China is expected to see a peak of railway passenger flow today.

● 解　释

rush hour 指城市上下班时的高峰时间。"铁路客流高峰"是中国特有的一种社会现象,可以译为 a peak of railway traffic 或 a peak of railway passenger flow。

"高峰"的第一个意思是"高的山峰"。英语可以译为 peak, height。例如:

1. 这条山脉有许多高峰和深谷。
   This mountain range has many high peaks and deep canyons.
2. 喜玛拉雅山珠穆朗玛峰是世界最高峰。
   Mount Qomolangma in the Himalayas is the highest peak of the world.
3. 今天下午,这个登山队胜利登上这座非洲最高峰。
   This afternoon, this mountaineering team succeeded in reaching the highest peak of Africa.
4. 今天上午,他们开始攀登这座高峰。
   1) This morning, they began to climb the heights of the mountain.
   2) This morning, they began to mount the heights of the mountain.
   3) This morning, they began to scale the heights of the mountain.

"高峰"的第二个意思是比喻"事物发展的最高点"。英语可以译为 heights, summit。例如:
5. 我们正在努力攀登科学高峰。
   We are striving to climb the heights of science.
6. 经过不懈努力,我们达到了科学成就的高峰。
   Through unremitting efforts, we reached the summit of scientific achievement.

"高峰期"指"事物发展的最兴旺时期"。英语可以译为 peak, peak period, height。例如:
7. 50 岁时,他达到了事业的高峰期。
   At the age of 50, he reached the peak of his career.
8. 我在事业的高峰期离开了公司。
   I left the company at the height of my career.
9. 旅游业在八月份处于高峰期。
   Tourism is at its peak in August.
10. 春天是流行病高峰期。
    Spring is the peak period of epidemic.

"高峰"的第三个意思是指"事物发生频率最高或数量最高"。英语可以译为 peak。例如：

11. 秋天是会议高峰季节。

    Autumn is the peak conference season.

12. 在这个城市，夏季的用电量达到高峰。

    In this city, demand for electricity has its peak in summer.

13. 失业率在 1990 年达到高峰，此后就逐年减少。

    The unemployment rate had its peak in 1990, and decreased every year since then.

动词 to peak 具有"达到高峰"的意思。例如：

14. 玩具销售额在圣诞节前夕达到高峰，现已逐渐下降。

    1) Toy sales peaked just before Christmas and are now decreasing.

    2) Toy sales reached its peak just before Christmas and are now decreasing.

15. 通常，黄昏时用电量达到高峰。

    1) Demand for electricity peaks in the early evening.

    2) Demand for electricity has its peak in the early evening.

"高峰"的第四个意思是指"车流最拥挤或人流最多"。英语可以译为 travel peak, traffic peak。例如：

16. 昨天，北京火车站迎来春节后第一个返程客流高峰。

    Yesterday, Beijing Railway Station saw the first return-trip travel peak after the Spring Festival.

17. 春节后返程客流高峰通常在正月初七出现。

    The return-trip travel peak usually appears on the seventh day of the first Lunar month.

18. 去年铁路春运最高峰时一天客流超过 500 万人。

    Spring Festival railway traffic peak saw more than five million passengers in one day last year.

"高峰时间"指"城市上下班时道路上车流最拥挤的时间"。英语可以

译为 peak hour, rush hour。例如:
19. 在高峰时间,道路上挤满了车辆。

    1) The roads are full of traffic at peak hours.

    2) The roads are full of traffic at rush hours.

20. 公共汽车在高峰时间常常晚点。

    Buses are often late in peak hours.

21. 我们正赶上高峰时间。

    We're hitting the rush hour.

22. 高峰时间已经过去了。

    The rush hour is over.

23. 在高峰时间超车是危险的。

    It is dangerous to cut in during the rush hour.

24. 交通高峰时间通常在早晨八、九点之间。

    1) Usually, traffic has its peak between eight and nine in the morning.

    2) Rush hour is usually between eight and nine in the morning.

25. 我不愿意在高峰时间出去。

    I don't like to go out during the rush hour.

26. 我觉得在高峰时间坐公共汽车很烦人。

    I think riding a bus during the rush hour is pretty awful.

27. 高峰时间污染会骤然上升。

    Pollution will suddenly increase during rush hours.

"高峰"的第五个意思是比喻"领导人员中的最高层"。英语可以译为 summit。"高峰会议"指"首脑会议;政界、企业界等方面高级领导人的会议",简称"峰会"。英语可以译为 summit meeting, summit conference, summit。例如:

28. 昨天,中法两国最高领导人在北京举行了高峰会议。

    Yesterday, the top leaders of China and France held a summit meeting in Beijing.

29. 中国希望即将召开的中美高峰会议将加强双边关系。
China hopes the upcoming Sino-US summit conference will boost bilateral relations.
30. 中欧峰会定于5月2日在巴黎举行。
The Sino-EU summit is to be held in Paris on May 2.

# 四十八、基　石

### ● 汉语关键词
基石、墓脚基石、墓碑、墓石、奠基石、拱顶石

### ● 英语关键词
headstone, footstone, footing stone, foundation stone, foundation, cornerstone, keystone

### ● 句　子
制造业是现代化的基石。

### ● 误　译
Manufacturing is the footstone of modernization.

### ● 正　译
Manufacturing is the footing stone of modernization.

### ● 解　释
footstone 的意思是 a gravestone placed at the foot of a grave, typically smaller than a headstone, and frequently resembling a large cobblestone, 即"墓脚基石"。与 footstone 相关的是 headstone, 它的意思是 a tombstone or gravestone which is a permanent marker, normally carved from stone, placed over or next to the site of a burial in a cemetery or a church yard, 即"墓碑、墓石"。headstone 和 footstone 一前一后, 都与坟墓有关。注意不要将 footstone 与 footing stone 混淆。footing stone 的意思是 a broad flat stone used as the base or bottom course of a wall, 即"基石", 它与坟墓无关。

# 100个热门话题汉译英
Chinese-English Translation of 100 Hot Topics

试比较:
1. 一块千年墓碑直立在这座古教堂的废墟旁。
   A thousand-year-old headstone stands next to the ruins of the ancient church.
2. 昨天,我在公墓东区发现了这块破碎不堪的墓脚基石。
   Yesterday I found this badly broken footstone in the east portion of the cemetery.
3. 没有基石,建筑物会坍塌。
   Without the footing stone, buildings will collapse.

"基石"的第一个意思是"泛指用作建筑物基础的石料"。英语可以译为 foundation stone, footing stone。例如:
4. 这座宫殿的基石是大理石。
   The foundation stones of the palace were marble.
5. 这座城墙的基石是用各种各样的宝石装饰的。
   The foundation stones of the city wall were adorned with every kind of precious stone.
6. 工人们安放好了这所房子的基石。
   The workers placed the foundation stones that the house would rest upon.
7. 在这次发掘中发现的建筑物废墟里有宫殿的基石。
   Among the building remains found in this excavation were the foundation stones of the palace.
8. 昨天,正式安放了这座新庙宇的基石。
   Yesterday, the footing stone of the new temple was officially laid.

"基石"的第二个意思是"专指建筑物奠基用的刻石,上面刻有奠基的年月日等",即"奠基石"。英语的 foundation stone 和 cornerstone 的意思是 a ceremonial masonry stone, or facsimile, set in a prominent location on the outside of a building, with an inscription on the stone,相当于"奠基石"。例如:
9. 这些著名艺术家正在为这座新博物馆奠定基石。
   These famous artists are laying a foundation stone for the new museum.

10. 许多著名人士出席了这座新建筑物的奠基仪式。
    Quite a lot of famous people were present at the foundation stone laying ceremony of the new building.
11. 今天上午,市长为新市政厅奠定基石。
    This morning, the mayor laid the cornerstone for the new city hall.

"基石"的第三个意思是"比喻事物的基础或中坚力量"。英语可以译为 foundation, foundation stone, cornerstone, keystone。例如:

12. 激情、动力和奉献是成功的基石。
    Passion, motivation and dedication are the foundation of success.
13. 在西方,希腊语和拉丁语曾一度被视为良好教育的基石。
    In the West, Greek and Latin were once viewed as the foundation stones of a good education.
14. 维护世界和平是我国外交政策的基石。
    The maintenance of world peace is the cornerstone of our country's foreign policy.
15. 意志、工作和等待是成功的金字塔基石。
    Will, work and wait are the pyramidal cornerstones for success.
16. 信赖与责任是任何婚姻的基石。
    Trust and commitment are the cornerstones of any marriage.

keystone 的原义是 the central stone at the top of an arch that keeps all the other stones in position,即"拱顶石"。例如:

17. 他操纵吊车将拱顶石放入拱顶。
    He operated the crane to place the keystone in the arch.

keystone 的比喻意义为 the most important part of a plan or argument that the other parts depend on,即"基石"。例如:

18. 勤劳是事业的灵魂,又是繁荣的基石。
    Industry is the soul of business and the keystone of prosperity.

19. 可持续能源是经济发展的基石。
    Sustainable energy is a keystone for economic development.
20. 电路理论的系统课程是工程师教育的基石。
    A systematic course in circuit theory is a keystone in the education of engineers.

# 四十九、草　　根

### 汉语关键词
草根、基层、基层民众、草根阶层、草根性、草根文化、草根艺人、草根工业

### 英语关键词
grass roots, grass roots level, grass-roots character, nature of grass roots, grass-rooted culture, grass-roots entertainer, grass-roots industry

### 句　子
网络具有新的特点,例如草根性。

### 误　译
The Internet has its new characteristics, for example, its nature of straw roots.

### 正　译
The Internet has its new characteristics, for example, its nature of grass roots.

### 解　释
straw 指的是农作物脱粒后剩下的茎,即"秸秆",如稻秸、麦秸、豆秸。稻草,就是"稻秸"或"稻秆",与"草"没有关系,与"根"也没有关系。

"草根"的第一个意思是"草的根部"。英语可以译为 grass roots。例如:
1. 非洲象吃草根、树皮、带叶的树枝和果实。
   The African Elephant eat grass roots, tree barks, leaved branches and fruits.

2. 与树根相比较，草根生长得非常快。
   Compared with roots of trees, grass roots grow very fast.
3. 这些饥荒难民靠吃草根和树皮充饥。
   The famine victims lived on grass roots and tree barks.

"草根"的第二个意思是"社会或组织中的普通群众，而不是领导人或决策者"，即"基层群众"。英语可以译为 grass roots。例如：
4. 这名候选人已赢得党内基层群众的支持。
   The candidate has won support from the grass roots of his party.
5. 基层群众的意见是赞成这个建议。
   1) Grass-roots opinion is in favour of the proposal.
   2) Opinion at grass roots is in favour of the proposal.
6. 这个党似乎正在失去与基层群众的联系。
   The party seems to be losing contact with the grass roots.

"草根阶层"或"基层"译为 grass roots, grass-roots level。例如：
7. 官员们应该注意草根阶层的生活状况。
   Officials should pay attention to the living conditions at the grass roots.
8. 我们需要赢得基层的支持。
   We need to win support at grass-roots level.
9. 草根阶层的舆论是同情这些罢工者。
   Opinion at grass-roots level is sympathetic to the strikers.

"基层单位"译为 grass-roots unit, unit at the grass roots。"基层组织"译为 grass-roots organization。"基层干部"译为 official at the grass-roots level, cadre at the grass-roots level。"基层选举"译为 election at the grass roots。例如：
10. 部长最近到一个基层单位调查研究。
    1) The minister has recently gone to make investigations in a grass-roots unit.
    2) The minister has recently gone to make investigations in a unit at

the grass roots.
11. 在过去5年里,这个基层组织经历了深刻变化。
    Over the past five years, this grass-roots organization has undergone profound changes.
12. 基层干部在抗雪灾斗争中起了作用。
    1) Officials at the grass-roots level played an important role in the fight against snow disasters.
    2) Cadres at the grass-roots level played an important role in the fight against snow disasters.
13. 基层直接选举已在农村成为当前的趋势。
    Direct election at the grass roots has become a current trend in the rural areas.

"草根"的第三个意思是"非主流的、与精英阶层相对应的弱势阶层"。英语可以译为 grass roots。"草根性"译为 grass-roots character, nature of grass roots。例如:
14. 他强调了博客文体的草根性。
    He emphasized the grass-roots character in the style of blogs.
15. 中国电子商务的最大特点是它的草根性。
    China's E-Business is best characterized with its nature of grass roots.

"草根文化"可以译为 grass-rooted culture。例如:
16. 草根文化,老百姓喜闻乐见。
    Grass-rooted culture is well liked by the ordinary people.
17. 草根文化根植于老百姓,对广大群众有一种天然的亲和力。
    Grass-rooted culture is rooted in ordinary people, and has a natural affability with the broad masses of people.
18. 草根文化贴近现实,而充满生机和活力。
    Grass-rooted culture is close to reality, and full of vigour and vitality.

"草根艺人"译为 grass-roots entertainer。例如:

19. 由于他作为一位草根艺人所取得的成功,这个演员受到观众的极大赞赏。
By virtue of his very success as a grass-roots entertainer, the actor won great acclaim from the audience.

"草根工业"的意思是 township enterprises which take root among farmers and grow like weeds。英语可以译为 grass-roots industry。例如:

20. 这些活动提供就业和收入给农村、小村庄、城镇,还有一个可以进一步发展的草根工业基地。
These activities provide employment and income to rural areas, small villages, towns and a grass-roots industry base that can be further developed.

# 五十、重 建

### 汉语关键词
重建、复原、修复、整修、恢复

### 英语关键词
rebuild, rebuilding, reconstruct, reconstruction, reestablish, reestablishment, restore, restoration, recover, recovery, rehabilitate, rehabilitation

### 句 子
村民们正在重建被大雪压塌的房屋。

### 误 译
The villagers are restoring the houses destroyed by heavy snow.

### 正 译
1) The villagers are rebuilding the houses destroyed by heavy snow.
2) The villagers are reconstructing the houses badly damaged by snow disasters.

3) The villagers are reestablishing the houses broken down during the snowstorm.

4) The villagers are rebuilding the houses which had been snowed down.

### 解 释

to restore 的意思是 to repair a building so that it looks as good as it did originally，即"复原"、"修复"或"整修"，强调的是"将依然存在的旧建筑物恢复原样"。与 to repair 和 to renovate 是同义词。例如：

1. 他们修复了这座古老的建筑物。

   1) They repaired the old building to its former appearance.
   2) They restored the old building to its original splendour.
   3) They renovated the old building to its previous condition.

"重建"的意思是"重新建造已被严重损坏或不再存在的事物"。英语可以用动词 to rebuild, to reconstruct 或 to reestablish 表示。例如：

2. 村民们在洪水过后重建了房屋。

   The villagers rebuilt their houses after the flood.

3. 他们已决定拆掉旧饭店，并就地重建一座新饭店。

   They have decided to raze the old hotel and reconstruct a new one on the site.

4. 这场天灾一发生，地方政府立即开始就重建本地区农业的计划展开工作。

   Immediately after the natural calamity occurred, the local government began the work on a project to reestablish agriculture in this area.

5. 雪灾之后，灾区农民开始重建家园。

   1) After the snow havoc, the farmers in the disaster-affected areas began to rebuild their homeland.
   2) After the snow havoc, the farmers in the disaster-afflicted areas began to reconstruct their homeland.
   3) After the snow havoc, the farmers in the disaster-hit regions started

to reestablish their homestead.

"重建"也可以用相应的名词 rebuilding, reconstruction 或 reestablishment 表示。例如：

6. 重建这座大桥花了两年时间。
   The rebuilding of the huge bridge took 2 years.
7. 重建那座建筑物是不可能的。
   A reconstruction of that building is impossible.
8. 市政府有一个重建被大火烧毁的城市博物馆的计划。
   The municipal government has a plan for the reconstruction of the city museum which was burned down in a fire.
9. 这场雪灾后的重建将增加国内对钢材、木材和其他建筑材料的需求。
   The reconstruction after the snow disasters will increase domestic demand for steel, wood and other building materials.
10. 这家电信营运商已在雪灾地区启动网络重建计划。
    The telecom operator has launched network reconstruction projects in snow-hit areas.
11. 在伊拉克，没有安全就不可能有重建，但是没有重建也不可能有安全。
    In Iraq, there could be no reconstruction without security, but there could also be no security without reconstruction.
12. 重建这个公司花了3年时间。
    The reestablishment of the business took three years.

"恢复"或"复原"的意思是"变成原来的样子、面貌或状态"。英语可以用动词 to restore, to recover 或 to rehabilitate 表示。例如：

13. 这个灾区的地方政府正在努力加紧重建以恢复生产秩序和人民生活。
    The local government in this disaster-hit area is trying to beef up reconstruction to restore order in production and people's life.

14. 经济最终开始回恢复。
    The economy is at last beginning to recover.
15. 他们正努力照原样复原这座房子。
    They are trying to recover the house as it was.
16. 他们正在实行一个复原这座古城的计划。
    They are carrying out a plan to rehabilitate the old town.

"恢复"或"复原"也可以用相应的名词 restoration, recovery 或 rehabilitation 表示。例如：

17. 这位专家在外国成功经验的基础上，阐明了复原该矿区景观对可持续发展的意义。
    On the basis of the successful experience of other countries, the expert illustrated the significance of the restoration of the landscape in the mining area for sustainable development.
18. 出于对历史性建筑复原的好奇心，他们决定重建这座古代宫殿。
    Out of the curiosity for the restoration of historical buildings, they decided to rebuild the ancient palace.
19. 我们不得不为修缮和复原这座房子付出代价。
    We have to pay for the repair and recovery of the house.
20. 他们正在执行一个复原这座古老城市的综合计划。
    They are implementing a comprehensive programme for the rehabilitation of the old city.

# 五十一、接　　轨

● 汉语关键词

接轨、连接、对接、联系、接触

● 英语关键词

contact, connect, link, link up with, dock on, dock with, be docked on, be docked with, integrate, become integrated with, get integrated with, be geared to, get geared to, switch over to, become compatible with, keep in line with

● 句 子

陇海线在郑州与京广线接轨。

● 误 译

The Lianyungang-Lanzhou Railway is contacted to the Beijing-Guangzhou Railway at Zhengzhou.

● 正 译

The Lianyungang-Lanzhou Railway is connected to the Beijing-Guangzhou Railway at Zhengzhou.

● 解 释

"接轨"的意思是"连接"。to contact 的意思是"联系"或"接触"; to connect 的意思才是"连接"。例如:
1. 救险队员们一直在设法联系被困的矿工。
The rescue crews have been trying to contact the trapped miners.

"接轨"的第一个意思是"连接铁轨"。英语可以译为 to link the rails, to connect the rails。"全线接轨"就是"全线贯通",英语可以译为 (the rails) to be linked up or to be connected。例如:
2. 2005 年 10 月 15 日在拉萨接轨,青藏铁路最终建成。
The Qinghai-Tibet Railway was finally completed when rails were linked at Lhasa on October 15, 2005.
3. 最后,全线接轨,铁路就可以通车了。
Finally, the rails were linked and the line was opened for traffic.
4. 在拉萨接轨,使得从内地到西藏完全乘火车旅行成为可能。
The rails were linked up at Lhasa, making it possible to travel from interior China to Tibet completely by train.

# *100*个热门话题汉译英
## Chinese-English Translation of 100 Hot Topics

5. 铁路线修到达西藏,最后在拉萨接轨。
   The railway line had reached Tibet, and the rails were finally connected at Lhasa.
6. 在这座小镇接轨,提供铁路服务,一路横跨全国,通向东海岸。
   Rails were linked together at this small town, providing train service all the way across the country to the east coast.
7. 胶济线在济南与京沪线接轨。
   The Qingdao-Jinan Railway is connected to the Beijing-Shanghai Railway at Jinan.

"接轨"的第二个意思是"使宇航器在太空相互衔接",即"对接"。英语可以译为 to link up with, to dock on, to dock with, to be docked on, to be docked with。例如:

8. 这架航天飞机已经与国际太空站接轨。
   1) The space shuttle has linked up with the international space station.
   2) The space shuttle has docked with the international space station.
   3) The space shuttle has been docked with the international space station.
9. 明年,一个技术舱将与太空站对接。
   Next year, a technology module will be docked on the space station.

"接轨"的第三个意思是比喻"使两种制度或方法相互衔接"。英语可以译为 to link up with, to integrate, to become integrated with, to get integrated with, to be geared to, to get geared to, to switch over to, to become compatible with, to keep in line with。例如:

10. 这位专家谈论到如何使我们的统计制度与国际标准接轨。
    The expert talked about how to make our statistical system link up with the international standards.
11. 随着加入世贸组织,中国国内的纺织市场和纺织机械市场已与国际市场接轨。
    With its entry into the WTO, China's domestic textile and textile machinery markets have integrated with the world market.

12. 随着农业市场与国际市场接轨,中国国内的农产品价格有所上涨。
China's prices of domestic agricultural products rose as its agricultural market became integrated with the international market.
13. 随着财务制度的改进,这家企业已逐渐与国际市场接轨。
With its financial systems being upgraded, the enterprise has gradually got integrated with the world market.
14. 越来越多的公司已经采用这个与国际标准接轨的新的质量管理体系。
A growing number of companies have adopted this new quality management system, which is geared to international standards.
15. 这个公司已经持续地改进管理,现在与国际惯例接轨了。
The company has constantly improved its management and is now geared to international conventions.
16. 对这些企业来说,提高他们产品的市场竞争力并与国际标准接轨是必要的。
It is necessary for the enterprises to increase the competitiveness of their products in the market and get geared to international standards.
17. 为了解决这些问题,我们应该与国际惯例接轨,并加速国际化的进程。
In order to solve these problems, we should switch over to international practices and accelerate the progress of internationalization.
18. 我国的银行运作已逐步与国际公认的惯例接轨。
Banking operation in our country has gradually become compatible with internationally accepted practices.
19. 中国展览界业内人士强调说中国的展览会应该与国际标准接轨。
Insiders from the Chinese exhibition industry emphasize that Chinese exhibitions should keep in line with international standards.

# 100个热门话题汉译英
Chinese-English Translation of 100 Hot Topics

# 五十二、排 行 榜

● 汉语关键词

排行榜、畅销书排行榜、流行歌曲排行榜、流行音乐排行榜、运动成绩排行榜、奖牌排行榜、名列榜首、名列首位、名列第一

● 英语关键词

best-seller list, list of best-sellers, list of best-selling books, charts, pop charts, music charts, hit parade, rankings, medal rankings, medal standings, medal tally, medal table, be Number One on the list, be top on the list, be top of the list, be on top of the list, top the list, come first, rank first, be ranked first, place first

● 句　子

这本书在畅销书排行榜上名列首位。

● 误　译

This book ranks first on the ranking list of best-sellers.

● 正　译

This book ranks first on the list of best-sellers.

● 解　释

list of best-sellers 自身已有序列的含义。ranking 作为形容词，意思是"高级别的"，用在这里是累赘，又与 ranks first 重复，应该删去。

"排行榜"是"公布出来的按某种统计结果排列顺序的名单"。排行榜涉及影视、音乐、娱乐、财经、房产、汽车、数码、教育、体育等多个领域。英语的各种排行榜都有固定译法。"排行榜"是"排序名单"，可以译为 list。"畅销书排行榜"可以译为 best-seller list, list of best-sellers, list of best-selling books。例如：

1. 这家书店定期公布畅销书排行榜。

The bookstore publishes a list of best-sellers regularly.

2. 《纽约时报》畅销书排行榜被广泛认为是美国最出色的畅销书排行榜之一。
   The New York Times Best Seller List is widely considered to be one of the preeminent lists of best-selling books in the United States.
3. 这里是本周10大畅销书排行榜。
   Here is a Top 10 list of best-selling books for this week.
4. 这篇文章展示了英国文学15大畅销书排行榜。
   This article presents a top fifteen list of best-selling books on English literature.
5. 畅销书排行榜是在一周时段内某些集团书店对特定书籍相关销售量的排序。
   A best-seller list is a ranking of the relative sales of particular kinds of books at certain groups of stores within a one-week period.

"名列榜首"可以译为 to be Number One on the list, to be top on the list, to be top of the list, to be on top of the list, to top the list。例如：

6. 《圣经》名列榜首不足为奇。
   1) It is not surprising that the Bible is Number One on the list.
   2) It is not surprising that the Bible is top on the list.
   3) It is not surprising that the Bible is top of the list.
   4) It is not surprising that the Bible is on top of the list.
   5) It is not surprising that the Bible tops the list.

"名列首位"或"名列第一"，可以用 to come first, to rank first, to be ranked first, to place first 表示。例如：

7. 这本书在本年度最佳儿童书籍排行榜名列首位。
   1) This book comes first on the list of the best children's books of the year.
   2) This book ranks first on the list of the best children's books of the

year.

3) This book is ranked first on the list of the best children's books of the year.

4) This book places first on the list of the best children's books of the year.

"排行榜"按照销售量多少排序。英语 charts 的意思是"销售图表",常常用来表示 a list produced each week of the pop music records or albums that have sold the most copies,即"每周流行音乐唱片或专辑排行榜"。pop charts 是"流行歌曲排行榜"。music charts 是"流行音乐排行榜"。例如:

8. 这首歌曲在排行榜名列榜首。

This song is on top of the charts.

9. 广播电台通常播放在排行榜名列榜首的歌曲。

Radio stations usually play songs that are top of the charts.

10. 这位歌手的最新专辑在流行音乐排行榜上节节攀升。

The singer's latest album is inching its way up the music charts.

11. 该乐队的首张专辑名列 13 个国家的流行音乐排行榜之首。

The band's first album topped the music charts in 13 countries.

12. 他的名列排行榜榜首的流行歌曲在青少年中间很受青睐。

His chart-topping pop song is popular among the youngsters.

13. 她的歌曲正在 10 大金曲排行榜上攀升。

Her song is climbing up the Top 10 charts.

hit parade 也有"每周流行音乐唱片排行榜"的意思。例如:

14. 去年,那首歌曲在每周流行音乐唱片排行榜上出现了三次。

That song appeared on the hit parade three times last year.

"运动成绩排行榜"可以用 rankings 表示。"奖牌排行榜"可以译为 medal rankings。例如:

15. 这个年青运动员的名字第一次出现在运动成绩排行榜上。
    The young athlete's name appeared on the rankings for the first time.
16. 在奖牌排行榜上,中国羽毛球队以四块金牌、三块银牌和两块铜牌名列榜首。
    On the medal rankings, the Chinese Badminton Team came first with four gold medals, three silvers and two bronzes.
17. 中国跳水队保持了在奖牌排行榜中的领先地位。
    The Chinese Diving Team has maintained their leading position in the medal rankings.

"奖牌排行榜"还可以用 medal standings, medal tally, medal table 表示。例如:

18. 我们队在奖牌排行榜上名列第三将没有困难。
    Our team will have no difficulty in achieving third place in the medal standings.
19. 两天比赛以后,海湾国家卡塔尔以两金、一银和两铜在奖牌排行榜上名列第二。
    After two days' competition, Gulf state Qatar ranked second on the medal standings with two golds, one silver and two bronzes.
20. 在2004年雅典奥运会上,中国队以32块金牌在奖牌排行榜上仅次于美国队名列第二。
    At the 2004 Athens Games, China finished second to the United States on the medal tally with 32 golds.
21. 在1996年亚特兰大奥运会上,中国队以50块奖牌(其中16块金牌)在奖牌排行榜上名列第四。
    At the 1996 Atlanta Games, China was fourth on the medal table with 50 medals, 16 of them gold.

## 五十三、造　假

### ● 汉语关键词
假、假货、造假、造假账、造假行为、造假术、打假

### ● 英语关键词
bogus, counterfeit, fake, fakery, false, forge, forged, forgery, fraud, sham, cheating, make fake things, cook the books, cook the accounts, crack down on

### ● 句　子
这张获奖的藏羚羊照片已被揭露是造假。

### ● 误　译
This award-winning photo of Tibetan antelopes has been exposed as making a fake.

### ● 正　译
1）This award-winning photo of Tibetan antelopes has been exposed as fake.

2）This award-winning photo of Tibetan antelopes has been exposed as a fake.

3）This award-winning photo of Tibetan antelopes has been exposed as being fake.

4）This award-winning photo of Tibetan antelopes has been exposed as being a fake.

### ● 解　释
fake既是形容词，也是名词。不能将"造假"字对字地译为 to make a fake，因为英语没有这样的搭配。但是"被揭露是造假"可以有 to be exposed as fake / a fake / being fake / being a fake 等四种说法。

真实只有一个，英语中表示"真"的词很少。伪造的、冒充的、冒牌的或仿造的东西有许许多多，英语中表示"假"的词很多，有 bogus, counterfeit,

fake, false, forged, fraud, sham 等。例如：
1. 这个外国旅客因持假护照而被拘留。
   The foreign passenger was detained for holding a bogus passport.
2. 两人因贩卖带有耐克和路易·威登等著名品牌的假商标的货物而被捕。
   Two people were arrested for selling counterfeit trademark merchandise marked with famous brand names such as Nike and Louis Vuitton.
3. 这位卫生专家警告说假药正在全球夺取成千上万人的生命。
   The health expert warns that fake medicines are killing many hundreds of thousands of people across the globe.
4. 这位专家正在给听众讲如何区别真假古瓷瓶。
   The expert is telling the audience how to distinguish authentic from fake antique vases.
5. 法庭最终证明被告伪造了假文件和假签名。
   The court finally proved that the defendant had made a false document and a false signature.
6. 这名男子被发现在黑市买卖假币。
   The man was buying and selling forged money in the black market.
7. 有时候，造假极难看出。
   Sometimes, fraud is terrifically hard to spot.
8. 这位鉴赏家发现这张假画上有一个假签名。
   The connoisseur found that there was a sham signature affixed to the sham picture.

"假货"，英语可以译为 counterfeit, fake。例如：
9. 当你去一家路易·威登专卖店，你花3,000美元买一个包；但是如果你去洛杉矶的市中心，你却能花50美元买一个假货。
   When you go to a Louis Vuitton shop, you pay $3,000 for a bag; but if you go to Los Angeles downtown, you can buy a counterfeit for $50.

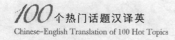

10. 每个想买古董而又不在行的人,都怕买到假货。
    Everybody who wants to buy antiques, but is not an expert, fears buying a fake.

"造假",英语可以译为 to make fake things, to counterfeit, to forge。例如:

11. 警方今天声称在本地区抓获一个制造假证件的团伙。
    The police today claimed to have busted a gang that made fake certificates in this district.

12. 最初,制造假钞的唯一方法是雕版印制。
    Originally, the only method of counterfeiting paper money was by engraving.

13. 警方声称这个契约上的签名是伪造的。
    The police claimed that the signatures on the contract had been forged.

"造假账",可以译为 to cook the books, to cook the accounts。例如:

14. 这个会计师因造假帐而被开除了。
    1) The accountant was sacked for cooking the books.
    2) The accountant was sacked for cooking the accounts.

"造假行为"和"造假术",可以译为 cheating, fakery, forgery, fraud。例如:

15. 这位教授在学术造假丑闻被揭露后就立即辞职了。
    The professor resigned immediately after his academic cheating scandal was exposed.

16. 这个摄影造假术包括将他的头连到别人身体的影象上,使他看上去瘦一些。
    The photo fakery includes a photo of his head attached to an image of a different body that makes him look thinner.

17. 警方继续调查他与这个公司签的合同中是否涉及造假。
    The police continued to investigate whether there was forgery involved in the contract that he signed with the company.

18. 近几年,一些国际公司由于会计造假连续倒闭。
    In recent years, some international companies went bankrupt successively because of accounting fraud.

"打假"的意思是"依法打击制造、销售假冒伪劣商品"。英语可以译为 to crack down on。例如:

19. 中国政府已采取各种有效措施打击假冒伪劣商品。
    The Chinese government has taken various effective measures to crack down on counterfeit goods.
20. 中国各级工商管理部门将继续打击假冒伪劣产品。
    The industrial and commercial authorities at various levels in China will continue to crack down on fake products.
21. 警方已立即采取行动在市场上打击盗版产品。
    The police have taken immediate actions to crack down on pirated goods in the market.

## 五十四、怀　　疑

● 汉语关键词

怀疑、不相信、疑惑、猜测、不信任

● 英语关键词

doubt that, have doubts that, be doubtful that, doubt whether, doubt if, be doubtful about, be doubtful whether, be doubtful if, be dubious about, be dubious of, be sceptical/skeptical about, be sceptical/skeptical of, suspect, mistrust, have a mistrust of, be mistrustful of, be suspicious about, be suspicious of

● 句　子

许多人怀疑这些华南虎照片是假的。

## 误 译

Many people doubt that these South China Tiger photos are fake.

## 正 译

Many people suspect that these South China Tiger photos are fake.

## 解 释

to doubt 和 to suspect 的意思相反。这句话的翻译全拧了。

"怀疑"的第一个意思是"不相信某事物是可能的",即否定某事物的可能性。英语用 to doubt that 表示,即 to think that sth is unlikely or improbable,或 not to think that sth is likely or probable。例如:
1. 我怀疑/不相信他会考试及格。
   I doubt that he'll pass the examination.

"怀疑/不相信"还可以用 to have doubts that, to be doubtful that 表示。例如:
2. 他怀疑/不相信他现在的职业适合他。
   He has doubts that his current career is right for him.
3. 我怀疑/不相信他们有什么意愿跟我谈判。
   I have doubts that they have any desire to negotiate with me.
4. 说还能找到这个失踪的孩子,令人怀疑/难以置信。
   It seems doubtful that the missing child will ever be found again.
5. 说设备到达时还能使用,令人怀疑/难以置信。
   It was doubtful that the equipment would be usable on arrival.

"怀疑"的第二个意思是"疑惑某事物是否可能",即不肯定某事物的可能性。英语用 to doubt whether, to doubt if 表示,即 to be uncertain that sth is likely or probable。例如:
6. 许多人怀疑/疑惑这些华南虎照片是否是真的。
   Many people doubt whether/if these South China Tiger photos are authentic.

7. 我开始怀疑自己是不是太敏感了。
   I began to doubt whether/if I had been too sensitive myself.

"怀疑/疑惑"还可以用 to be doubtful about, to be doubtful whether/if, to be dubious about/ of, to be sceptical/ skeptical about/ of 表示。
例如：

8. 当地居民怀疑/疑惑这位官员说过的话。
   The local inhabitants were doubtful about what the official had said.
9. 刚拿起来开始用，我就怀疑/疑惑这个产品是否好用。
   Just by picking it up and starting to use it, I was doubtful about the viability of this product.
10. 我仍然怀疑/疑惑我是否该接受这个工作。
    I'm still doubtful whether/if I should accept this job.
11. 她怀疑/疑惑她是否能赶上一趟下午的航班。
    She was doubtful whether/if she would catch an afternoon flight.
12. 这个病人动手术能否活下来，是令人怀疑/疑惑的。
    It was doubtful whether/if the patient would survive the operation.
13. 这家公司能否从财务困境中复苏，是令人怀疑/疑惑的。
    It was doubtful whether/if the company could recover from its financial difficulties.
14. 我依然怀疑/疑惑他选择教师职业的动机。
    I remain dubious about/of his motives in choosing a teaching career.
15. 我对是否应该信任他，有点怀疑/疑惑。
    I was a little dubious about/of whether or not to trust him.
16. 比尔·盖茨曾一度怀疑/疑惑互联网，现在已经改变了看法。
    Bill Gates, once sceptical/skeptical about/of the Internet, has now changed his mind.
17. 这位科学家依然怀疑/疑惑这个研究计划的价值。
    The scientist remains sceptical/skeptical about/of the value of this research programme.

"怀疑"的第三个意思是"猜测某事物(大部分是负面的事情)是可能的"。英语用 to suspect that 表示，即 to think that sth is likely or probable。例如：

18. 如果你真的怀疑/不相信某件事是真的，那么你就是怀疑/猜测它是假的。
    If you really doubt that something is true, then you suspect that it's false.
19. 她怀疑/猜测这种化妆品能够致癌。
    She suspected that this cosmetic product might cause cancer.
20. 我怀疑/猜测他今天来不了。
    I suspect that he won't come today.
21. 他怀疑/猜测他从取款机上取到了假钞。
    He suspected that he had got forged money from the ATM (automatic teller machine).
22. 这位科学家怀疑/猜测那两个人死于禽流感。
    The scientist suspected that the two people had died from bird's flu.

"怀疑"的第四个意思是"不信任某个可能错误或有问题的人或事"。英语用 to mistrust, to have a mistrust of, to be mistrustful of, to be suspicious about/of 表示。例如：

23. 这对老夫妻自结婚以来，从没有彼此怀疑/不信任过。
    The old couple have never mistrusted each other since they got married.
24. 当他还是个小小孩时，就学会了怀疑/不信任大人。
    As a very small child, he had learned to mistrust adults.
25. 这些老人怀疑/不信任他们不相识的外来人。
    1) These old people mistrust outsiders with whom they are not acquainted.
    2) These old people have a mistrust of outsiders with whom they are not acquainted.
    3) These old people are mistrustful of outsiders with whom they are not acquainted.

26. 他怀疑/不信任所有跟他谈话的人。
    He is suspicious about/of everybody who talks with him.
27. 人们怀疑这个百万富翁财富的来源。
    People are suspicious about/of the source of the millionaire's wealth.

# 五十五、形　　象

### ● 汉语关键词

形象、形象年龄、图像时代、视觉形象、公众形象、形象设计师、形象代言人、文学形象、艺术形象、形象思维、英雄形象、生动

### ● 英语关键词

image, image age, visual image, public image, image designer, image spokesman, image spokeswoman, literary image, thinking in terms of images, artistic image, heroic image, vivid, expressive

### ● 句　子

有人认为中国的形象年龄是33岁。

### ● 误　译

Some people think that China's image age is 33 years old.

### ● 正　译

Some people think that China's image age is 33 (years).

### ● 解　释

英语表示年龄,用了 age,再用 old,就是累赘。years 可以用,也可以省略。例如:

1. 他的年龄是20岁。
   1) He is twenty (years old).
   2) He is twenty years of age.
   3) He is aged twenty (years).
   4) His age is twenty (years).

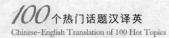
100个热门话题汉译英
Chinese-English Translation of 100 Hot Topics

英语表示"实际年龄",用 current age;表示"形象年龄",用 image age。例如:
2. 她的形象年龄是 15 岁,而实际年龄是 18 岁。
   Her image age is 15, while her current age is 18.

由于 age 除了当"年龄"讲,还有"时代"的意思。因此,image age 具有歧义,还有"图像时代"的意思。例如:
3. 在当今图像时代,绘画艺术已变成它昔日辉煌的阴影。
   In this image age, the art of painting has become a shadow of its past glory.
4. 随着数码图像时代的到来,如何利用形象改进企业已成为其发展的关键。
   With the advent of the Digital Image Age, the issue of how to use images to improve business has become a key point in its development.
5. 图像时代的到来为教育研究带来了许多新课题。
   The advent of image age has brought many new topics for the study in education.

"形象"的第一个意思是"能引起人的思想或感情活动的具体形状或姿态"。英语可以译为 image。例如:
6. 她的话语开始在我的脑海里建立起一个形象。
   Her words began to create an image in my mind.
7. 医生测试了这个孩子的视觉形象能力。
   The doctor tested the child's visual image ability.
8. 他将他的设计基于一个孩子的天真形象,双手向外伸展,正在放飞一只鸟。
   He based his design on the innocent image of a child, hands outstretched, setting free a bird.
9. 这个组织具有强烈的公众形象。
   The organization has a strong public image.

10. 这个政客试图通过亲吻婴儿来改善形象。

    The politician tries to improve his image by kissing babies.
11. 他发现企业形象设计师从来没有如此重要过。

    He finds a business image designer has never been so important.
12. 这位形象代言人对评论没有回应。

    The image spokesman did not return calls for comment.
13. 这位女演员以前曾推广过许多产品和企业,但是这是她第一次充当媒体形象代言人的角色。

    The actress previously promoted many products and businesses, but it's the first time she has played the role of a media image spokeswoman.

"形象"的第二个意思是指"文艺作品中创造出来的生动具体的、能激发人的思想或感情的生活图景"。英语可以译为 image。例如:

14. 这位作家主张生动的文学形象不一定是有趣的文学形象。

    The writer holds that a vivid literary image is not necessarily an interesting one.
15. 我们通常要区分三类形象:艺术形象、文献记载的形象和普通形象。

    We usually distinguish three main categories of images: the artistic image, the documentary image and the ordinary image.
16. 形象思维与逻辑思维之间没有不可逾越的鸿沟。

    There is no impassable chasm between thinking in terms of images and logic thinking.
17. 阿基里斯,这部英雄史诗的主要人物,呈现出一个英雄形象。

    Achilles, the main character in this epic poem, exhibits a heroic image.

"形象"的第三个意思是"描绘或表达具体生动"。英语可以译为 vivid, expressive。例如:

18. 这位教师在谈话中用了一个形象的比喻。

    The teacher used a vivid figure of speech in his talk.

19. 这位演说家的语言精练而形象。

　　The orator's language is concise and expressive.

"形象逼真"有歧义,可以是"形象是逼真的",也可以是"又形象,又逼真"。例如:

20. 这个形象逼真。

　　The image is true to life.

21. 这幅画形象逼真。

　　The picture is vivid and true to life.

22. 这个人物形象逼真。(这个人物形象是逼真的。)

　　The character image is true to life.

23. 这个人物形象逼真。(这个人物又形象又逼真。)

　　The character is vivid and true to life.

# 五十六、事　　业

● 汉语关键词

　　事业、事业心、事业单位、福利事业、公用事业、事业费

● 英语关键词

　　undertaking, cause, career, devotion to one's work, dedication to one's work, public institution, welfare services, public utilities, operating expenses

● 句　子

　　他在一家事业单位工作。

● 误　译

　　He works at an undertaking unit.

● 正　译

　　He works at a public institution.

### 解 释

"事业单位"是与"企业单位"而言的,应该译为 public institution。

"事业"的第一个意思是"人们为实现某个目标而从事的、具有一定规模和体系、对社会发展具有一定影响的经常性活动"。英语可以译为 undertaking, cause 或 career。undertaking 强调"承担的任务"。例如:

1. 这位科学家才年仅30岁,但是已经事业有成。
   Though the scientist is only thirty years old, he is already quite successful in his undertaking.
2. 他下决心完成父亲未完成的事业。
   He has made up his mind to fulfill the undertaking that his father had failed to.

cause 强调"支持或捍卫的经常性活动"。例如:

3. 这位教师把一生都献给了教育事业。
   The teacher has dedicated his whole life to the cause of education.
4. 中国人民正在继续为世界和平事业而战斗。
   The Chinese people are continuing to fight for the cause of world peace.
5. 我们将共同努力推进人类和平与发展的崇高的事业。
   1) We'll make joint efforts to advance the lofty cause of peace and development for mankind.
   2) We'll make joint efforts to forward the lofty cause of peace and development for mankind.
6. 这个学术团体的宗旨是促进科学发展,维护科学事业。
   This academic society aims at promoting the progress of science and upholding the cause of science.
7. 该组织致力于推动科学教育事业。
   This organization is dedicated to furthering the cause of science education.
8. 这家公司非常积极从事慈善事业。
   The corporation is very active in the cause of charity.

9. 这些环境保护主义者都支持环境保护事业。
   1) These environmentalists all support the cause of environmental protection.
   2) These environmentalists all champion the cause of environmental protection.
10. 他终生为正义事业而斗争。
    He has fought for the cause of justice all his life.

career 强调"从事的职业"。例如:
11. 为了适应未来事业发展的需要,我已决定继续深造。
    To meet the needs of career development in the future, I have decided to further my studies.
12. 你应该把自己培养成一个搞事业的人。
    You should train yourself to be a career-minded person.
13. 作为一个搞事业的人,他把自己的工作视为受不断拓展自己的思想、知识、能力和原创力的驱使而不断进步的过程。
    As a career man, he regards his work as constant progress, driven by the constant expansion of his mind, his knowledge, his ability and his creative ingenuity.

"事业心",英语可以译为 devotion to one's work, dedication to one's work。例如:
14. 他的事业心和全心全意服务为他公司的每个人树立了典范。
    His devotion to his work and his whole-hearted service have set a good example for everyone in his company.
15. 他的朋友们都敬佩他的事业心和他面临困难时的勇气。
    His friends all admire him for his dedication to his work and also his courage when faced with difficulties.

"事业"的第二个意思是"特指没有或仅有少量生产或经营收入,主要由国家经费开支的事业"。"事业单位",英语可以译为 public institution。例如:
16. 事业单位由国家提供经费,并向公众提供服务。
    Public institutions are state-funded and offer services to the public.

17. 博物馆是一个独立的行政事业单位。
    The museum is an independent administrative institution.
18. 行政事业部门有权行使政府给予的行政管理权。
    Administrative departments have the power over administrative management that is given by the government.

"福利事业",英语可以译为 welfare services。例如:
19. 志愿者正在帮助他们的社区发展为贫困老人的福利事业。
    The volunteers are helping their community to develop welfare services for the needy elderly people.

"公用事业",英语可以译为 public utilities。例如:
20. 城市公用事业包括城市公共交通、电力供应、燃气供应、给排水和电信等方面。
    Urban public utilities include urban public transportation, supply of electricity and natural gas, supply and drainage of water, and telecommunications.

"事业费",英语可以译为 operating expenses。例如:
21. 事业费包括销售费用和行政管理费。
    Operating expenses consist of selling and administrative expenses.

# 五十七、架　　子

● 汉语关键词

架子、衣裳架子、摆架子、拿架子、没有架子

● 英语关键词

stand, rack, shelf, frame, skeleton, clothes-horse figure, outline, framework, put on airs, assume great airs, be haughty in one's manner, stand on one's dignity, ride the high horse, mount the high horse, be easy of approach, be modest and unassuming in one's manner, stance, posture, way

● 句 子

你是个衣裳架子,穿什么都好看。

● 误 译

You are a clothing rack. You would look good in anything.

● 正 译

You've got a clothes-horse figure. You would look good in anything.

● 解 释

clothing rack 指晾晒衣服的架子,没有比喻意义。clothes horse 与"马"无关,除了指晾晒衣服的架子以外,还可以比喻"穿戴讲究、衣着时髦的人"。例如:

1. 这个晒衣架用来晾晒衣服和毛巾。

   The clothes horse was used for drying clothes and towels.

2. 她是沿街最引人注目的衣着时髦的人。

   She is the most striking clothes horse along the street.

"衣裳架子"比喻"窈窕身材",可以译为 clothes-horse figure。例如:

3. 她有两只大的黑眼睛,一副笑脸和一副窈窕身材。

   She has huge dark eyes, a smiling face and a clothes-horse figure.

4. 这位老妇人仍然保持着她的窈窕身材。

   The old lady still retains her clothes-horse figure.

"架子"的第一个意思是"支撑物体的构件或放置器物的用具"。英语可以译为 stand, rack, shelf, frame, skeleton。例如:

5. 这个花瓶架子自身就是一件艺术品。

   This vase stand is an art piece in itself.

6. 这个花盆架子的装饰图案令人赏心悦目。

   The ornamental design of the flower pot stand is pleasing to the eye.

7. 织物陈列在铁丝架子上。

   The fabric was displayed on a wired stand.

8. 她洗完盘子,然后放到盘子架子上去晾干。

   She washed the dishes and then put them in the plate rack to dry.

9. 请不要随便从架子上拿取书籍。

   Please do not help yourself to books from this shelf.

10. 他被从墙上伸出的架子碰伤了。

    He was hurt by a shelf protruding from the wall.

11. 笔记本放在最高的架子上。

    The notebook is on the topmost shelf.

12. 她小心翼翼地把杯子放在架子边上。

    She carefully placed the cup on the edge of the shelf.

13. 我的书太多,架子装不下。

    I have too many books for my shelves.

14. 昨天她把一个架子装在墙上。

    Yesterday she fixed a shelf to the wall.

15. 架子在那么大的重压之下开始弯了下去。

    The shelf is beginning to yield under that heavy weight.

16. 他们缺少搭藤蔓攀爬的架子用的杆儿,而没有架子,葡萄产量就会减少一半。

    They were short of sticks to make frames for the climbing vines, without which the yield would be halved.

17. 他瘦得几乎变成了一个骨头架子。

    He is reduced almost to a skeleton.

"架子"的第二个意思是"比喻事物的组织或结构"。英语可以译为 outline, framework。例如:

18. 你应该先搭好架子再开始写文章。

    You are supposed to work out an outline before starting writing.

19. 小说的架子已经搭好了。
    The framework of the novel has been worked out.
20. 这所新学校正在搭架子。
    This new school is setting up its framework.

"架子"的第三个意思是"自高自大的神态、装腔作势的作风"。"摆架子"或"拿架子",英语译为 to put on airs, to assume great airs, to be haughty in one's manner, to stand on one's dignity, to ride the high horse, to mount the high horse。例如:

21. 因为爱摆架子,所以他不受欢迎。
    He is unpopular because he likes to put on airs.
22. 不要对老百姓摆官僚架子。
    Don't put on airs like a bureaucrat in front of the masses of people.
23. 你最好不要对我拿架子。我不喜欢那一套。
    You had better not put on airs with me. I won't like it.
24. 她老拿架子,因为她自以为比别的什么人都好。
    She is always putting on airs because she thinks she's better than everybody else.
25. 他和群众打成一片,从来不摆架子。
    He mixed freely with the people, never putting on airs.
26. 我的邻居总是摆架子,装出她认识重要人物,被邀请出席豪华宴会。
    My neighbour is always assuming great airs, pretending she knows important people and is invited to rich parties.
27. 他只是个科长,官不大,架子却不小。
    He is only a section chief, who takes a minor post, but is haughty in his manner.
28. 她没拿架子,没把我们当作仆人对待。
    She didn't stand on her dignity or treat us as servants.

29. 只有道德形象不高的人才会摆架子。

It is only people of small moral stature who have to stand on their dignity.

30. 他这个人有点太喜欢摆架子。

1) He is a bit too fond of riding the high horse.

2) He is a bit too fond of mounting the high horse.

"没有架子",就是"平易近人,谦和"。英语可以译为 to be easy of approach, to be modest and unassuming in one's manner。例如:

31. 那位部长一点儿没有官架子。

That minister is easy of approach.

32. 那位要人一点儿没有架子。

That important man is very unassuming in his manner.

33. 尽管有名,她仍然是个没有架子的人,就像她以前当学生时那样。

Despite her fame, she remained the modest, unassuming person she had been as a student.

"架子"的第四个意思是"架势、姿势"。英语可以译为 stance, posture, way。例如:

34. 他摆出要大干一场的架子。

He took the stance of going all out to do the work.

35. 一看他锄地的架子,就知道他是个庄稼里手。

Judging from the posture he takes when he works with a hoe, we know he is a good farmhand.

36. 一看架子,就看出他是个好木匠。

From the way he works, you can see he is a good carpenter.

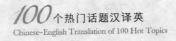

## 五十八、摩 擦

- 汉语关键词

  摩擦、摩擦力、摩擦音

- 英语关键词

  rub, friction, frictional force, force of friction, fricative, brush, clash

- 句 子

  中国官员建议应妥善解决两国经贸关系中的分歧和摩擦。

- 误 译

  A Chinese official suggests that the differences and rubbings between the two countries in economy and trade should be resolved appropriately.

- 正 译

  A Chinese official suggests that the differences and frictions between the two countries in economy and trade should be resolved appropriately.

- 解 释

  rubbing 表示物体之间的摩擦,不表示人与人、或国与国之间的冲突。而 friction 既可以表示物体之间,也可以表示人与人、或国与国之间的冲突。

"摩擦"的第一个意思是"物体和物体紧密接触,来回移动"。英语可以译为 to rub。例如:

1. 他在不停地摩擦双手来生热。

   He was constantly rubbing his hands, which generated heat.

2. 这两块漂浮在水面上的木头互相摩擦。

   The two pieces of wood that floated on the surface of the water were rubbing against each other.

3. 木炭屑同玻璃棒刚一摩擦,棒上就出现了电。

   No sooner had the pieces of charcoal been rubbed against the glass rod than electricity appeared on the rod.

"摩擦"的第二个意思是"两个相互接触的物体,当进行相对运动或有相对运动趋势时,在接触面上产生的阻碍运动的作用"。英语可以译为 friction。例如:
4. 我们走路和跑步时都依靠摩擦。
   We depend on friction when we walk or run.
5. 金属表面应该涂润滑脂,以减少摩擦。
   Metallic surfaces should be greased so as to decrease friction.
6. 与岩石之间的摩擦加上攀登者的重量,把绳子弄断了。
   Friction against the rock, combined with the weight of the climber, caused his rope to break.
7. 没有摩擦,皮带传动的机器就无法使用。
   In the absence of friction, belted machinery would not be used.
8. 摩擦使一个滚动的球最终停了下来。
   Friction causes a rolling ball to stop finally.
9. 摩擦使滑动的箱子逐渐慢了下来,然后停住。
   Friction gradually caused the sliding box to slow down and stop.
10. 两块粗糙厚木板如果经过打磨,它们之间的摩擦会减小。
    The friction between two rough planks can be lessened if they are made smooth.

"摩擦力",可以译为 frictional force, force of friction 或 friction。例如:
11. 因摩擦而产生的力称为摩擦力。
    The forces due to friction are called frictional forces.
12. 这种我们称为摩擦力的力总是阻碍运动。
    This force, which we call friction, always opposes motion.
13. 静摩擦力大于滑动摩擦力。
    Static friction is greater than sliding friction.

14. 摩擦力能影响航天器返回地球大气层的速度。
    The force of friction affects the speed at which spacecraft can re-enter the earth's atmosphere.

    "摩擦音",可以译为 fricative。例如:
15. 语音治疗包括听力辨别、行为训练、唇音训练、送气音和摩擦音训练、舌外伸训练、以及综合训练。
    Speech treatment includes audio discrimination, behaviour training, lip phone training, aspirates and fricatives training, tongue lolling out, and comprehensive training.

    "摩擦"的第三个意思是"个人、党派、团体或国家间因彼此利害矛盾而引起的冲突"。"轻微摩擦"英语可以译为 brush;"严重摩擦"可以译为 clash 或 friction。例如:
16. 昨天,他与邻居发生了摩擦。
    Yesterday, he had a brush with his neighbour.
17. 今天早晨,这小俩口有点小摩擦。
    This morning, the young couple had a little brush.
18. 这些示威者与警察有了一点小摩擦。
    1) The demonstrators had a brush with the law.
    2) The demonstrators had a brush with the police.
19. 中国已尽力用各种可能的方法避免与邻国发生边界摩擦。
    China has tried every possible way to avoid border clashes with her neighbouring countries.
20. 这两个派别正在闹摩擦。
    The two factions are in for a clash.
21. 这兄弟俩常常在意见上有摩擦。
    The two brothers often have a clash of opinions between them.
22. 这两个国家正试图通过谈判解决它们之间的冲突和摩擦。
    The two countries are trying to resolve the conflicts and frictions

between them through negotiations.
23. 由于玛丽爱干净,而埃玛邋遢,因此在她们合住一个房间时常常发生摩擦。
As Mary was neat and Emma was untidy, there were often frictions between them when they shared a room.

# 五十九、出　轨

● 汉语关键词

出轨、出轨行为、越轨、行为越轨

● 英语关键词

derail, be derailed, go off the rails, run off the rails, jump (off) the rails, jump the track, run off the lines, exceed the bounds, overstep the bounds, escapade, adultery, go beyond the limits, exceed the limits, commit an act of indiscretion, commit an act of decency, commit an act of transgression, transgress the bounds of decency, act improperly

● 句　子

据报导这列火车因超速行驶而出轨。

● 误　译

The train was reported to go off the rails because of exceeding the speed limits.

● 正　译

The train was reported to have gone off the rails because of exceeding the speed limits.

● 解　释

"报导"在后,用过去时;"出轨"在先,应该用不定式的完成体表示。

"出轨"或"脱轨"的第一个意思是"火车或有轨电车等轨道交通工具在

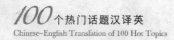

# 100个热门话题汉译英
Chinese-English Translation of 100 Hot Topics

行驶时脱离轨道"。英语可以译为 to derail, to be derailed, to go off the rails, to run off the rails, to jump (off) the rails, to jump the track, to run off the lines。例如：

1. 昨天郊区有列火车出轨了。

   A train was derailed in the suburbs yesterday.

2. 今天早晨一列地铁出轨了。

   A subway train went off the rails this morning.

3. 从山坡上掉下的一块巨石造成火车出轨。

   A boulder which had gone off the hillside derailed the train.

4. 一棵横在铁轨上的树造成机车出轨。

   The engine was derailed by a tree lying across the line.

5. 在日本北方，一列火车出轨两天后，救援人员从火车残骸中拖出了第五具尸体。

   Rescue workers pulled a fifth body from a train wreck two days after it derailed in northern Japan.

6. 这列火车由于碰上放在铁轨上的石块而出轨了。

   The train was derailed by rocks placed on the line.

7. 星期三，一列满载假日游客的巴基斯坦特快火车出轨，造成58人死亡和120多人受伤。

   A Pakistani express train packed with holiday travelers derailed on Wednesday killing 58 people and injuring more than 120.

8. 在西班牙，星期一有列地铁出轨致使至少30人丧生，10多人受伤。

   In Spain, a subway train derailed on Monday, killing at least 30 people and injuring a dozen more.

9. 由于受到破坏，一列火车出轨了。

   Owing to sabotage, a train jumped the rails.

10. 如果白蚁侵蚀了铁路枕木，火车就有出轨的危险。

    Trains are in danger of running off the rails if white ants have invaded the supporting beams.

11. 火车在靠近城镇边缘的地方出轨，结果导致了一场可怕的事故。
    The train jumped the track near the edge of the town and there was a terrible accident.
12. 一段破损的轨道使这列火车的尾部车厢出轨。
    A broken section of track caused the rear carriage of the train to jump off the rails.
13. 当这辆有轨电车出轨时，许多人受了伤。
    When the tram ran off the lines, many people were injured.

"出轨"的第二个意思是"比喻言语行动超出常规"。英语可以译为 to exceed the bounds, to overstep the bounds。例如：

14. 这的话说得出轨了。
    What he had said exceeded the bounds.
15. 他的行为出轨了。
    His behaviour has overstepped the bounds.
16. 他一向言行小心翼翼，惟恐出轨。
    He always speaks and behaves carefully lest he should overstep the bounds of decency or propriety.
17. 他办事稳妥，从不出轨。
    He acts reliably, never exceeding the bounds.

"出轨行为"，如果指冒险的事，可以译为 escapade。如果指偷情的事，可以译为 adultery。例如：

18. 他们用未成年酗酒狂欢和其它的出轨行为来表达对不负责任的父亲的愤恨。
    They acted out their resentment at their irresponsible father with underage drinking binges and other escapades.
19. 这个妇女公开指责她丈夫的出轨行为。
    The woman publicly accused her husband of adultery.

"越轨"的意思是"行为超出规章制度或公共道德所允许的范围"。英语可以译为 to go beyond the limits, to exceed the limits。例如:
20. 我们要按规矩办事,不要越轨。

　　We must act according to the rules, and mustn't go beyond the limits.
21. 如果你越轨了,你将会受到惩罚。

　　If you exceed the limits, you will be punished.

"行为越轨",可以译为 to commit an act of indiscretion, to commit an act of decency, to commit an act of transgression, to transgress the bounds of decency, to act improperly。例如:
22. 他们必须保持沉默,要不就行为越轨了。

　　They must keep silence, otherwise they will commit an act of indiscretion.
23. 最终,他们改变了进程,而且行为越轨了。

　　Finally, they changed their course and committed an act of decency.
24. 实际上,他并没有行为越轨。

　　Actually he didn't commit an act of transgression.
25. 她的决定没有影响别人,也没有行为越轨。

　　Her decision did not affect others or transgressed the bounds of decency.
26. 一位好公民不应该行为越轨。

　　A good citizen should not act improperly.

# 六十、妖　魔　化

● 汉语关键词

　　恶魔、妖魔、妖魔化

● 英语关键词

　　demon, turn sb into a demon, change sb into a demon, alter sb into a demon, convert sb into a demon, transform sb into a demon, demonize

● 句 子

美国正在妖魔化伊朗,将其当作下一个军事打击的目标。

● 误 译

The United States is turning Iran into a demon as the next target of a military strike.

● 正 译

The United States is demonizing Iran as the next target of a military strike.

● 解 释

demon 的意思是"恶魔"或"妖魔"。to turn sb into a demon 的意思是"用魔法使……变成妖魔",经常出现在神话鬼怪故事里,不是现实中的事情。它还有"变成恶魔一样的人"的意思。也可以用 to change sb into a demon, to alter sb into a demon, to convert sb into a demon, to transform sb into a demon 表示。例如:

1. 孙悟空摇身一变,成了个小妖怪。

   1) The Monkey King instantly turned himself into a little demon.
   2) The Monkey King instantly changed himself into a little demon.
   3) The Monkey King instantly altered himself into a little demon.
   4) The Monkey King instantly converted himself into a little demon.
   5) The Monkey King instantly transformed himself into a little demon.

2. 这只猫被变成了一个妖精,并赋予了九条命。

   The cat was turned into a demon and given nine lives.

3. 希特勒变成了杀了那么多犹太人的恶魔。

   Hitler converted himself into a demon that had so many Jews killed.

"妖魔化"的意思是"把人、团体或政党说成像妖魔一样邪恶"。英语可以译为 to demonize。例如:

4. 某些外国媒体妖魔化中国,伤害了中国人民的感情和尊严。

   Some foreign media demonized China, hurting the feeling and dignity of

the Chinese people.

5. 从1949年中华人民共和国成立时起,西方报界一直在妖魔化中国。
   Since the founding of the People's Republic of China in 1949, Western press has always demonized China.

6. 一些外国组织歪曲事实,妖魔化中国制造的产品。
   Some foreign organizations distorted the true facts, demonizing the products made in China.

7. 报纸的大字标题是:西方正在试图妖魔化中国。
   The headline of the newspaper is the West is trying to demonize China.

8. 丑化甚至妖魔化医生,既是我们社会的悲哀,也是我们社会的耻辱。
   To vilify and even demonize medical doctors is both a sorrow and a shame of our society.

9. 没有必要刻意神圣化一个行业,也没有必要妖魔化一个行业。
   It is unnecessary either to intentionally make a trade sacred, or to demonize it.

10. 这个公司的销售人员被揭露曾妖魔化他们的竞争对手。
    The salesmen from this company were exposed to have demonized their competitive rivals.

11. 在这本书里,神圣的女性被妖魔化,并被称为不洁。
    In this book, the sacred feminine was demonized and called unclean.

12. 我不认为他是那种任意妖魔化其他人的人。
    I don't think he is the type to demonize other people at will.

13. 他在报纸上发表了一篇文章妖魔化这位总统候选人。
    He published an article in the newspaper to demonize the presidential candidate.

14. 这位有偏见的政客把亚洲移民妖魔化为潜在的或现实的罪犯。
    The prejudiced politician has demonized the Asian immigrants as potential or actual criminals.

15. 战争时期的宣传总是妖魔化敌人。
    Wartime propaganda always demonizes the enemy.

16. 政客们在竞选活动中倾向于妖魔化他们的对手,而不是走到一起。
    Politicians tend to demonize their opponents instead of coming together in the election campaigns.
17. 这个政党的领导人对另一个政党的领导人说他们不应该互相妖魔化。
    The leader of this political party said to his counterpart from another party that they should not demonize one another.
18. 艺术使政治妖魔化的东西人性化。
    Art humanizes what politics demonizes.
19. 对待东方一直存在着两种明显不同的态度:一种是轻蔑和仇视,即丑化和妖魔化东方;另一种是赞赏和向往,即美化和诗意化东方。
    There are always two apparently different attitudes towards the Orient: one is contempt and enmity, that is to vilify and demonize the Orient; and the other is appreciation and aspiration, that is to beautify and poeticize the Orient.

# 六十一、地　　震

● 汉语关键词

地震、发生、大地震、地震灾区、政治地震、人事地震

● 英语关键词

earthquake, happen, occur, arise, take place, break out, big earthquake, great earthquake, large earthquake, huge earthquake, major earthquake, powerful earthquake, massive earthquake, earthquake-battered area, earthquake-jolted area, earthquake-stricken area, political earthquake, personnel earthquake

● 句　子

2008年5月12日,四川汶川发生大地震。

● 误　译

On May 12, 2008, a major earthquake was occurred in Wenchuan

County, Sichuan Province.

● 正 译

On May 12, 2008, a major earthquake occurred in Wenchuan County, Sichuan Province.

● 解 释

to occur 是个不及物动词，不能用被动语态，而应该用主动语态。

地震的"发生"，英语可以用 to happen, to occur, to arise, to take place, to break out 表示。例如：
1. 1976 年 7 月 28 日，河北唐山发生大地震。
   1) On July 28, 1976, a major earthquake happened in the city of Tangshan, Hebei Province.
   2) On July 28, 1976, a major earthquake occurred in the city of Tangshan, Hebei Province.
   3) On July 28, 1976, a major earthquake arose in the city of Tangshan, Hebei Province.
   4) On July 28, 1976, there arose a major earthquake in the city of Tangshan, Hebei Province.
   5) On July 28, 1976, a major earthquake took place in the city of Tangshan, Hebei Province.
   6) On July 28, 1976, a major earthquake broke out in the city of Tangshan, Hebei Province.

to hit, to jolt 也可以表示地震的"发生"。例如：
2. 1906 年 4 月 18 日，美国旧金山发生大地震。
   1) On April 18, 1906, a major earthquake hit San Francisco, U.S.
   2) On April 18, 1906, a major earthquake jolted San Francisco, U.S.

从"大地震"到"特大地震"，英语可以依次用 big earthquake, great earthquake, large earthquake, huge earthquake, major earthquake,

powerful earthquake, massive earthquake 表示。例如：
3. 1923年9月1日，日本东京发生大地震。
   1) On September 1, 1923, a big earthquake happened in Tokyo, Japan.
   2) On September 1, 1923, a great earthquake happened in Tokyo, Japan.
   3) On September 1, 1923, a large earthquake happened in Tokyo, Japan.
   4) On September 1, 1923, a huge earthquake happened in Tokyo, Japan.
   5) On September 1, 1923, a major earthquake happened in Tokyo, Japan.
   6) On September 1, 1923, a powerful earthquake happened in Tokyo, Japan.
   7) On September 1, 1923, a massive earthquake happened in Tokyo, Japan.

下面是一些与地震相关的表达方法：
4. 地震的发生是一种复杂现象，涉及很多偶然因素，是无法准确预测的。
   Earthquake occurrence is a complex phenomenon, which involves many accidental factors, and cannot be accurately predicted.
5. 甚至发达国家的地震专家也无法预报地震。
   Even seismologists from developed countries are unable to predict the earthquake happening.
6. 地震发生可能引起动物反常行为，但是动物反常行为不一定意味着地震发生。
   An earthquake occurrence may cause abnormal behaviour of animals, but abnormal behaviour of animals does not necessarily mean an earthquake occurrence.
7. 四川汶川大地震为里氏8.0级。
   The major earthquake that jolted Wenchuan County, Sichuan Province measured 8.0 on the Richter scale.
8. 如果地震发生在靠近人口密集的地区，它会造成许多人员伤亡，并造成巨大财产损失。
   If an earthquake occurs near populated areas, it may cause many deaths and injuries, and extensive property damage.

9. 中国政府正在采取有效措施防止和减少地震灾害。
   The Chinese Government is adopting effective measures to prevent and reduce earthquake disasters.
10. 汶川大地震发生以后立即开始了救援工作。
    Rescue work started immediately after the Wenchuan earthquake.
11. 这支救援队将用专业的方法和设备救援、搜寻和定位在地震灾害中的幸存者。
    The rescue team will use professional methods and equipment to rescue, search and locate the survivors in the earthquake disasters.

"地震灾区",英语可以译为 earthquake-battered area, earthquake-hit area, earthquake-jolted area, earthquake-stricken area。例如:

12. 今天,中国政府加快了在地震灾害地区的救援和救济工作。
    1) The Chinese government has today scaled up the rescue and relief efforts in the earthquake-battered areas.
    2) The Chinese government has today scaled up the rescue and relief efforts in the earthquake-hit areas.
    3) The Chinese government has today speeded up the rescue and relief efforts in the earthquake-jolted areas.
    4) The Chinese government has today speeded up the rescue and relief efforts in the earthquake-stricken areas.

"地震"还可以比喻"造成巨大震动的社会现象"。"政治地震",英语可以译为 political earthquake。"人事地震",英语可以译为 personnel earthquake。例如:

13. 这个高官的丑闻在这个欧洲国家引起了一场政治地震。
    The scandal of the high official caused a political earthquake in this European country.
14. 这次政治地震给这个欧洲国家的发展造成了负面影响。
    This political earthquake produced a negative influence upon the development of this European country.

15. 总经理的辞职在公司里引起了一场人事地震。
   The resignation of the general manager led to a personnel earthquake in the company.
16. 这个公司的首席执行官尽力阻止一场人事地震。
   The CEO of the corporation tried his best to prevent a personnel earthquake.

# 六十二、第一时间

- 汉语关键词

  第一、第一时间、第一地点

- 英语关键词

  first, primary, primary time, primary place, most important, most significant, come first

- 句子

  解放军救援队在第一时间奔赴地震灾区。

- 误译

  The PLA rescue teams hastened to the earthquake-stricken areas at the first time.

- 正译

  The PLA rescue teams hastened to the earthquake-stricken areas at primary time.

- 解释

  first time 的意思是"第一次"。而"第一时间"的意思指"距事情发生后最近的时间"。英语应该译为 primary time。例如:

1. 工厂厂长在第一时间赶到了事故现场。
   The factory director hurried to the accident scene at primary time.
2. 消防队员在第一时间赶到了火灾现场。
   The firefighters rushed to the fire scene at primary time.

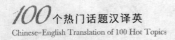
## 100个热门话题汉译英
### Chinese-English Translation of 100 Hot Topics

3. 记者在第一时间从震中地区发回了报道。
   The reporter sent back a dispatch from the epicentral area at primary time.
4. 地震发生之后,这位作家在第一时间向灾区人民捐款10万元。
   After the earthquake occurrence, the writer donated one hundred thousand *Yuan* to the people in the disaster-stricken area at primary time.
5. 医疗队在第一时间给伤员实施现场急救。
   The medical team gave emergency treatment on the spot to the wounded people at primary time.

"第一地点"指"某事最初发生或最初发现的地点"。英语可以译为 primary place。例如:
6. 广播电台播放了第一地点的现场新闻。
   The radio station broadcast the spot news from the primary place.
7. 超市经理要求售货员在第一时间和第一地点对顾客的需求做出快速反应。
   The supermarket manager demanded that the salespersons should make quick responses to the requirements of the customers at primary time and in primary place.

"第一"的第一个意思是"在一系列事物中排在等级或次序首位的"。英语可以译为 first。例如:
8. 他在学校数学竞赛中得了第一名。
   1) He got a first in the school math contest.
   2) He came first in the school math contest.
9. 美国"第一夫人"是白宫女主人的非正式称号。
   First Lady of the United States is the unofficial title of the hostess of the White House.
10. 我知道一家供应第一流美食的饭馆。
    I know a restaurant where first-class food is available.

11. 他已从一个权威的来源获取了足够的第一手材料。
    He has obtained enough firsthand information from an authoritative source.
12. 凡事都有第一次。
    There is a first for everything.

在两个紧密相关的事物比较时,英语可以用 primary 表示"第一",用 secondary 表示"第二"。例如:

13. 物质是第一性的,而意识是第二性的。
    Matter is primary while consciousness is secondary.
14. 第一产业包括农业、林业、渔业和畜牧业;第二产业包括采矿业、制造业、电子业和建筑业。
    Primary industry includes agriculture, forestry, fishery and husbandry, while secondary industry includes mining, manufacturing, electronics, and construction.
15. 有些专家认为既然科学技术构成第一生产力,那么管理就是第二生产力。
    Some experts hold that since science and technology constitute the primary productive force, then management is the secondary productive force.
16. 在银行抢劫案中,银行是第一现场,而逃跑的汽车和盗贼的藏身处是第二现场。
    In a bank robbery, the bank is the primary scene, but the get-away car and the thief's hiding place are secondary scenes.

"第一"的第二个意思是比喻"最重要的"。英语可以译为 most important, most significant 或 to come first。例如:

17. 百年大计,质量第一。
    1) For a project of vital and lasting importance, quality is most significant.
    2) For a project of vital and lasting importance, quality comes first.

· 205 ·

18. 生命可贵,健康第一。

1) Life is precious, and health is most important.

2) Life is precious, and health comes first.

19. 在高速公路上行车,安全第一。

1) When you drive on the expressway, safety is most important.

2) When you drive on the expressway, safety comes first.

20. 由于国家安全第一,我们必须加强国防建设。

1) As national security is most important, we must reinforce our national defence.

2) As national security comes first, we must reinforce our national defence.

# 六十三、救　　灾

● 汉语关键词

　　救、救灾、救荒、救火、救险、救急

● 英语关键词

　　save, rescue, come to sb's rescue, relieve famine, help sb to tide over a crop failure, fight a fire, put out a fire, extinguish a fire, carry out a salvage operation, help sb to cope with an emergency

● 句　子

　　全国人民正在为抗震救灾捐款捐物。

● 误　译

　　The Chinese people are donating money and materials to fight the earthquake and save the disaster.

● 正　译

　　The Chinese people are donating money and materials to fight the earthquake and provide disaster relief.

### 解 释

"救灾"的意思是"援助灾难中的人,使其免于灾难"。救的对象是人,不是灾难。不可以字对字译为 to save the disaster。"救灾"的字面意思是 to save sb from a natural disaster, 实际上经常译为 to provide disaster relief, to help people to tide over a natural disaster, to fight a disaster。例如:

1. 地震发生后,各级政府已投入大量资金抗震救灾。
   Since the occurrence of the earthquake, the governments at all levels have put in large amounts of funds to fight the earthquake and help people to tide over the disaster.
2. 装载救灾物资的汽车陆续抵达地震灾区。
   Trucks loaded with disaster relief materials have arrived successively in the earthquake-hit areas.
3. 地震灾区急需抢险器械和救灾基金。
   Equipment for rush repairs and funds for disaster relief are badly needed in the earthquake-battered areas.

"救"的意思是"营救或援助人,使其脱离或免于危险或灾难"。"救"的第一个用法是后面跟被救的对象,即受害者。英语可以译为 to save sb, to rescue sb, to come to sb's rescue。例如:

4. 如果有一线希望,就要千方百计救性命。
   Every effort will be made to save lives if there is the slightest hope.
5. 这位解放军战士跳入湍急的江水中去救这个儿童。
   The PLA soldier plunged into the rushing river to rescue the child.
6. 救援队员清除瓦砾将婴儿从废墟中救了出来。
   The rescue workers removed the rubble and saved the baby from the debris.
7. 一位60多岁的老太太在地震195个多小时后从岩石裂缝中被救出来。
   A woman in her 60s was rescued from a rock crack, more than 195

hours after the earthquake.

8. 尽管困难重重,救援队员们仍继续尽最大努力抢救被埋在瓦砾堆里的人。

   In spite of all difficulties, the rescuers continued to try their best to save people who had been buried in the piles of rubble.

9. 这支救险队曾经从大火和洪水中救过许多人。

   The emergency team has rescued many people from fires and floods.

10. 救险队员们继续在倒塌的楼房中搜寻遇难者并成功地救出了几名幸存者。

    The emergency workers continued to search ruined buildings for victims and succeeded in saving a few survivors.

"救"的第二个用法是后面跟表示灾难的名称,即造成危害的事物。"救"的字面意思是 to save sb from sth, to rescue sb from sth。但是,这类用法都有独特的译法。"救荒"的意思是"采取措施或帮助度过灾荒"。可以译为 to relieve famine, to help sb to tide over a crop failure。例如:

11. 政府采取了一系列有效措施救荒。

    1) The government adopted a series of effective measures to relieve famine.

    2) The government adopted a series of effective measures to help people to tide over a crop failure.

"救火"的意思是"灭火,并从火中救人和财物"。英语可以译为 to fight a fire, to put out a fire, to extinguish a fire。例如:

12. 他家房子着火了,他的邻居都来帮助救火。

    1) When his house was on fire, his neighbours came to help to fight the fire.

    2) When his house was on fire, his neighbours came to help to put out the fire.

    3) When his house was on fire, his neighbours came to help to extinguish the fire.

"救险"的意思是"从险境中救人和财物"。英语可以译为 to carry out a salvage operation。例如:

13. 救险队员们赶往瓦斯爆炸的煤矿进行救险。

    The emergency workers hastened to the coal mine where there had been firedamp explosions to carry out a salvage operation.

"救急"的意思是"帮助人脱离急难"。英语可以译为 to help sb to cope with an emergency。例如:

14. 正如俗话所说:"救急不救穷。"

    As a common saying goes, you can help a person to cope with an emergency but you can't save him from poverty.

# 六十四、断　　层

### 汉语关键词

断层、断层地震、地震断层、地壳断层、海底断层、断层作用、断层带、人才断层、文化断层、知识断层

### 英语关键词

fault, fault earthquake, earthquake fault, seismic fault, crust fault, submarine fault, faulting, fault zone, break in a continuum, gap in a continuum, break in continuity, gap in continuity, discontinuity

### 句　子

四川汶川发生大地震,地下断层延伸三百多公里。

### 误　译

A major earthquake occurred in Wenchuan County, Sichuan Province, with its underground fault stretched over 300 kilometres.

### 正　译

A major earthquake occurred in Wenchuan County, Sichuan Province,

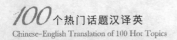

with its underground fault stretching over 300 kilometres.

### ● 解　释

　　to stretch 是不及物动词，在 with 引导的短语中要用现在分词，不能用过去分词。

　　"断层"的第一个意思是地质学名称，指"地壳岩石沿断裂面发生明显位移的地质现象"。英语可以译为 fault。例如：
1. 有些地震学家推测这条地震断层会引发大地震。
　　Some seismologists predicted that this seismic fault might cause major earthquakes.
2. 断层作用可以诱发地震，而地震发生又可能反过来促成断层的生成与发育。
　　Faulting may lead to earthquake happening, and earthquake happening may in turn promote the formation and growth of faults.
3. 这些科学家最近获得了地壳断层岩石样本，有助于科学家预测地震。
　　These scientists have recently obtained rock samples of crust fault, which is of help to the prediction of earthquakes.
4. 台湾的那次地震是由海底断层破裂所引起的。
　　The earthquake that occurred in Taiwan was caused by submarine fault rupture.
5. 这座桥梁遭受了断层地震的严重损害。
　　The bridge was seriously damaged by the fault earthquake.
6. 这个断层带能够造成具有极大破坏性的地震。
　　The fault zone is capable of generating significantly destructive earthquakes.

　　"断层"的第二个意思是"连续性的事业或人员的层次中断，不相衔接"。英语可以译为 break in a continuum, gap in a continuum, break in continuity, gap in continuity, discontinuity。例如：

7. 我们要避免我们的事业出现断层。
   1) We must avoid a break in the continuum of our undertakings.
   2) We must avoid a gap in the continuum of our undertakings.
8. 人才断层会阻碍科学技术的发展。
   The break in intellectual lineage will hinder the development of science and technology.
9. 我们必须培养大批优秀专业人员来弥补人才断层。
   We must train large numbers of excellent professionals to fill the gap in intellectual lineage.
10. 这个地区的高层次人才供应正出现结构性断层。
    In this region there has arisen a structural discontinuity in high-level talents supply.
11. 到目前为止还没有文化断层的迹象。
    Up to now, there has been no sign of a break in cultural continuity.
12. 越来越高的文盲率在最不发达国家形成了文化断层。
    The growing illiteracy rate has formed a gap in cultural continuity in the least developed countries.
13. 在文章中,作者讨论了文化传承与文化断层的问题。
    In the article, the author discusses the issue of cultural continuity and discontinuity.
14. 忽视基础教育,必将导致知识断层。
    The neglect of fundamental education will lead to a break in the continuum of knowledge.
15. 学习困难的学生通常存在知识断层。
    There is usually a break in the continuum of knowledge among the students with difficulties in their studies.
16. 问题是在我们的知识中存在断层。
    The problem is that there is a break in the continuum of our knowledge.
17. 一些青年学生感到他们面临知识断层危机。
    A few young students feel that they are faced with the crisis of knowledge

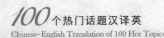

discontinuity.

18. 这位专家发现儿童教育中存在知识断层。
The expert finds that there is knowledge discontinuity in the children's education.

# 六十五、加　　油

> **汉语关键词**
> 
> 加油、加油站、火上加油、火上浇油、加油加醋、加油添醋

> **英语关键词**
> 
> fuel, refuel, filling station, petrol station, gas station, oil, lubricate, make an extra effort, work with added vigour, cheer sb on, root for sb/sth, go, come on, play up, cheer up, lighten up, pour oil on the flames, be fuel to sth, add highly-coloured details to sth

> **句　子**
> 
> 观众朝运动员们高声喊道:"加油!加油!"

> **误　译**
> 
> The spectators shouted loudly to the athletes, "Cheers!"

> **正　译**
> 
> 1) The spectators shouted loudly to the athletes, "Go! Go! Go!"
> 2) The spectators shouted loudly to the athletes, "Play up! Play up!"

> **解　释**
> 
> cheer 的意思是 a shout of joy, support or praise,即欢呼声或喝彩声。Cheers 是祝酒用语,即"干杯"。给运动员鼓劲儿,常喊"Go! Go! Go!"或"Play up! Play up!",就是"加油"的意思。

"加油"的第一个意思是"给运输工具添加燃料油"。英语可以译为 to fuel, to refuel。例如:

1. 所有的飞机在长途飞行前都必须加油。
   All aircraft must fuel before a long flight.
2. 直升机已经加满油,并准备起飞。
   The helicopter was already fuelled up and ready to go.
3. 公共汽车停下来加油。
   The bus made a stop to refuel.
4. 飞机在北京加油后继续飞行。
   The plane refueled at Beijing and flew on.
5. 飞机在执行下次任务之前需要加油。
   The plane needs to refuel before the next mission.
6. 飞机需要加燃油。请叫一辆加油车来。
   The aircraft needs refueling. Please call a refueling tender.

"加油站",可以译为 filling station, petrol station, gas station。例如:
7. 20公里之外有一个加油站。
   There is a filling station twenty kilometres away.
8. 我们可以到最近的加油站给汽车加满汽油。
   We can fill the car up with petrol at the nearest petrol station.
9. 我们最后驶近一个加油站。
   We finally drove up to a gas station.

"加油"的第二个意思是"给机器添加润滑油"。英语可以译为 to oil, to lubricate。例如:
10. 如果你不给机器加好(润滑)油,它就不会正常运转。
    The machine won't function properly if you don't oil it well.
11. 我给自行车加了(润滑)油,又给轮胎打足了气。
    I oiled my bike and pumped up the tyres.
12. 我定期给机器加(润滑)油,但是这无济于事。
    I have lubricated the machine regularly but this doesn't help at all.

# 100个热门话题汉译英
Chinese-English Translation of 100 Hot Topics

注意,"汽车需要加油"和"给汽车加油"有歧义:
13. 这辆汽车需要加(燃料)油。
    1) The car needs fueling.
    2) The car needs refueling.
14. 这辆汽车需要加(润滑)油。
    1) The car needs oiling.
    2) The car needs lubricating.
15. 他正在给汽车加(燃料)油。
    1) He is fueling the car.
    2) He is refueling the car.
16. 他正在给汽车加(润滑)油。
    1) He is oiling the car.
    2) He is lubricating the car.

"加油"的第三个意思是"在工作中或比赛中进一步努力或加劲儿"。英语可以译为 to make an extra effort, to work with added vigour。例如:
17. 在学习中,你必须加油。
    1) You must make an extra effort in your studies.
    2) You must work with added vigour in your studies.

"加油"的第四个意思是"鼓励在工作中或比赛中进一步努力或加劲儿"。英语可以译为 to cheer sb on, to root for sb/sth。例如:
18. 观众为赛跑运动员加油。
    The spectators cheered the runners on.
19. 他们为自己的足球队高声喊加油。
    They cheered loudly for their football team.
20. 观众都在给他们最心爱的运动员加油,希望他赢。
    The spectators were cheering their favourite athlete on, wishing him to win.
21. 祝你好运!我会为你加油。
    Good luck! I'll be rooting for you.

22. 他们正在给他们的队加油,争取胜利。
    They were rooting for their team to victory.
23. 观众们在给姚明加油。
    The spectators are rooting for Yao Ming.

"加油"的第五个意思是"鼓励进一步努力或加劲儿干的感叹语"。英语可以译为 to go, to come on, to play up, to cheer up, to lighten up。例如:

24. 几万人在天安门广场异口同声喊道:"中国,加油!"
    On Tian'anmen Square, tens of thousands of people shouted in the same voice," Go, China!"
25. 观众们高喊:"北京队,不要气馁。加油!"
    1) The spectators shouted loudly, "Beijing Team, don't lose heart. Please come on."
    2) The spectators shouted loudly, "Beijing Team, don't lose heart. Please cheer up."
    3) The spectators shouted loudly, "Beijing Team, don't lose heart. Please lighten up."

"火上加油"或"火上浇油",英语可以译为 to pour oil on the flames, to be fuel to sth。例如:

26. 这几句话起了火上加油的作用。
    These words served to pour oil on the flames.
27. 他的漠不关心使她的仇恨火上加油。
    His indifference was a fuel to her hatred.

"加油加醋",或"加油添醋"英语可以译为 to add highly-coloured details to sth。例如:

28. 他在叙述自己的经历时,总爱加油加醋。
    When recounting his experiences, he is fond of adding highly-coloured details to them.

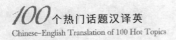

# 六十六、搜 索

### 汉语关键词
搜索、搜索飞行、搜索枯肠、搜索工具、搜索引擎、人肉搜索

### 英语关键词
search, search for, hunt for, comb a place for sth, scout around, scouting flight, search one's mind for sth, rack one's brain for sth, cudgel one's brain for sth, beat one's brain over sth, search tool, search engine

### 句 子
救援队员正在原始森林里搜索失踪的直升机。

### 误 译
The rescue workers were searching the missing helicopter in the primitive forest.

### 正 译
The rescue workers were searching for the missing helicopter in the primitive forest.

### 解 释
to search 的宾语是"被搜索的处所"; to search for 的宾语才是"被搜索的人或物"。

"搜索"的第一个意思是"仔细寻找隐藏或失踪的人或物"。英语可以译为 to search, to search for, to hunt for, to comb a place for sth, to scout around。例如：
1. 调查人员正在飞机残骸中进行搜索，试图找出造成悲惨事件的原因。
Investigators are searching the wreckage of the plane to try and find the cause of the tragedy.

2. 警方搜索了半径6公里以内树林的每个地方。
   1) The police searched all the woods within a radius of six kilometres.
   2) The police searched all the woods within a six-kilometre radius.
3. 救援队正在搜索海难中的幸存者。
   The rescue team was searching for the survivors of the shipwreck.
4. 调查人员仍在搜索直升机部件。
   Investigators were still searching for parts of the helicopter.
5. 调查人员今天搜索线索以探究这架班机在起飞后刚几秒钟就失事的原因。
   1) Investigators searched for clues today as to why the airliner crashed just seconds after takeoff.
   2) Investigators hunted for clues today as to why the airliner crashed just seconds after takeoff.
6. 这架侦察机正在搜索空中目标和地面目标。
   The reconnaissance plane was searching for aerial targets and ground targets.
7. 士兵在整个山坡上成扇形散开，搜索空降特务。
   The soldiers fanned out across the hillside and searched for the airborne spy.
8. 她继续忙为她的设计搜索新的理念。
   She keeps busy searching for new ideas for her designs.
9. 警方找遍群山搜索失踪的孩子。
   The police officials combed the hills for the missing child.
10. 警方搜索了这个地区，寻找爆炸的线索。
    The police combed the area for clues in bombing.
11. 我们将在树林里搜索丢失的羊。
    We'll go and scout around for the lost sheep in the woods.
12. 这个年轻人四处搜索生火用的木柴。
    The young man scouted around for wood for the fire.

"搜索飞行",英语译为 scouting flight。例如:
13. 这位飞行员受指令进行搜索飞行调查这次飞机失事。
The pilot was commanded to fly with a scouting flight to investigate this airplane crash.

"搜索枯肠"的意思是形容"写诗文时竭力思索"。英语可以译为 to search one's mind for sth, to rack one's brain for sth, to cudgel one's brain for sth, to beat one's brain over sth。例如:
14. 他搜索枯肠想找到几句安慰的话。
He searched his mind for some words of comfort.
15. 我搜索枯肠数日,试图选择一个可以写作的题目。
I racked my brain for days trying to choose a topic to write about.
16. 他搜索枯肠三天三夜,努力想找到一种解释。
He cudgeled his brain for three days and nights struggling for an explanation.
17. 这个博士生为写学位论文而搜索枯肠。
The PhD student beat his brain over his dissertation.

"搜索"的第二个意思是"利用网上搜索工具查找信息"。英语可以译为 to search, to search for。例如:
18. 我将演示给你看如何搜索互联网。
I'll show you how to search the Internet.
19. 他经常通过谷歌或雅虎搜索信息。
He often searches for information through Google or Yahoo.
20. 我搜索你的名字时,什么也找不到。
Nothing's coming up when I search for your name.

"搜索工具",英语可以译为 search tool。"搜索引擎",英语可以译为 search engine。例如:
21. 这种搜索工具能让你用你想用的任何关键词搜索谷歌。
The search tool allows you to search Google using any keyword(s) you wish.

22. 这是一个搜索本地网站和远处网站的容易安装的搜索引擎。
    This is an easy-to-install search engine for local and remote sites.
23. 这种搜索引擎能帮助你准确找到你在寻找的信息。
    The search engine may help you find exactly what you're looking for.

"人肉搜索",可以译为 cyber manhunt。"人肉搜索引擎",可以译为 human-powered search engine, human search engine。例如:

24. 有人认为人肉搜索可能会侵犯公民的隐私权。
    Some people think that cyber manhunt may violate a citizen's privacy.
25. 人肉搜索引擎依靠人力提交信息。
    Human-powered search engines rely on humans to submit information.
26. 今天早晨,在这个网站上出现了一个名叫《召唤人肉搜索引擎》的帖子。
    This morning, there appeared a post entitled *Calling for the human search engine* at this website.

# 六十七、干 预

### 汉语关键词

干预、干涉、心理干预、危机干预

### 英语关键词

interfere, intervene, meddle, psychological intervention, mental intervention, psychological interference, mental interference, crisis intervention, crisis interference

### 句 子

应该对地震灾区小学生的心理障碍进行干预。

### 误 译

The mental disorders of the elementary school students in the earthquake-hit areas should be intervented.

● 正 译

The mental disorders of the elementary school students in the earthquake-hit areas should be intervened.

● 解 释

英语没有 intervented 这个单词。中国学生常常误认为 intervention 的动词是 to intervente 或 to intervent，其实应该是 to intervene。

"干预"的第一个意思是"过问别人的事"，带有贬义。"干涉"的意思是"强行过问或制止别人的事，尤其是不应该管而硬管的事"，也带有贬义。英语可以译为 to interfere，to intervene，to meddle。例如：

1. 他希望他的母亲停止干预，让他自己做决定。
   He wishes his mother would stop interfering and let him make his own decisions.
2. 我们不要干预这些涉及隐私的事情。
   We mustn't interfere in these things that involve privacy.
3. 我劝你不要干预他人的家务事。
   I advise you not to intervene in other people's family matters.
4. 他无权干预你的事情。
   He has no right to meddle in your affairs.
5. 他从不干预政治事务和政治问题。
   He has never meddled in political affairs and political issues.
6. 父母不应过多干预子女的婚姻。
   Parents shouldn't interfere too much in their children's marriage.
7. 警方非常不愿意干预家务事。
   The police are very unwilling to interfere in family problems.
8. 你最好不要干涉别人的私事。
   1) You'd better not interfere in other people's private affairs.
   2) You'd better not meddle in other people's private affairs.
   3) You'd better not poke your nose into other people's private affairs.

9. 任何一个国家都不应该干涉别国的内政。
   No country should interfere in the internal affairs of other countries.
10. 我们反对任何国家用武力干涉中国统一的企图。
    We are opposed to the attempt of any country to intervene by force in China's unification.

"干预"的第二个意思是"通过引导、启发、转移、排解等方法达到缓解心理压力的目的,并能给予积极的治疗",带有中性义。英语可以译为 to interfere, to intervene。例如:

11. 他在讲演中就如何干预一些大学生的自杀心理提出了建议。
    In his talk, he made suggestions on how to interfere in some college students' suicidal psychology.
12. 他就如何干预消防队员在大火现场的心理危机进行了一系列的研究。
    He has made a series of studies on how to intervene in the psychological crisis of firemen at the scene of fire.
13. 在地震灾区,心理医生已经采取了一些必要措施对失去父母的孩子们进行心理危机干预。
    In the earthquake-stricken areas, psychiatrists have adopted some necessary measures to intervene in the psychological crisis of those children who had lost their parents.

"心理干预",可以译为 psychological intervention, mental intervention, psychological interference, mental interference。"危机干预",可以译为 crisis intervention, crisis interference。例如:

14. 四川大地震发生以后,中国将帮助受精神创伤的幸存者进行心理干预。
    China will help traumatized survivors with psychological intervention after the massive quake that occurred in Sichuan Province.
15. 在早期阶段,心理干预治疗有助于患者的康复。
    In early stage, mental intervention treatment is helpful to the recovery

of the patient.
16. 这位医生研究了心理干预对癌症病人的影响。
    The doctor has studied the effects of psychological interference on patients with cancer.
17. 这位研究者使用一种新技术检测对人脑的心理干预。
    The researcher used a new technique to detect mental interference to the human mind.
18. 在灾难发生以后,有效的心理危机干预可以帮助人们获得生理和心理上的安全感。
    After a disaster occurs, effective psychological crisis intervention can help people obtain the sense of security physiologically and psychologically.
19. 心理危机干预的主要目的是避免自伤或伤及他人,和恢复心理平衡与动力。
    Psychological crisis intervention is mainly aimed at helping people to avoid doing harm to themselves or to others, and to recover their mental balance and mental power.
20. 在高校,心理咨询师在危机干预中正起着重要作用。
    Psychological consultants are playing an important role in crisis interference at universities and colleges.

# 六十八、封　　杀

## 汉语关键词

封杀、封禁、取缔、抵制、扼杀、制止

## 英语关键词

ban, boycott, nip, drive sb out of the entertainment business, forbid sb to participate in a contest, ban sb from entering a contest, force out

## 句　子

这所英国大学因公然支持"藏独"而遭到中国网民封杀。

● 误 译

This British university was banned by the Chinese netizens for it had openly supported Tibetan independence.

● 正 译

This British university was boycotted by the Chinese netizens for it had openly supported Tibetan independence.

● 解 释

to ban sth 的意思是 to forbid sth officially,即"官方明令禁止"。普通民众无权禁止,只能抵制。to boycott 的意思是 to refuse to buy, use or take part in sth as a way of protesting,即"抵制"。这里应该用 to boycott。

"封杀"的第一个意思是"权威部门用封禁或取缔的办法使人或物在某一个领域不能存在"。英语可以译为 to ban。例如:

1. 想不到这样一部优秀文学作品竟遭封杀。

It is unexpected that such an excellent literary work has been banned.

2. 本市有关部门将封杀翻译错误和不规范的英文标志。

The concerning department of this city will ban those mistakenly translated and non-standard signs in English.

3. 有关部门已经封杀了这些不健康广告。

The concerning department has banned these unhealthy advertisements.

4. 我市公安和工商管理部门将封杀没有资质的职业中介机构。

The department of public security and administrative department of industry and commerce in our city will ban those unqualified employment agencies.

5. 上海电影节组委会将永久封杀莎朗·斯通本人及其影片,以抗议她对四川地震发表的不当言论。

The organizing committee of the Shanghai International Film Festival will permanently ban Sharon Stone and her films in protest against her for the improper comments she made about the Sichuan earthquake.

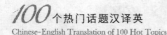

6. 据报道,美国政府封杀了这家来自伊朗的商业公司。
   It is reported that the U. S. Government has banned this commercial company from Iran.
7. 据报载,美国网络服务供应商将联手封杀全国范围内的儿童色情网站及论坛。
   According to the newspaper, American network service providers will ban the child sex websites and forums across the country in a joint effort.

"封杀"的第二个意思是"群众用抵制的办法使人或物在某一个领域不能存在"。英语可以译为 to boycott。例如:
8. 这些学生正在呼吁人们封杀这家使用童工的公司的产品。
   These students are asking people to boycott goods from the company that uses child labour.
9. 有些青年人通过网络号召顾客们封杀这家据说曾资助"藏独"的外国企业。
   Through the web, some young people called on the customers to boycott the foreign enterprise, which was said to have aided Tibetan independence.

"封杀"的第三个意思是"扼杀或制止,以使事情不能发生"。英语可以译为 to nip。例如:
10. 这股歪风一冒头即遭封杀。
    The evil trend was nipped in the bud.

"封杀"的第四个意思是"逼迫艺人退出演艺界或禁止运动员参加比赛"。英语可以译为 to drive sb out of the entertainment business, to forbid sb to participate in a contest, to ban sb from entering a contest。例如:
11. 这个演员因"艳照门"丑闻而被封杀。
    The actor was driven out of the entertainment business due to his "sex photo" scandal.
12. 这名运动员因在体育运动中服用兴奋剂而遭封杀。
    1) The athlete was forbidden to participate in the contest for having

taken dopes in sport.

2) The athlete was banned from entering the contest for having taken dopes in sport.

"封杀"的第五个意思是棒球术语,即"守场员对击跑员进行传杀或对由于击跑员击球上垒而被迫进垒的跑垒员进行传杀的防守行为"。英语可以译为 to force out。例如:

13. 当守场员在跑垒员进垒之前已将球传至跑垒员被迫所进之垒,跑垒员即被封杀。

A base runner is forced out when a fielder with the ball touches the runner's force base before the runner reaches that base.

14. 跑垒员因未能跑至被迫所进之垒而被封杀。

The base runner was forced out for failing to touch the base to which he was forced.

# 六十九、领　　养

● 汉语关键词

领养、认养、收养、代养

● 英语关键词

foster, adopt, adoption, take in and bring up, take in and provide for

● 句　子

这对中年夫妇决定从地震灾区领养一个孤儿。

● 误　译

The middle-aged couple decided to foster an orphan from the earthquake-hit area.

● 正　译

The middle-aged couple decided to adopt an orphan from the

earthquake-hit area.

### ● 解 释

英语 to foster 的意思是 to take sb else's child into your home for a period of time, without becoming his or her legal parent(s), 即"帮助抚养别人寄养的孩子, 但不成为其法定父母", 实际上是"代养一段时间", 不是"领养"。to adopt 的意思是 to take sb else's child into your family and become its legal parent(s), 即"收养别人的孩子, 成为其法定父母", 才是"领养"。

"领养"、"认养"和"收养"的第一个意思是"通过法定手续认领别人的孩子, 当作自己的子女抚养"。英语可以译为 to adopt, adoption, to take in and bring up。例如:

1. 这对无子女夫妇从孤儿院认养了一个女儿。
   This childless couple adopted a daughter from the orphanage.
2. 根据法律, 一名收养人只能收养一个孩子, 或男或女。
   According to the law, an adopter may adopt one child only, male or female.
3. 这个小女孩被收养成为我家的一员。
   The little girl was adopted into our family.
4. 由于这对已婚夫妇无法生育, 他们领养了一个私生子。
   As the married couple couldn't have children, they adopted a child born out of wedlock.
5. 20 多年来, 这个收破烂儿的老汉收养了几十个弃婴。
   Over the past twenty years or more, the old rag-and-bone man has taken in and brought up dozens of foundlings.
6. 许多不能生育的美国夫妇来亚洲领养婴孩。
   Many American couples that can't have a baby come to Asia to adopt babies.
7. 在很多地方, 同性的伴侣不能领养小孩。
   In many places, same-sex partners can't adopt children.
8. 这个穷苦的妇女被迫把婴儿给别人领养。
   The poor woman was forced to have her baby adopted.

9. 我不是汤姆的亲生父亲。他是我的养子。
   I'm not Tom's real father. He is my adopted son.
10. 他不是我们的亲生儿子。他三岁时我们领养了他。
    He's not our natural son. We adopted him when he was three.
11. 她太穷了,养不起她的婴儿,就不得不提出让别人领养。
    She was too poor to keep her baby alive and had to put it up for adoption.
12. 如果你自己不能生孩子,为什么不考虑领养呢?
    If you can't have children of your own, why not consider adoption?

"领养"、"认养"和"收养"的第二个意思是"通过法定手续认领别的老人,当作自己的亲人赡养"。英语可以译为 to adopt, to take in and provide for。例如:

13. 这个教师认养了一位孤寡老头。
    1) This teacher adopted a wifeless and childless old man.
    2) This teacher took in and provided for a wifeless and childless old man.

"领养"或"认养"的第三个意思是"经有关部门确认负责养护动物、绿地、树木、公共设施等"。英语可以译为 to adopt。例如:

14. 这对老夫妇在动物园领养了一只大熊猫。
    This old couple adopted a giant panda in the zoo.
15. 她从一个动物福利组织认养了一只无家可归的宠物猫。
    She adopted a homeless pet cat from an animal welfare organization.
16. 黑猫比起其他种类的猫不容易被领养。
    Black cats tend to be adopted less often than other felines.
17. 最近,本市开展了认养绿地的活动。
    We have recently launched a campaign for the adoption of greenbelt in our city.
18. 我在我们住宅小区的花园里认养了一棵树。
    I adopted a tree in the garden of our residential area.

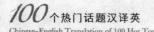

19. 据报载,旧金山市政府计划认养中国地震灾区2至3个城镇,以帮助重建。
According to the newspaper, San Francisco Municipal Government planned to adopt two to three towns in China's earthquake-stricken areas, so as to aid their reconstruction.

"收养"的第三个意思是"收容被遗弃的动物,负责喂养"。英语可以译为 to take in and provide for abandoned animals。例如:

20. 这位老太太在家里收养了十几只流浪狗。
This old lady took in and provided for a dozen of stray dogs in her house.

# 七十、疏　导

● 汉语关键词

疏导、心理疏导

● 英语关键词

dredge, channel, direct, lead, guide, regulate, guide by persuasion, persuade by reason, psychological counseling, psychological persuasion

● 句　子

我们要疏导大学生,以解决他们的思想问题。

● 误　译

We should channel the university students by persuasion so as to solve their ideological problems.

● 正　译

We should guide the university students by persuasion so as to solve their ideological problems.

● 解　释

to channel 的意思是 to direct money, ideas, feelings, etc. towards a

particular thing or purpose,即"将金钱、思想、感情等引导到一个特定事物或目的上来",其宾语是事物,而不是人。例如:
1. 老师把这个学生的思想引导到实践和行动上来。
   The teacher channeled the student's ideas into practice and action.
2. 父亲把这个男孩的精力引导到有用的事情上来。
   His father channeled the boy's energies into something useful.
3. 教练把这个青年人的好斗情绪引导到体育上来。
   His coach channeled the young man's aggression into sport.

"疏导"的第一个意思是"开通壅塞的水道,使水流通畅"。英语可以译为 to dredge。例如:
4. 科学家们发现有必要疏导这条河流。
   The scientists found it necessary to dredge the river.
5. 他们疏导了这条运河以阻止洪水。
   They dredged the canal to stop flooding.
6. 我们疏导了这条沟以减缓洪水。
   We dredged the ditch to mitigate flooding.

"疏导"的第二个意思是"引导气体或液体,使之流动顺畅"。英语可以译为 to channel。例如:
7. 这个竖井用来将沼气疏导至表面。
   The vertical shaft is used to channel marsh gas to the surface.
8. 植物茎中的筛管能够疏导水分。
   The sieve tubes of a plant stem can channel moisture.
9. 他们疏导水流引进沙漠。
   They channeled water into the desert.

"疏导"的第三个意思是"引导拥堵的车辆,使交通顺畅"。英语可以译为 to direct, to channel, to lead, to guide, to regulate。例如:

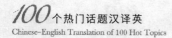

10. 他的工作是早高峰时疏导交通。
    His job is to direct the traffic during the morning rush hour.
11. 高峰时,这名志愿者在交通拥堵处帮助疏导车辆。
    During rush hours, the volunteer helps to direct the flow of cars in places with heavy traffic.
12. 这些交通设施已经成功地发挥了有效疏导交通的功能。
    These transportation facilities have successfully performed their function to channel the traffic flow efficiently.
13. 在一些地方,警车被用来疏导交通。
    In some places, police cars are used to lead traffic.
14. 在这个城市,他们已在街道上安装了智能交通标识来疏导交通。
    In this city, they have installed intelligent traffic signs on the streets to guide traffic.
15. 在这个地区,交通警察有许多志愿者帮助他们疏导交通。
    The traffic police have many volunteers to help them regulate traffic in this area.

"疏导"的第四个意思是"通过讲道理开导,使思想或心理问题得到解决"。英语可以译为 to guide by persuasion, to persuade by reason。例如:
16. 这位官员不厌其烦地对群众做疏导工作。
    The official takes the trouble to guide the masses by persuasion.
17. 对不满的人进行疏导是必要的。
    It's necessary to persuade the disgruntled people by reason.
18. 他正在对那些抱怨的人进行疏导。
    He was persuading by reason those people who had made complaints.

"心理疏导",英语可以译为 psychological counseling, psychological persuasion。例如:
19. 我们应该给大学生提供更多的心理疏导。
    We should offer more psychological counseling to university students.

20. 地震灾区的救援人员也需要心理疏导。
    The rescue workers in the earthquake-stricken areas also need psychological counseling.
21. 这个妇女有心理障碍,需要接受心理疏导。
    The woman suffers from mental disorder and needs psychological counseling.
22. 这位心理咨询师正在通过心理疏导治疗患抑郁症的病人。
    The psychological consultant was treating the patient who suffered from depression with psychological persuasion.
23. 只有通过持续的心理疏导,他的焦虑才能消除。
    Only through constant psychological persuasion, can his anxiety be relieved.

# 七十一、公　　害

## 汉语关键词

公害、侵扰公共利益罪、柴鸡蛋、散养鸡蛋、笼养鸡蛋

## 英语关键词

public nuisance, free-range egg, cage-free egg, battery egg, serious environmental pollution, serious pollution to the environment, public harm to the environment, hazard, public hazard, plague, public plague

## 句　子

刚才我在超市买了一袋无公害柴鸡蛋。

## 误　译

Just now I bought a bag of non-public nuisance fresh eggs in the supermarket.

## 正　译

Just now I bought a bag of organic free-range eggs in the supermarket.

## 解　释

public nuisance 的意思是 an offence by sb in a public place or affecting

the morals, safety, or health of the community, 即"侵扰公共利益罪", 是一个法律专有名词, 有严格的界定, 与食品无关。例如:
1. 他被控犯有侵扰公共利益罪。
   He was charged with causing a public nuisance.

"无公害鸡蛋"是"没有受到污染的鸡蛋", 但是不能直译为 pollution-free egg, 因为英语不用这样的说法。"无公害鸡蛋"就是"有机鸡蛋", 可以译为 organic egg。fresh egg 是"鲜蛋", 不等于柴鸡蛋。"柴鸡蛋"是散养鸡蛋, 译为 free-range egg 或 cage-free egg, 区别于笼养鸡蛋(battery egg)。例如:
2. 她总是吃柴鸡蛋, 而不吃笼养鸡蛋。
   She always eats free-range eggs rather than battery ones.

"公害"的第一个意思是"各种污染源对社会公共环境造成的严重污染和破坏"。英语可以译为 serious environmental pollution, serious pollution to the environment, public harm to the environment。例如:
3. 废气、废水、废渣、噪声污染、恶臭、振动和光污染都会造成公害。
   Waste gas, wastewater, waste residue, noise pollution, foul smelling, vibration, and light pollution may all cause serious environmental pollution.
4. 这家化工厂的项目已经造成了公害, 并损伤了附近居民的健康。
   The project of this chemical plant has caused serious pollution to the environment and harmed the health of the residents in the neighbourhood.
5. 这些危险的化学品在万一燃烧时可能产生有毒气体和气味, 构成二次公害。
   These hazardous chemicals may produce toxic gas and odour in case of burning, making up a second public harm to the environment.

"公害"的第二个意思是比喻"对公众健康、安全和道德观念造成威胁的有害事物"。英语可以译为 hazard, public hazard, public plague。例如:
6. 在全世界, 环境污染已成为一大公害。
   Environment pollution has become a serious public hazard all over the world.

7. 国家保护和改善我们的生存环境和生态环境,并防治污染和其他公害。

    The state protects and improves our living environment and ecological environment, and also prevents and controls pollution and other public hazards.

8. 毒品是全人类面对的世界性公害。

    Drugs are a worldwide public hazard confronted by the whole humankind.

9. 堆积如山的垃圾已成为威胁这个地区居民健康的公害。

    The piles of rubbish have become a serious public hazard that endangers the health of the inhabitants in this area.

10. 世界卫生组织称,遭遇环境公害造成的危险时,儿童远比成年人脆弱。

    The World Health Organization says that children are far more vulnerable than adults when it comes to the dangers posed by environmental hazards.

11. 世界卫生组织称,环境公害能引起流产、死胎、低出生体重和先天缺陷。

    The World Health Organization says environmental hazards can cause miscarriage, still birth, low birth weight and birth defects.

12. 城市宠物狗泛滥会造成公害。

    That people raise pet dogs in an unchecked way in urban areas will give rise to public hazards.

plague 的本义是 any infectious disease that kills a lot of people,即"死亡率高的传染病"或"瘟疫"。例如:

13. 欧洲在中世纪多次遭受瘟疫。

    Europe suffered many plagues in the Middle Ages.

14. 科学家们在努力开发医治艾滋病这种新的严重传染病的药物方面已取得重大进展。

    The scientists have made great progress in the effort to develop drugs against the new plague of Aids.

plague 具有 widespread(广泛传播的)、uncontrollable(不可控制的)、harmful(有害的),甚至 fatal(致命的)等特点。public plague 具有比喻意义,也可以译为"公害"。例如:

15. 人们公认赌博是一大公害。
    It is generally acknowledged that gambling is a public plague.
16. 政府采取了严厉措施扫黄打非,以清除这些公害。
    The government has adopted strict measures to eliminate pornography and illegal publications so as to remove these public plagues.
17. 在当今世界,邪教已成为一大公害。
    Cults have become a public plague in today's world.
18. 嫉妒是什么人都不放过的公害。
    Envy is a public plague that spares no one.

# 七十二、泛　滥

### 汉语关键词
泛滥

### 英语关键词
be in flood, flood, overflow, inundate, be flooded with, be deluged with, be awash with, spread unchecked, spread in an unchecked way, unchecked spread, unchecked spreading, reach epidemic levels, reach epidemic proportions

### 句　子
目前市场上假文物泛滥,欺骗了很多顾客。

### 误　译
At present, forged relics are spreading unchecked in the market, which have deceived many customers.

### 正　译
At present, the market is flooded with forged relics, which have

deceived many customers.

### 解 释

to spread unchecked 的意思是"不受限制地自由传播",指的是像思想或疾病等一种东西的广泛散布。"市场上的文物"是数量众多的商品,"假文物泛滥"是大量的东西充斥市场。例如:

1. 我们决不能让错误思想和言行自由泛滥。

   We won't allow erroneous ideas and actions to spread unchecked.

"泛滥"的第一个意思是"江河湖泊的水溢出而淹没"。英语动词可以译为 to be in flood, to flood, to overflow, to inundate; 名词可以译为 overflow。例如:

2. 这条河泛滥了。

   The river has flooded.

3. 我们不能从那里穿过草地,因为河水泛滥了。

   We can't cross the meadow there because the river is in flood.

4. 每年春天,这条河都泛滥。

   Every spring, the river overflows.

5. 这条河泛滥,直到街道被水淹没。

   The river overflowed until the streets were awash.

6. 他们修筑了一道临时堤坝以防止河流泛滥。

   They built a temporary dam to prevent the river from overflowing.

7. 南方一些人口稠密的省份洪水泛滥成灾。

   Some populous provinces in South China were seriously inundated with flood.

8. 在古埃及,繁荣与人民的生存依靠尼罗河每年一次的泛滥。

   In ancient Egypt, both the prosperity and the very existence of the people depended on the annual overflow of the Nile.

"泛滥"的第二个意思是"事物数量太多而充斥"。英语可以译为 to be flooded with, to be deluged with, to be awash with。例如:

# 100个热门话题汉译英
## Chinese-English Translation of 100 Hot Topics

9. 解放前,中国一些沿海城市外国货泛滥。
   1) In the pre-liberation days, some coastal cities in China were flooded with foreign goods.
   2) Before liberation, some coastal cities in China were deluged with foreign goods.
10. 这个城市毒品泛滥。
    The city is awash with drugs.
11. 这些日子,书店里关于如何养宠物的书泛滥。
    These days, the bookshops are flooded with books on how to keep pets.
12. 市场上声称具有减肥作用的健康补品泛滥。
    The market is awash with health supplements claiming to have slimming properties.
13. 不幸的是,市场上假冒、谬误和伪造的证书泛滥。
    Unfortunately the market is awash with phony, erroneous, and fraudulent certificates.
14. 根据这本书,一个半世纪以前在美国假冒伪劣产品泛滥。
    According to this book, America was awash with counterfeit and shoddy products one and a half century ago.
15. 这个地区盗版光盘泛滥。
    This area is deluged with pirated compact discs.

"泛滥"的第三个意思是比喻"一种坏的思想、不良现象或疾病等不受限制地到处扩散"。英语动词可以译为 to spread unchecked, to spread in an unchecked way, to reach epidemic levels, to reach epidemic proportions;名词可以译为 unchecked spread, unchecked spreading。例如:

16. 我们决不能让淫秽作品泛滥。
    We can by no means allow pornography to spread unchecked.
17. 我们应该采取行动阻止这种不良现象泛滥。
    We should take actions to stop this unhealthy phenomenon from spreading in an unchecked way.
18. 少数人的陋习导致了流言蜚语泛滥。
    A few people's bad habits have given rise to the unchecked spreading of

rumours and gossips.

19. 美国私人拥有枪支泛滥使得犯罪人员更加容易获得暴力工具。
    In the United State, the unchecked spread of privately owned guns has made it easier for the criminals to get violence tools.

20. 网上淫秽作品泛滥对正在成长的青年人产生消极影响。
    The unchecked spreading of Internet pornography is producing passive impact on the younger people who are growing up.

21. 毒品泛滥造成社会财富的极大浪费,对我国经济发展产生了严重的影响。
    The unchecked spreading of drugs has caused great waste of social wealth, producing serious influence upon the economic development of our country.

22. 这个非洲国家政府已采取了一些措施制止艾滋病的泛滥。
    The government of the African country has adopted some measures to halt the unchecked spreading of Aids.

23. 在有些电影和电视剧里,暴力正在泛滥成灾。
    Violence is reaching epidemic levels in some of the films and TV plays.

24. 在那个城市,偷车正在泛滥成灾。
    Car theft is now reaching epidemic proportions in that city.

# 七十三、曝 光

● 汉语关键词
  曝光、暴光、曝丑

● 英语关键词
  expose, exposure, lay bare, expose one's defects or shortcomings

● 句 子
  这个网民希望通过在网上自我曝光的方式引起全社会关注。

### 误 译

The netizen hopes to arouse the attention of the whole society by means of exposing himself on line.

### 正 译

The netizen hopes to arouse the attention of the whole society by means of exposing his own shortcomings and mistakes on line.

### 解 释

"自我曝光"的意思是"暴露自己的缺点、错误或问题"。而 to expose oneself (of a man) 的意思是 to show one's sexual organs in public on purpose, in the hope of exciting or shocking people, 即"男子故意当众裸露性器官", 是一种触犯公众的行为, 不是"暴露缺点"的意思。例如:

1. 他故意当众裸露性器官以后被指控当众耍流氓。
   He was charged with public lewdness after he exposed himself in public.
2. 这名男子在小酒馆故意当众裸露性器官以后名誉扫地。
   The man's reputation is in tatters after exposing himself in a pub.

"曝光"或"暴光"的第一个意思是"使照相底片或感光纸感光, 形成潜影"。英语可以译为 to expose。例如:

3. 这个胶卷已经曝光。
   This reel of film has been exposed.
4. 他学会了两种简单的方法, 能使阴暗、曝光不足的照片非常好看。
   He learned two simple techniques that can make dark, under-exposed photos look great.
5. 这张照片光线太强, 一定是曝光过度了。
   The photograph is too light; it must have been over-exposed.
6. 他教我如何使胶卷曝光和冲洗胶卷。
   He taught me how to expose a film and develop a film.
7. 这些实例表明曝光不足的影像、正确曝光的影像和曝光过度的影像都是什么样子。
   These examples illustrate what under-exposed images, correctly exposed

images and over-exposed images look like.

名词 exposure 的第一个意思是 the length of time for which light is allowed to reach the film when taking a photograph, 即"曝光时间"。例如：
8. 这张相片我用了长曝光时间。
   I used a long exposure for this photo.
9. 百分之一秒的曝光时间就足够了。
   An exposure of one-hundredth of a second will be enough.
10. 我可能是把风景的参数误认为是曝光不足。
    I may have been mistaking the parameters of landscape for under exposure.
11. 他正在做大量测试，力图避免或改正曝光过度。
    He was doing a number of tests trying to avoid or correct the over exposure.

exposure 的第二个意思是 a length of film in a camera that is used to take a photograph, 即"底片"。例如：
12. 这个胶卷上剩下三张底片没拍。
    There are three exposures left on this roll of film.

"曝光"的第二个意思是比喻"不光彩的隐秘事暴露出来，被众人知道"。英语可以译为 to expose, to lay bare。例如：
13. 这个政客的丑闻在报纸上曝光后，在政坛引起了轰动。
    After the newspapers laid bare the politician's scandal, it produced a sensation in the political arena.
14. 这个官员的丑事曝光后，激起了公众的强烈反应。
    After the official's scandal was exposed, it aroused strong public resentment.
15. 这家外国公司走私汽车的事件被媒体曝光。
    The car smuggling incident of the foreign company was exposed by the media.
16. 这个教授的剽窃行为在学术界被曝光。
    The plagiarist behaviour of the professor was exposed in the academic circles.

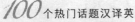

"曝丑"的意思是"公开暴露自身的缺点或错误,以接受群众监督"。英语可以译为 to expose one's defects or shortcomings, to lay bare one's flaws, mistakes or problems。例如:

17. 我认为这个电影明星向公众曝丑纯粹是为了新闻炒作。

I think that when the film star exposed his defects and shortcomings to the public, he was purely intended to create news sensationalism.

18. 我看不出他有什么理由要向他的同事们曝丑。

I see no reason why he should lay bare his flaws, mistakes and problems to his colleagues.

# 七十四、单 双 号

● 汉语关键词

单个的、双倍的、成双的、双人的、双重的、单号、单数、奇数、双号、双数、偶数、单日、双日

● 英语关键词

single, double, odd number, even number, odd day, even day

● 句 子

由于我的车牌尾数为双号,我只能在双日行驶。

● 误 译

As my car license plate ends in a double number, I can travel in my car only on double days.

● 正 译

As my car license plate ends in an even number, I can travel in my car only on even days.

● 解 释

double 的第一个意思是 twice as much or as many as usual,即"双倍的";第二个意思是 having or made of two things or parts that are equal or similar,即"成双的";第三个意思是 made for two people,即"双人的";第四个意思是 composed of two unlike parts,即"双重的"。double 与 single(单个的)相对立,是数量概念,而与单双数没有关系。例如:

1. 她竟然在19秒钟吃了一个双份的冰激凌,令人惊讶。

   It was surprising that she ate a double ice cream in 19 seconds.

2. 这是一个双黄蛋。

   It's an egg with a double yolk.

3. 我想要预订一个有一张双人床的单人房间。

   I'd like to book a single room with one double bed.

4. 我认为这个词有双重意思。

   I think the word has a double meaning.

"单号"、"单数"或"奇数"译为 odd number;"双号"、"双数"或"偶数"译为 even number,都是序列概念,与数量无关。例如:

5. 1,3,5,7和9是奇数。

   1, 3, 5, 7 and 9 are odd numbers.

6. 奇数不能被2整除。

   An odd number cannot be divided exactly by the number two.

7. 2,4,6,8和10是偶数。

   2, 4, 6, 8 and 10 are even numbers.

8. 偶数能被2整除。

   An even number can be divided exactly by the number two.

9. 我家门牌号码以单数开头。

   My street address starts with an odd number.

10. 他的车牌尾数为双号。

    His car license ends with an even number.

"单日"译为 odd day;"双日"译为 even day。例如:

11. 从7月20日到9月20日,北京机动车将按牌照尾号实行单号单日行驶,双号双日行驶。

    From July 20 to September 20, those vehicles with license plates

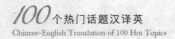

ending in odd numbers shall be allowed on the road on odd days, while those with license plates ending in even numbers shall be allowed on the road on even days in Beijing.

12. 这列火车每个单日驶往成都,每个双日返回。

The train runs to Chengdu on every odd day and returns on every even day.

与"单双号限行"相关的表达方法有:

13. 北京奥运会机动车管理方案规定从7月20日起依据车牌尾数单双号限制私家车隔日行驶。

Beijing Olympic vehicle control plan bans private cars on alternate days from July 20, depending on whether their number plates end in odd or even numbers.

14. 7月20日,一项单双号限行规定生效,将允许北京330万私家车拥有者隔日才能上路行驶。

An odd-and-even license plate rule came into effect on July 20, which would allow the 3.3 million private car owners of Beijing to drive into the city only on alternate days.

15. 根据单号单日、双号双日允许私家车隔日行驶的限行规定,每天大约200万辆机动车不能上路。

Every day, about two million vehicles are forced off the roads in a scheme that allows private vehicles to be used on alternate days, according to whether their license plates correspond to the odd or even numbered days of the month.

16. 从7月20日到9月20日,具有单双号牌照的机动车将只能隔日上路行驶。

From July 20 to September 20, vehicles with odd and even plates will hit the roads only on alternate days.

17. 市政当局已警告司机们不要无视单双号限行规定,因为高科技监控摄影机能够很容易监测到他们的牌照号码。

The city authorities have warned drivers not to flout the even-and-odd

plate rule because hi-tech surveillance cameras can easily detect their numbers.
18. 北京市交通管理局宣称每日0时至3时将解除单双号限行规定。
Beijing Municipal Traffic Administration Bureau said that it would lift the even-and-odd ban between midnight and 3 a.m. every day.

# 七十五、洗　　钱

● 汉语关键词
洗、洗钱、反洗钱

● 英语关键词
wash，launder，launder money，money laundering，anti-money laundering

● 句　子
这个官员以洗钱罪被捕。

● 误　译
The official was arrested on the charge of washing money.

● 正　译
The official was arrested on the charge of money laundering.

● 解　释
to wash 的原义是 to make sb/sth clean using water and usually soap，即"用水和肥皂洗涤"。衣服、水果和汽车可以用水洗，而钱是不能用水洗的。例如：
1. 这些衣服需要洗了。
   These clothes need washing.
2. 她把水果彻底洗干净了再吃。
   She washed the fruit thoroughly before eating.
3. 因为今天有大雨，不适宜洗车。
   As there is heavy rain today, it is not suitable for car washing.

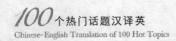

"洗钱"是从英语 to launder money 直译过来的。to launder 的第一个意思是 to wash, dry and iron clothes, etc., 即"洗、晒和熨衣物"。例如：

4. 我们必须把这些床上用品洗一洗。

    We must have these bedclothes laundered.

5. 这个孩子喜欢刚洗的床单的气味和感觉。

    The child loves the smell and feel of freshly laundered sheets.

6. 这种布料耐洗吗？

    Will this fabric launder well?

to launder 的第二个意思是 to move money that has been obtained illegally into foreign bank accounts or legal businesses so that it is difficult for people to know where the money came from, 即"洗钱"，指"通过存入银行等方法将非法所得钱款改变名义和性质，使其成为合法收入"。"洗钱"的动词可以译为 to launder money。例如：

7. 逃税者洗钱，为的是他们能就其钱款和财产来源说谎而逃税。

    Tax evaders launder money so that they can lie about where money and assets came from in order to evade tax.

8. 银行经理们通过拉斯维加斯赌场洗钱。

    Bank managers launder money through Las Vegas casinos.

9. 需要洗钱的最常见的罪犯类型有贩毒者、挪用公款者、贪污的政客与公职官员、匪徒、恐怖主义分子和行骗高手。

    The most common types of criminals who need to launder money are drug traffickers, embezzlers, corrupt politicians and public officials, mobsters, terrorists and con artists.

"洗钱"的名词可以译为 money laundering。例如：

10. 这家餐馆正是一个洗钱的掩护场所。

    This restaurant is just a front for money laundering.

11. 这些交易涉及洗钱活动。

    These transactions involved money laundering.

12. 洗钱之类的犯罪活动已在我国引起极大重视。

    Such crimes as money laundering have drawn great attention in our country.

13. 他们跟洗黑钱活动没有任何关系。

    They have nothing to do with laundering dirty money.

14. 他已被控告犯诈骗、逃税和洗钱罪,并定于8月份出庭。

    He has been charged with fraud, tax evasion and money laundering and is due in court in August.

15. 他是个洗钱老手。他已在毒品走私团伙中混了30多年。

    He is an expert at laundering money. He has been in the gang smuggling drugs for over thirty years.

16. 世界上几乎每个国家都会发生洗钱活动。

    Money laundering happens in almost every country in the world.

17. 现代的贩毒者能在境外洗钱。

    Modern drug traffickers can launder their money offshore.

18. 这个政客在一家外国银行转移秘密竞选基金。

    The politician laundered secret campaign money in a foreign bank.

"反洗钱",可以译为 anti-money laundering。例如:

19. 中国将加强反洗钱控制和监测。

    China will strengthen anti-money laundering checks and monitoring.

20. 中国于2003年在中国人民银行设立了一个反洗钱局,于2006年通过第一部反洗钱法。

    China set up an anti-money-laundering bureau in the People's Bank of China in 2003 and passed its first anti-money-laundering law in 2006.

21. 这个反洗钱法使洗钱活动变得更加困难。

    The anti-money-laundering law makes it more difficult for money to be laundered.

22. 最近,中国人民银行发布了《2007年中国反洗钱报告》。

    The People's Bank of China has recently issued *China Anti-Money-Launde-*

*ring Report* 2007.

23. 中国在过去5年里建立起了较为完整的反洗钱制度。
China has established a relatively integrated system against money-laundering in the past five years.

# 七十六、障　　碍

## 汉语关键词

障碍、语言障碍、障碍物、障碍比赛、障碍赛跑、心理障碍、精神障碍、性障碍、言语障碍、功能性障碍、听觉障碍、代谢障碍、人格障碍、心境障碍、学习障碍、无障碍、无障碍环境、无障碍设施

## 英语关键词

obstacle, barrier, hindrance, impediment, obstruction, language barrier, obstacle race, steeplechase, disorder, psychological disorder, mental disorder, sexual disorder, speech disorder, functional disorder, hearing disorder, metabolic disorder, personality disorder, mood disorder, learning disorder, barrier-free, obstacle-free, barrier-free environment, obstacle-free environment, barrier-free facilities, obstacle-free facilities

## 句　子

我市已为残疾人修建了许多条无障碍道路。

## 误　译

In our city, we have built a lot of no-obstacle roads for the handicapped people.

## 正　译

In our city, we have built a lot of obstacle-free roads for the handicapped people.

## 解　释

英语没有 no-obstacle road 的说法。一般来说，no 加上名词很少用来

构成当形容词用的修饰语;但是用 non 是可以的。有人将"无障碍道路"译为 non-obstacle road,是可以接受的。但是"无障碍"最好译为 barrier-free, obstacle-free。"无障碍环境"可以译为 barrier-free environment, obstacle-free environment。"无障碍设施"可以译为 barrier-free facilities, obstacle-free facilities。例如:

1. 无障碍环境建设作为社会进步的一个象征,在我国已成为公众讨论的一个热门话题。
The building of an obstacle-free environment, as a symbol of social progress, has become a heated topic for public discussion in our country.
2. 市政府正不遗余力改造北京的无障碍设施。
The Municipal Government is sparing no efforts to reconstruct the obstacle-free facilities in Beijing.
3. 这个大型购物广场配有永久性和临时性无障碍设施,给残疾人提供了方便。
The shopping mall is quipped with permanent and temporary obstacle-free facilities, offering convenience to the people with disabilities.

"障碍"的第一个意思是指"阻挡通行、前进或交流的东西"。英语可以译为 obstacle, barrier, hindrance, impediment。例如:

4. 这项法律旨在为经济增长扫除障碍。
This law is designed to remove obstacles for economic growth.
5. 这支救援队伍扫清了障碍,成功地打开了通往震中地区的道路。
The rescue team removed the barriers and succeeded in opening up the road to the epicentre area.
6. 这次耽搁已给我们的计划造成一些障碍。
This delay has caused some hindrance to our plan.
7. 缺乏足够的资金对我们的研究进展是一个严重的障碍。
Lack of adequate funding is a serious hindrance to the progress of our research.
8. 这个非洲国家发展的主要障碍是它的大量外债。
The main impediment to the development of the African country is its

huge foreign debt.

"语言障碍",英语可以译为 language barrier。例如:
9. 他已克服了语言障碍。

He has got over the language barrier.
10. 语言障碍使得我们无法跟他谈话。

Language barrier made it impossible for us to talk with him.

"障碍物",英语可以译为 obstacle, barrier, obstruction, hindrance。例如:
11. 那些障碍物未能拦住群众。

1) The barriers failed to hold the crowds back.

2) The barriers failed to keep the crowds back.
12. 警方设置了障碍物,以控制人群。

The police put up barriers to control the crowd.
13. 这堆石头充当了障碍物。

This heap of stones acted as a barrier.
14. 他纵马跳过所有的障碍物。

He leaped his horse over all the obstacles.
15. 你必须小心滑行,因为滑行道两边有障碍物。

You must taxi with caution, as there are obstructions on both sides of the taxiway.
16. 入口处没有障碍物。

The entrance is clear of obstruction.

"障碍比赛",英语可以译为 obstacle race。"障碍赛跑",英语可以译为 steeplechase。例如:
17. 学生们学会了障碍赛跑的基本技能,而且他们通过这些基本技能提高了平衡与协调的能力。

The students learned the basic skills of obstacle race, through which they improved their ability of balance and coordination.

18. 200米障碍游泳比赛在学校附近的河里举行。
    The 200-metre swimming obstacle race took place in the river near the school.
19. 他已准备好障碍赛跑。
    He is ready for the steeplechase.
20. 这名非洲运动员在障碍赛跑中轻而易举地赢得了金牌。
    The African athlete waltzed off with gold medal in the steeplechase.

"障碍"的第二个意思是"心理或生理上由于受到抑制或阻碍等原因而产生的不适应或不正常的现象或疾病"。英语可以译为 disorder。"心理障碍",可以译为 psychological disorder。例如:

21. 近年来大学生中出现了许多不同程度的心理障碍,这对大学生的健康与成长起了消极作用。
    In recent years, psychological disorder in varying degrees has appeared among college students, which has made a negative effect on their health and growth.
22. 他已克服了对他的心灵发展可能有害的心理障碍。
    He has overcome the psychological disorder that can be detrimental to the development of his mind.

"精神障碍",可以译为 mental disorder。例如:

23. 最近一项调查表明我国63%的自杀者患有精神障碍。
    A recent investigation indicates that 63% of the people who committed suicide in our country had suffered from mental disorder.

"性障碍",可以译为 sexual disorder。例如:

24. 这位医生向病人解释如何消除性障碍。
    The doctor explained to the patient how to remove sexual disorder.

"言语障碍",可以译为 speech disorder。例如:

25. 这个人由于言语障碍而完全不能说话,因而被认为是哑巴。
    The man is totally unable to speak due to a speech disorder and so he is

considered mute.

"功能性障碍",可以译为 functional disorder。例如：
26. 他的疾病被误诊为功能性障碍。
His disease was misdiagnosed as functional disorder.

"听觉障碍",可以译为 hearing disorder。例如：
27. 听觉障碍是儿童语言障碍的主要原因。
Hearing disorder is the main cause of language disorder in children.

"代谢障碍",可以译为 metabolic disorder。例如：
28. 当你体内的异常化学反应打乱了正常的代谢进程时,代谢障碍就发生了。
A metabolic disorder occurs when abnormal chemical reactions in your body disrupt the normal metabolic process.

"人格障碍",可以译为 personality disorder。例如：
29. 这项测试旨在测定你是否患有人格障碍。
The test is intended to help determine if you have a personality disorder.

"心境障碍",可以译为 mood disorder。例如：
30. 在像美国这样的高收入国家,抑郁等心境障碍是属于最强烈的风险因素。
In such high-income countries as the United States, mood disorders like depression are among the strongest risk factors.

"学习障碍",可以译为 learning disorder。例如：
31. 由受过培训的专业人员进行评估和测试,可以帮助辨识学习障碍。
Evaluation and testing by a trained professional can help identify a learning disorder.

# 七十七、破　　产

### 汉语关键词
破产、政治破产、智力破产、道德破产、精神破产、情感破产

### 英语关键词
bankruptcy, insolvency, political bankruptcy, intellectual bankruptcy, moral bankruptcy, spiritual bankruptcy, emotional bankruptcy, go bankrupt, go into bankruptcy, become impoverished, come to naught, be exploded, fall through

### 句　子
西方某些媒体将北京奥运会政治化的图谋破产了。

### 误　译
Some West media's schemes to politicalize Beijing Olympics went bankrupt.

### 正　译
Some West media's schemes to politicalize Beijing Olympics came to naught.

### 解　释
这里的"破产"是比喻意义，指"彻底失败"。to go bankrupt 的意思是 to have no money to pay what you owe，指公司破产，而不指计划、阴谋或谣言破产。

"破产"的第一个意思是"丧失全部财产"。英语可以译为 to become impoverished。例如：

1. 这场大火使他破了产，而且差一点死了。
   The great fire made him impoverished and nearly dead.
2. 村上的许多农家因这场洪水而破产。
   Many farmer families in the village became impoverished because of the

flood.

"破产"的第二个意思是法律名词,即"债务人不能偿还债务时,法院根据本人或债权人的申请,做出裁定,把债务人的财产变卖,按比例归还各债权人,不足数额不再偿付"。英语名词可以译为 bankruptcy, insolvency。动词可以译为 to go bankrupt, to go into bankruptcy。例如:

3. 连续亏损两年之后,这家公司宣告破产。
   After losing money for two successive years, the firm declared bankruptcy.
4. 这家公司在法院被宣布破产。
   1) The company was declared bankrupt in the court.
   2) The company was declared insolvent in the court.
5. 这家公司申请破产。
   The company made a petition for its bankruptcy.
6. 星期一,雷曼兄弟申请破产保护,对美国金融体系的恐惧冲击了全世界的股票市场。
   On Monday, Lehman Brothers filed for bankruptcy protection and fears about the US financial system knocked equity markets down across the world.
7. 经济衰退时,破产是种常见的现象。
   Bankruptcy is a common phenomenon in an economic recession.
8. 去年,这个城镇有十起破产事件记录在案。
   Last year, there were ten bankruptcies recorded in this town.
9. 根据法院裁决,这家企业破产了。
   According to the court's ruling, the company went bankrupt.
10. 政府已通过拨款给这家公司挽救其免于破产。
    The government has rescued the firm from bankruptcy by giving them a grant.
11. 破产的前景已经减弱了。
    The prospect of bankruptcy has now receded.
12. 如果你的负债超过你的资产,你就会破产。
    If your liabilities exceed your assets, you may go bankrupt.

13. 他挥霍掉了大部分钱财，而濒于破产。

    He dissipated most of his money and was on the brink of bankruptcy.

14. 这家公司因经营管理不善而破产。

    The company went bankrupt because of poor management.

15. 他因无能，已使公司濒于破产。

    His incompetence has brought the company to the brink of bankruptcy.

16. 国会通过了一项新的破产法。

    1) The Congress passed a new bankruptcy law.

    2) The Congress passed a new law of bankruptcy.

    3) The Congress passed a new insolvency law.

17. 这家公司受到破产的威胁。

    The company is threatened with bankruptcy.

18. 他父亲的破产使他过上了困苦的日子。

    His father's bankruptcy led him a dog's life.

19. 银行亏损和合作伙伴不守信用把他逼得破产了。

    The failure of the bank and the dishonesty of a partner drove him into bankruptcy.

20. 他们爱挥霍的生活方式导致了破产。

    Their profligate lifestyle resulted in bankruptcy.

"破产"的第三个意思是 a state of complete lack or loss of some abstract property such as political bankruptcy, intellectual bankruptcy, moral bankruptcy, spiritual bankruptcy and emotional bankruptcy 即"政治、智力、道德、精神和情感等抽象事物的匮乏或丧失"。英语名词可以译为 bankruptcy。例如：

21. 这个政客不讲诚信，最终导致他的政治破产。

    The politician's dishonesty finally led to his political bankruptcy.

22. 官员腐败成为政治破产的重要标志。

    The corruption of the officials has become an important sign of political bankruptcy.

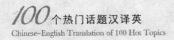

23. 这位专家指出美国政治已达到智力破产。
    The expert points out that U. S. politics has reached intellectual bankruptcy.
24. 他指出了今日美国电视与好莱坞电影的道德破产。
    He pointed out the moral bankruptcy of television and Hollywood from USA today.
25. 有人说这个社会在道德上破产了。
    Some people say the society is morally bankrupt.
26. 这部电影是对道德破产、精神破产和情感破产的探索。
    This film is an exploration of moral, spiritual and emotional bankruptcy.

"破产"的第四个意思是比喻"事情彻底失败,多含贬义"。英语可以译为 to come to naught, to be exploded, to fall through。例如:

27. 我们必须使他们的阴谋破产。
    We must bring their schemes to naught.
28. 尽管有某些改进,他们的计划还是破产了。
    In spite of certain improvements, their plan came to naught.
29. 不知何故,他的绑架阴谋破产了。
    His kidnapping plot fell through for some unknown reason.
30. 这个谣言在紧要关头破产了。
    The rumour was exploded in the nick of time.

# 七十八、行　　走

## 汉语关键词

行走、太空行走、太空服、航天服、舱外航天服、行走江湖

## 英语关键词

walk, spacewalk, make a spacewalk, take a spacewalk, walk in space, spacesuit, EVA spacesuit, travel to live, travel to survive, go from place to place

● 句 子

今天中国航天员已实现在太空行走的梦想。

● 误 译

Today, Chinese astronauts have come true their dream of walking in space.

● 正 译

Today, Chinese astronauts have realized their dream of walking in space.

● 解 释

to come true 是不及物动词,后面不能跟宾语。"实现梦想"应该译为 to realize one's dream。"梦想实现了"可以译为 One's dream has come true。例如:

1. 这名来自穷困家庭的学生圆了上大学的梦。

The student from an impoverished family has realized his dream of entering a university.

2. 这名贫困学生上大学的梦想实现了。

1) The impoverished student's dream of attending university has come true.

2) The impoverished student's dream of attending university has been realized.

"行走"的第一个意思是"走动"或"走路"。英语可以译为 to walk。例如:

3. 我们行走或奔跑都要依赖摩擦。

We depend on friction when we walk or run.

4. 我爷爷依然非常健壮,行走如飞。

My grandfather is still very strong and he walks as if winged.

5. 无障碍设施为坐轮椅的人和行走不便的人提供了方便。

Obstacle-free facilities are accessible to those people in wheelchairs and those who have difficulty walking.

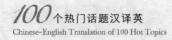

6. 他在意外事故中幸存,但终身残废,永远不能再行走了。

    He survived the accident but he was maimed for life and will never walk again.

7. 他左脚痛得厉害,因而几乎不能行走。

    His left foot hurt so badly that he could barely walk.

"太空行走"的意思是指"航天员离开载人航天器乘员舱,只身进入太空的出舱活动"。英语名词可以译为 spacewalk;动词可以译为 to make a spacewalk, to walk in space, to spacewalk。例如:

8. 你在太空行走的感觉是什么?

    What do you feel about spacewalk?

9. 这两位俄罗斯航天员已开始在空间站外太空行走。

    The two Russian astronauts have started the spacewalk outside the space station.

10. 中国于2008年9月25日成功地发射第三个载人飞船进入太空,以进行第一次太空行走。

    China successfully launched its third manned spacecraft into space on September 25, 2008, to carry out its first spacewalk.

11. 这位美国航天员正在月球上进行太空行走。

    The American astronaut was making a spacewalk on the moon.

12. 这两位航天员正在载人飞船外进行太空行走。

    The two astronauts were walking in space outside the manned spacecraft.

13. 这位航天员在载人舱外进行了了半小时太空行走。

    The astronaut spacewalked outside the manned cabin for half an hour.

14. 到了这位航天员结束他太空行走的时候了。

    It was time for the astronaut to end his spacewalk.

"航天服",又称"太空服",译为 spacesuit。"舱外航天服"译为 EVA spacesuit。例如:

15. 当这位航天员进行太空行走时,他身穿航天服。
    The astronaut wore his spacesuit when he was taking a spacewalk.
16. 他们穿着厚厚的航天服,学习如何对付一个既没有重量又没有引力,也没有"上"或"下"的环境。
    Wearing their thick spacesuits, they learned to deal with an environment where there is neither weight nor gravity, neither 'up' nor 'down'.
17. 这位航天员正穿着臃肿的航天服在轨道舱外工作。
    The astronaut was working outside the orbital module in a bulky spacesuit.
18. 这两位中国航天员正在组装舱外航天服,准备第一次太空行走。
    The two Chinese astronauts were assembling EVA spacesuit for the first spacewalk.

"行走"的第二个意思是"到处走动以求生存",是一种生活方式。英语可以译为 to travel to live, to travel to survive。例如:

19. 我靠自己在世上行走。
    I travel to live by myself in the world.
20. 他孤独地在世上行走。
    He travels alone to survive in the world.
21. 因为他们没有农田,不得不狩猎和四处行走以求生存。
    As they have no farmland, they have to hunt and travel here and there to survive.

"行走江湖",英语可以译为 to go from place to place。例如:

22. 这个民间艺人行走江湖以混口饭吃。
    The folk craftsman goes from place to place to earn a living.

# 七十九、问 题

● 汉语关键词

问题、问题奶粉、问题儿童

● 英语关键词

problem, problematic, problematic milk powder, problem milk powder, problematic child, problem child, question, questionable, issue, key, point, thing, something wrong, trouble, mishap

● 句 子

问题奶粉已经严重伤害了许多婴儿的健康。

● 误 译

The questionable milk powder has done great harm to the health of many infants.

● 正 译

The problematic milk powder has done great harm to the health of many infants.

● 解 释

questionable 和 problematic 都可以译为"有问题的",但是意思完全不同。questionable 的意思是 that you have doubts about because you think it is not accurate or correct,即"主观上觉得可疑的",指的是可能性。problematic的意思是 full of problems and difficult to deal with,即"客观上造成困难或麻烦而不好对付的",指的是事实。例如:

1. 他们已得出的结论是很有问题的。

The conclusions that they have reached are highly questionable.

2. 这是一个极度被人忽视,然而很有问题的地区。

This is a much overlooked and very problematic area.

"问题奶粉"可以译为 problematic milk powder 或 problem milk

powder。例如:
3. 地方政府已经封存了公司里的问题奶粉制品,从商店货架上撤下了问题奶粉制品,并召回了已售出的问题奶粉制品。
   1) The local government has sealed the problematic milk powder products in companies, or removed them from store shelves and recalled all those sold.
   2) The local government has sealed the problem milk powder products in companies, or removed them from store shelves and recalled all those sold.
4. 那些因问题奶粉而患肾结石的婴儿真是不幸。
   1) It's so unfortunate for those babies who have suffered from kidney stones because of the problematic milk powder.
   2) It's so unfortunate for those babies who have suffered from kidney stones because of the problem milk powder.
5. 政府已采取有效措施保证不会让问题奶粉流入市场。
   1) The government has taken effective measures to ensure that no problematic milk powder is going to the market.
   2) The government has taken effective measures to ensure that no problem milk powder is going to the market.
6. 不久以前,这个女婴因喂问题奶粉而生病,但是她现已痊愈,并已出院。
   1) Not long ago, the baby girl fell ill after being fed problematic milk powder but she has recovered and been discharged from hospital.
   2) Not long ago, the baby girl fell ill after being fed problem milk powder but she has recovered and been discharged from hospital.

"问题儿童",英语可以译为 problematic child 或 problem child。例如:
7. 他是个问题儿童,总是给警察找麻烦。
   1) He is a problematic child, always in trouble with the police.
   2) He is a problem child, always in trouble with the police.

8. 她正在观察和研究问题儿童的行为。

   1) She was observing and studying problematic child behaviour.

   2) She was observing and studying problem child behaviour.

"问题"的第一个意思是"要求回答或解释的题目"。英语可以译为question。例如：

9. 我可以向你问一个关于英语语法的问题吗？

   May I ask you a question about English grammar?

10. 我愿意简单回答你的问题。

    I'd like to answer your question briefly.

11. 你能详细解释一下这个问题吗？

    Can you explain the question in detail?

"问题"的第二个意思是"有待解决的矛盾或疑难"。英语可以译为problem。例如：

12. 政治体制改革需要解决思想问题。

    The reform of the political system requires the solution to the ideological problem.

13. 在许多国家，很难买得起房子被广泛认为是最常见的住房问题。

    In many countries, difficulty affording housing is widely acknowledged as the most common housing problem.

14. 如果你看到下列报错信息之一时，请参照下面的操作指南以学会如何解决问题。

    If you see one of the following error messages, please refer to the instructions below to learn how to resolve the problem.

"问题"的第三个意思是"有争议的重大或关键事件"。英语可以译为issue。例如：

15. 西藏问题不是一个民族问题，也不是一个宗教问题，更不是一个人权问题,而是一个保卫国家统一或分裂祖国的问题。
The Tibet issue is not an ethnic issue, not a religious issue, nor a human rights issue, but an issue either to safeguard national unification or to split the motherland.

16. 西藏问题完全是中国的内政问题,它关系到国家主权。
The Tibet issue is entirely an internal issue of China, which concerns the country's sovereignty.

17. 移民在美国已变成一个热门政治问题。
Immigration has become a hot political issue in the United States.

"问题"的第四个意思是"要点"或"关键"。英语可以译为 key, point, thing。例如:

18. 问题在于善于向别人学习。
The key lies in being good at learning from others.

19. 计划已经订好了,问题是怎样落实。
Now that the plan has been worked out, the point is how to put it into effect.

20. 问题在于你是否会做具体分析。
The thing lies in whether you can make concrete analysis.

"问题"的第五个意思是"事故"、"故障"、"毛病"或"可疑情况"。英语可以译为 something wrong, trouble, mishap。例如:

21. 我的汽车出问题了。
Something has gone wrong with my car.

22. 你的电脑出什么问题了?
What's wrong with your computer?

23. 最近他发现他的心脏有问题。
He has recently found there is something wrong with his heart.

24. 这个老人害怕他的听力、甚至脑子有问题。
The old man fears there is something wrong with his hearing or even

his brain.
25. 我认为你的这种想法有问题。
   I think there is something wrong with this idea of yours.
26. 我恐怕这项工作已经出了问题。
   I am afraid the work has run into trouble.
27. 这次长途旅程走完了,而没有发生问题。
   The long journey passed without mishap.

# 八十、危　机

● 汉语关键词

　　危机、金融危机、经济危机、政治危机、人才危机、信用危机、能源危机、石油危机、粮食危机、生态危机、环境危机、住房危机、信心危机、认同危机、危机点、危机处理、危机感、危机意识

● 英语关键词

　　crisis, financial crisis, economic crisis, political crisis, talent crisis, credibility crisis, energy crisis, oil crisis, food crisis, ecological crisis, environmental crisis, housing crisis, confidence crisis, identity crisis, crisis point, crisis management, sense of crisis, crisis awareness, danger, peril, threat, menace

● 句　子

美国人制造的次贷危机已在全世界引起一系列金融危机。

● 误　译

　　The subprime crisis created by the Americans has brought about a series of financial crisis in the whole world.

● 正　译

　　The subprime crisis created by the Americans has brought about a series of financial crises in the whole world.

### 解 释

一般来说,a series of 后面要跟名词复数,而 crisis 是单数形式,应改为 crises。源自希腊语的具有词尾词素-sis 的英语名词,其复数形式为-ses。例如:thesis → theses(论文)。

"危机"的第一个意思是"严重危险或危难的紧急关头"。英语可以译为 crisis。例如:

1. 美国现正面临严重金融危机。

   The United States is now faced with a serious financial crisis.

2. 这位专家认为房地产泡沫是金融危机的根源。

   The expert thinks that the real estate bubble is the source of financial crisis.

3. 石油价格的爆炸性上涨引起了经济危机。

   1) An explosion of oil prices caused an economic crisis.

   2) A sudden rise in oil prices led to an economic crisis.

4. 这个政治家敦促所有的政党联合起来以度过政治危机。

   The statesman urged all political parties to get united to tide over the political crisis.

5. 由于人才流失,这个发展中国家正遭受人才危机。

   As a result of brain drain, the developing country is suffering from a talent crisis.

6. 由于问题奶粉事件,我们的乳制品产业正在经历信用危机。

   As a consequence of the problematic milk powder incident, our dairy product industry is going through a credibility crisis.

7. 新能源的开发具有在不久的未来缓和能源危机的巨大潜力。

   The development of new energy has enormous potential to ease the energy crisis in the near future.

8. 经济萧条紧随石油危机而来。

   The recession trod on the heels of the oil crisis.

9. 保持贸易壁垒可能延续和加剧世界粮食危机。
   Keeping the trade barriers may prolong and deepen the world's food crisis.
10. 快速的发展正在加快生态危机威胁到我国的未来。
    Rapid development is spurring an ecological crisis that threatens our country's future.
11. 工业化在大量增进人类财富的同时,也制造了空前的环境危机。
    Industrialization has produced unprecedented environmental crisis while it is immensely building up human wealth.
12. 目前的住房危机是多年忽视这一问题的结果。
    The present housing crisis is the result of years of neglect.
13. 这个政党在其支持者之中正遭受信心危机。
    The political party was suffering a confidence crisis among its supporters.
14. 这个政党正面临严重的认同危机。
    The political party was facing a serious identity crisis.
15. 两国关系已达到危机点。
    Relations between the two countries have reached crisis point.
16. 小心那些提出解决危机方案的人。通常他们是危机的始作俑者。
    Beware of those who offer solutions to a crisis. Usually, they are the ones who instigated the crisis to begin with.
17. 这家公司依然处于危机之中,但是它已挺过了经济衰退的最糟糕的日子。
    The business is still in crisis but it has survived the worst of the recession.
18. 在危机时刻,我知道我可以找哪些朋友求助。
    In times of crisis I know which friends I can turn to.
19. 这本书的作者是一个从特别专业的视角看问题的危机处理专家。
    The author of the book is an expert in crisis management from a particular professional perspective.
20. 这两个国家之间的战争给该地区带来了危机感。
    The war between the two countries has brought a sense of crisis to the region.

21. 没有危机意识是最大的危机。

    Having no crisis awareness is the greatest crisis.

"危机"的第二个意思是"潜伏的危险、危难或祸患"。英语可以译为 danger, peril, threat, menace。例如：

22. 他们的处境艰难，危机四伏。

    They are beset with danger lurking in every direction.

23. 这个地方危机四伏。

    The place is pitted with peril.

24. 这个孩子是在一个危机四伏的环境里成长的。

    The child was raised in an environment where threat lurks.

25. 危机四伏，每一步都是危险的。

    Menace lurks everywhere, and every step is dangerous.

# 八十一、承　包

## 汉语关键词

承担、承包、分包、承包制、承包人、承包商

## 英语关键词

undertake, contract, subcontract, contracting, contracting responsibility system, contractor

## 句　子

这个农民承包了山脚下的一个果园。

## 误　译

The farmer undertook a fruit garden at the foot of the hill.

## 正　译

The farmer contracted a fruit garden at the foot of the hill.

# 100个热门话题汉译英
Chinese-English Translation of 100 Hot Topics

### ● 解　释

　　"承包"是按照合同进行的,应该译为 to contract。而 to undertake 的意思是 to make oneself responsible for sth and start doing it,即"承担",其宾语是一项负责和从事的工作或任务,可以说 to undertake a task(承担任务),to undertake a project(承担项目),to undertake research (承担研究工作),to undertake an investigation(承担调查任务)。to undertake 后面不能跟一个地点或单位名词做宾语,不能说 to undertake a factory, to undertake a company 或 to undertake a school。例如:

1. 他具有足够的知识和经验来承担这项任务。
   He has enough knowledge and experience to undertake the task.
2. 在我看来,没有理由让你承担这样一个项目。
   To my mind, there is no reason for you to undertake such a project.
3. 大学教授既教书,又承担研究工作。
   University professors both teach and undertake research.
4. 该公司已宣布对这个事故承担全部调查任务。
   The company has announced it will undertake a full investigation into the accident.

　　"承包"的意思是"接受工程、订货或其他生产经营活动并且按照合同负责完成",即"承包经营管理"。作为动词,"承包"可以译为 to contract。例如:

5. 这个建筑公司已承包在这条河上修建一座大水坝。
   The construction company has contracted to build a big dam across the river.
6. 这个制造商最近在我市承包了一个生产汽车零件的工厂。
   The manufacturer has recently contracted a factory to produce car parts in our city.
7. 这对夫妇在我们小区里承包了一个饭馆。
   The husband and wife contracted a restaurant in our residential area.
8. 这个公司在本地区承包了一项修建儿童医院的工程。
   The firm has contracted a project to build a hospital for the children in

this area.
9. 这个承包商将所承包工程的一部分交给了第三方。
   The contractor assigned part of the contracted project to a third party.

"分包"可以译为 to subcontract。例如：
10. 这个承包商不得将整个工程分包出去。
    The contractor had to subcontract the whole of the works.
11. 禁止分承包商将其承包的工程再分包出去。
    A subcontractor is prohibited from further subcontracting its contracted work.
12. 电气工程已分包给我们公司。
    The electrical work has been subcontracted to our company.

作为名词或名词修饰语，"承包"可以译为 contracting。例如：
13. 在全世界范围内正在进行一场劳务承包的激烈竞争。
    A keen competition on labour service contracting is going on all over the world.
14. 他在建筑工地管理一个分承包单位。
    He managed a subcontracting unit in the construction field.
15. 我们的承包费比城里其他承包商的承包费低得多。
    Our contracting fees are much lower than those of other contractors in town.

"承包制"，即"承包经营责任制"，可以译为 contracting responsibility system。例如：
16. 我国农村经济制度是建立在家庭承包经营责任制之上的。
    In our country, the rural economic system is based on the household contracting responsibility system
17. 家庭承包经营责任制通过长期承包将公有农田的生产和管理交给单个家庭去做。
    The household contracting responsibility system entrusts the production and management of public-owned farmland to individual households through

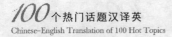

long-term contracts.
18. 我们必须努力稳定和完善家庭承包责任制。
We must do our best to steady and perfect household contracting responsibility system.
19. 家庭承包经营责任制已极大地激发了农民的农业生产热情。
The household contracting responsibility system has greatly boosted the farmers' enthusiasm for agricultural production.

"承包人"或"承包商",英语可以译为contractor。例如:
20. 所有的承包人都必须签定责任保证书。
All the contractors must sign responsibility pledges.
21. 承包商的责任是有限度的。
There are limitations to the contractor's liability.

# 八十二、海 啸

### 汉语关键词
海啸、金融海啸、经济海啸、政治海啸、人事海啸、生态海啸

### 英语关键词
tidal wave, tsunami, financial tsunami, economic tsunami, political tsunami, personnel tsunami, ecological tsunami

### 句 子
各国政府都在试图采取措施应对席卷全球的金融海啸。

### 误 译
The governments of various countries are trying to take measures to cope with the financial tidal wave that has swept the globe.

### 正 译
The governments of various countries are trying to take measures to

cope with the financial tsunami that has swept the globe.

● 解 释

  tidal wave 的意思是 an abnormally large and destructive wave caused by a storm, earthquake, or other natural event, 即"海啸", 在日语里叫做 tsunami(意思为 harbour wave)。tidal wave 和 tsunami 都可以指自然现象的"海啸"。但是,比喻激烈动荡的政治或经济形势时,只能用 tsunami。

  "海啸"的第一个意思是"由海底地震、火山爆发或海上风暴引起的海水剧烈波动。海水冲上陆地,往往造成严重灾害",指自然现象。英语可以译为 tsunami。例如:
1. 海啸有时威力很大,足以摧毁它所冲击的沿岸建筑,更能摧毁途中的船只。
Tsunami is sometimes powerful enough to destroy a coastwise building it strikes, still more a ship in its path
2. 2003 年年底,南亚发生海啸,造成 18 万人死亡,180 万人无家可归。
At the end of 2003, a tsunami occurred in South Asia, causing 180,000 people dead and 1.8 million people homeless.
3. 当海啸袭来时,珊瑚礁可能遭受严重损害。
When a tsunami hits, coral reefs may suffer severe damage.
4. 这次地震促使当局发出海啸警报。
The earthquake prompted the authorities to issue a tsunami warning.
5. 许多人捐钱给海啸受害者。
Many people donated money to the victims of the tsunami.
6. 一场可怕的海啸跟随地震而来。
A terrible tsunami followed the earthquake.
7. 许多人在泰国发生的那次海啸中丧生。
Many people died in the tsunami that took place in Thailand.
8. 海啸发生后,许多人淹死了。
After the tsunami happened, many people were drowned.

9. 一场地震引起了这次海啸。
   An earthquake triggered the tsunami.
10. 大海啸正从远处海面袭来。
    A huge tsunami was coming from the faraway sea.
11. 这次海啸地震的威力被大大低估了。
    The power of the tsunami earthquake was heavily underestimated.
12. 这个国家正在受海啸侵袭最严重的地区建筑一道海啸防波堤。
    The country was building a tsunami barrier in its worst tsunami-hit area.

"海啸",还可以译为 tidal wave。例如:
13. 海啸形成了一道令人恐怖的水墙。
    The tidal waves formed a terrifying wall of water.
14. 一阵猛烈的爆发使这个火山岛裂开,引起一场海啸,使许多人丧生。
    A violent explosion blew the volcanic island apart and caused a tidal wave that killed a lot of people.
15. 报纸说我们必须当心海啸。
    The newspaper says we must be cautious about tidal waves.

"海啸"的第二个意思是"经济或政治形势的剧烈震荡",指社会现象。"金融海啸",英语可以译为 financial tsunami。"经济海啸",英语可以译为 economic tsunami。"政治海啸",英语可以译为 political tsunami。"人事海啸",英语可以译为 personnel tsunami。"生态海啸",英语可以译为 ecological tsunami。例如:
16. 在过去的几周内,世界经历了一场史无前例的金融海啸。
    In the past few weeks, the world has seen an unprecedented financial tsunami.
17. 美国的次贷危机引发了一场世界范围的破坏性金融海啸。
    The American subprime crisis gave rise to a worldwide destructive

financial tsunami.

18. 一场经济海啸正在横扫华尔街,动摇美国金融的堡垒直至核心,并使久负盛名的投资银行陷入破产。
An economic tsunami is ravaging Wall Street, shaking the citadels of American finance to their core, and sinking celebrated investment banks into insolvency.

19. 目前的这场经济海啸将会在世界范围急剧地增加贫困和饥饿。
The current economic tsunami will sharply increase poverty and hunger worldwide.

20. 在这个亚洲国家,总统选举导致了一场政治海啸。
In this Asian country, the presidential election led to a political tsunami.

21. 一场政治海啸席卷了这个东南亚国家。
A political tsunami swept the Southeast Asian country.

22. 今天当一个说20%的职员要被解雇的消息传给每位雇员时,这家公司发生了人事海啸。
The company had a personnel tsunami today when a message went out to every employee saying that 20% of its staff would be laid off.

23. 最近华尔街的金融衰退已在许多金融机构引起人事海啸。
Recently, the financial meltdown in Wall Street has provoked personnel tsunami in a lot of banking institutions.

24. 我们的气候正在以像生态海啸席卷我们一样的方式变化着。
Our climate is changing in ways that will sweep over us like an ecological tsunami.

25. 这个国家海岸线的大部分被去年发生的生态海啸摧毁了。
Most of the country's coastline was destroyed from the ecological tsunami that occurred last year.

# 八十三、两　岸

● 汉语关键词

两岸、海峡两岸、两岸关系、两岸四地

● 英语关键词

two sides, both sides, either side, two banks, both banks, either bank, two sides of the Taiwan Straits, both sides of the Straits, across the Taiwan Straits, cross-Straits, relations between China's mainland and Taiwan, relations between the two sides of the Straits, cross-Straits relations; China's mainland, Taiwan, Hong Kong and Macao

● 句　子

海峡两岸的民众都是中国人。

● 误　译

People on the both sides of the Taiwan Straits are all Chinese.

● 正　译

People on both sides of the Taiwan Straits are all Chinese.

● 解　释

both, all, either 和 neither 等词作定语用时，规范的用法是前面不加定冠词 the。笔者在 Google 上搜索时，发现有些中文网页用 on the both sides of 的说法，而英美人的网页上罕见这样的搭配。看来 on both sides of 才是地道的英语。

"两岸"的第一个意思是泛指江河、湖泊、海湾、海峡等水域两边的地方。英语可以译为 two sides, both sides, either side, two banks, both banks, either bank。例如：

1. 有几百万人民生活在这条河的两岸。

There are millions of people living on the two sides of the river.

2. 这个海湾两岸的植被和花卉是非常相似的。

The vegetation and flora on the two sides of the gulf are very similar.

3. 河两岸都有一条自行车道。
   There is a bike trail on both sides of the river.
4. 你在湖的两岸都可以找到船只登陆的地方。
   You can find boat landings on either side of the lake.
5. 这座城市位于河的两岸。
   1) The city lies on the two banks of the river.
   2) The city is situated on the two banks of the river.
6. 河两岸有许多垂柳。
   There are many weeping willows on both banks of the river.
7. 两岸猿声啼不住,轻舟已过万重山。
   1) Monkey cries were heard on either bank all through the way while the boat passed by mountains swiftly in a row.
   2) The screams of monkeys on either bank had scarcely ceased echoing in my ear, when my skiff had left behind it ten thousand ranges of hills.

"两岸"的第二个意思是特指台湾海峡两边的地方,即我国大陆和台湾省,也称"海峡两岸"。英语可以译为 two sides of the Taiwan Straits, both sides of the Straits。例如:

8. 中国是两岸同胞共同的家园。
   China is the common homeland for the compatriots on both sides of the Straits.
9. 陈云林访台将推动两岸经济贸易合作。
   Chen Yunlin's visit to Taiwan will promote the economic and trade cooperation between the two sides of the Taiwan Straits.
10. 两岸的冲突与争议可以在和平发展进程中通过平等协商解决。
    Conflicts and disputes between the two sides of the Straits could be resolved by equal consultations in the process of peaceful development.
11. 两岸政治分歧不应该被当作阻止"三通"的借口或障碍。
    Political differences between the two sides of the Straits should not be used as a pretext or obstacle for obstructing the "three direct links".

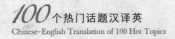
Chinese-English Translation of 100 Hot Topics

"两岸"作定语用，可以译为 across the Taiwan Straits, cross-Straits。例如：

12. 双方都希望进行更紧密的两岸金融合作以抵抗全球金融危机。
    Both sides hope to have a closer cross-Straits financial cooperation to withstand the global financial crisis.
13. 两岸会谈将避免敏感的政治问题，而集中谈经济合作。
    The cross-Straits talks will avoid sensitive political issues and focus on economic cooperation.
14. 两岸客运包机服务范围的扩大可以节省台商生产成本。
    The extension of the cross-Straits charter passenger flight service will save Taiwan traders' production cost.
15. 我相信海峡两岸具有智慧，而且能够通过会谈和谈判克服现存的问题。
    I believe that the two sides across the Taiwan-Straits are wise and capable of overcoming the existing problems through talks and negotiations.

"两岸关系"可以译为 relations between China's mainland and Taiwan, relations between the two sides of the Straits, cross-Straits relations。例如：

16. 海峡两岸"三通"将有助于推动两岸关系的发展。
    The "three direct links" across the Taiwan Straits will help to promote the development of the relations between the two sides of the Straits.
17. 坚持"一个中国"原则，是发展两岸关系和实现和平统一的基础。
    Adherence to the One-China Principle is the basis for the development of the cross-Straits relations and the realization of peaceful reunification.
18. 在他们的会谈中将不涉及与两岸关系相关的政治问题。
    In their talks, no political issues pertaining to cross-Straits relations will be involved.
19. 两岸空中与海上直航将有助于改善两岸关系。
    The direct transport links by air and sea between China's mainland and Taiwan will help improve the relations between the two sides of the Straits.

"两岸四地",特指我国大陆、台湾、香港和澳门。英语可以译为 China's mainland, Taiwan, Hong Kong and Macao。例如:

20. 我们将做出具体努力推进两岸四地的经济合作。
We will make concrete efforts to boost economic cooperation between China's mainland, Taiwan, Hong Kong and Macao.

21. 今天,两岸四地的几十名大学生在我市举行了一场演讲比赛。
Today, dozens of college students from China's mainland, Taiwan, Hong Kong and Macao held a speech contest in our city.

## 八十四、下　水

● 汉语关键词

下水、下水道、下水管、下水道系统

● 英语关键词

go into the water, get into the water, move into the water, launch, downstream, soak in water, engage in evil doing, fall into evil ways, offal, entrails, sewer, drain, sewer pipe, sewer system, sewerage

● 句　子

这个官员被犯罪团伙拖下水。

● 误　译

The official was dragged into the water by a criminal gang.

● 正　译

The official was enticed into evil doings by a criminal gang.

● 解　释

to be dragged into the water 指的是实际被拉入水中的动作。这句话的"被拖下水"是比喻意义,指"被诱惑做坏事",应译为 to be enticed into evil doings。

# 100个热门话题汉译英
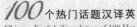

"下水"的第一个意思是泛指"进入水中"。英语可以译为 to go into the water, to get into the water, to move into the water。例如：

1. 这个游泳者慢慢从游泳池边上的梯子下水。
   The swimmer slowly got into the water from the ladder against the wall of the swimming pool.
2. 这个女孩坐在沙滩上脱鞋，准备下水。
   The girl sat on the beach, taking off her shoes and being prepared to move into the water.
3. 他一下水，右腿就抽筋了。
   As soon as he got into the water, his right leg went into spasm.
4. 汤姆是个胆小鬼，他不肯下水。
   Tom was a coward and he wouldn't go into the water.

"下水"的第二个意思是专指"船体在陆上造好后进入水中"。英语可以译为 to launch。例如：

5. 这艘船历经许多困难和拖延后，已准备好下水。
   After many difficulties and postponements, the ship was ready for launching.
6. 这艘新造的潜艇刚下水，就发生了事故。
   As soon as the newly-built submarine was launched, an accident occurred.
7. 这位工程师目睹了他亲自设计的豪华客轮下水的全过程。
   The engineer witnessed the whole process of the launching of the luxury passenger liner that he had personally designed.
8. 交通部长参加了这艘新造的远洋货轮的下水典礼。
   The Minister of Transport was present at the launching ceremony for the newly-built ocean-going cargo ship.
9. 新船下水通常用香槟酒来庆祝。
   The launching of a new ship is usually celebrated with champagne.

"下水"的第三个意思是"向下游航行或处于下游"。英语可以译为 downstream。例如：

10. 我们乘坐下水船欣赏沿岸风光。
    We took a boat downstream to enjoy the scenery along the river.
11. 这个村庄位于这个城市的下风下水。
    The village lies in the downwind and downstream location of the city.

"下水"的第四个意思是"把某些纺织品或纤维浸入水中使其收缩"。英语可以译为 to soak in water。例如:

12. 妈妈把新买的花布下水，打算给女儿做裙子。
    Mother soaked in water the flowery cotton print she had just bought, intending to make her daughter a skirt.
13. 新布最好先下水，晒干后再裁剪。
    It is advisable to soak new cotton print in water first and then have it dried before cutting.
14. 所有的毛料衣服，下水后都会缩水。
    All wool clothing will shrink after being soaked in water.

"下水"的第五个意思是比喻"干坏事"。英语可以译为 to engage in evil doing, to fall into evil ways。例如:

15. 既然他已下水，就一定会暴露自己。
    Since he is engaged in evil doing, he is bound to expose himself.
16. 杰克唆使狄克下水，现在他们俩都变成贼了。
    Jack made Dick fall into evil ways, and they are both thieves now.
17. 一个教唆犯拖这个青年下水。
    An abettor made the young man fall into evil ways.
18. 那些小流氓先请他吃喝，然后拉他下水。
    Those petty hooligans wined and dined him and then made him engage in evil doing.
19. 他糊里糊涂地被坏人拉下水。
    He was made to fall into evil ways by bad people before he had realized it.

"下水"的第六个意思是指"可以食用的牲畜内脏"。英语可以译为 offal, entrails。例如:

20. 下水的胆固醇含量高。
    Offal contains high cholesterol.
21. 这个食客认为下水很有营养。
    This eater thinks that offal is very nutritious.
22. 有些人爱吃猪下水。
    Some people like to eat pig's entrails.
23. 这些外国人不吃猪下水。
    These foreigners refrain from eating pig's offal.

"下水道",英语可以译为 sewer, drain。"下水管",英语可以译为 sewer pipe。"下水道系统",英语可以译为 sewer system, sewerage。例如:

24. 他们在住宅区周围修建了下水道。
    They put in sewers around the residential districts.
25. 下水道在日常使用过程中可能会被堵塞。
    Drains can be stopped in the course of everyday use.
26. 楼上堵塞的下水道可能会引起淹水。
    On upper floors, plugged drains may cause flooding.
27. 我们不得不叫管工来通一通下水道。
    We have to call a plumber to unblock the drains.
28. 由于下水管破裂了,这里有许多积水。
    As the sewer pipe is broken, there is a lot of accumulated water here.
29. 专家们正在讨论如何修复这座城市被地震毁坏的下水道系统。
    The experts were discussing how to repair the sewer system in this city that was damaged by the earthquake.
30. 饮用水服务设施和下水道系统服务设施对保证人民健康至关紧要。
    Drinking water and sewerage services are essential in ensuring the health of the people.

# 八十五、封　口

### 汉语关键词
封口、封口费

### 英语关键词
seal, heal, heal over, heal up, seal sb's mouth, close one's mouth about, shut one's mouth about, keep silent about, keep quiet about, speak with a tone of finality, close one's door to further compromise, shut one's door to further negotiation, set it as the maximum limit, flap, hush money

### 句　子
这个矿主给记者们发封口费,使他们对这次矿难封口。

### 误　译
1) The mine owner paid the journalists hush money, so as to close their mouth about the mine accident.

2) The mine owner paid the journalists hush money, so as to shut their mouth about the mine accident.

### 正　译
The mine owner paid the journalists hush money, so as to seal their mouth about the mine accident.

### 解　释
to close/shut one's mouth 的意思是"当事人封自己的口"即"闭嘴"或"闭口";而 to seal one's mouth 的意思是"当事人封别人的口"。在这句话里,矿主是当事人。他发封口费的目的是封别人的口。

"封口"的第一个意思是"封闭信封或容器开口的地方"。英语可以译为 to seal。例如:
1. 这封信还没有封口。
1) The letter is not sealed.

2) The letter is unsealed.
2. 这是一封还没有封口的信,而不是封口的信。
    This is an unsealed letter, instead of a sealed letter.
3. 我们寄信时要用浆糊、胶水或胶棒给信封封口。
    We must seal the envelope with paste, glue or glue stick before posting the letter.
4. 他用稀泥给坛子封口。
    He sealed the jar with mud.

"封口"的第二个意思是"伤口愈合"。英语可以译为 to heal, to heal over, to heal up。例如:
5. 我腿上的伤已经封口了。
    The wound in my leg has healed over.
6. 如果你保持伤口干净,很快就会封口。
    The wound will soon heal up if you keep it clean.
7. 疮还没有封口。
    The sore has not healed yet.

"封口"的第三个意思是"堵住别人的嘴,不让呼吸或说话",也可以说"封嘴"。英语译为 to seal sb's mouth。例如:
8. 绑匪用破布给不停叫喊的人质封住口。
    With rug, the kidnapper sealed the mouth of the hostage who had been crying.
9. 我用双手封住病人的口,形成一个管道,通过这个管道向他的鼻子吹气。
    I used my hands to seal the patient's mouth and to form a tube through which to blow air into his nose.

"封口"的第四个意思是"闭嘴不说,保持缄默"。英语可以译为 to close one's mouth about, to shut one's mouth about, to keep silent about, to keep quiet about。例如:

10. 关于这个政治丑闻,他决定封口。
    He decided to close his mouth about this political scandal.
11. 这件事不是我想封口,实在是头头儿不让我说。
    It is not that I wanted to shut my mouth about the incident, but that our boss didn't allow me to talk about it.
12. 关于这个新的商业计划,公司总经理叫他的员工们封口。
    The general manager of the company told his staff to keep silent about this new commercial plan.
13. 关于他跟他哥哥的争议,他一直试图封口。
    He has tried to keep quiet about his dispute with his brother.

"封口费",可以译为 hush money。例如:
14. 目击者从地下团伙那里拿了"封口费",就对他所见到的事守口如瓶了。
    Taking hush money from the underworld gang, the witness kept his mouth shut about what he saw.
15. 他因为揭露了一个贪官给记者"封口费"的事实而出了名。
    Because he exposed a corrupt official's offer of "hush money" to journalists, he became well known.

"封口"的第五个意思是"把话说死,不再改口"。也可以说"封嘴"或"封门"。英语可以译为 to speak with a tone of finality, to close one's door to further compromise, to shut one's door to further negotiation。例如:
16. 由于对方已经封口了,我们没法儿再谈了。
    As the other side has spoken with a tone of finality, we can't have any more discussion.
17. 说话不要轻易封口,要留有余地。
    You mustn't speak with a tone of finality, and you should leave room for further consideration.
18. 谈判双方都已封口了。
    Both parties have closed the door to further negotiation.

19. 他没有封口,还有商量的余地。
    As he hasn't shut the door to further compromise, there is still room for discussion.

"封口"的第六个意思是比喻"使规定的限度不突破"。英语可以译为 to set it as the maximum limit。例如:

20. 银行给我们的贷款就是这20万,已经封口了。
    The bank has made a loan of only two hundred thousand yuan to us and set it as the maximum limit.

"封口"的第七个意思是"信封、封套等可以封起来的地方"。英语可以译为 flap。例如:

21. 当我收到这封信时,信封的封口是没粘住的。
    The flap of the envelope was unstuck when I received the letter.

22. 他粘上信封的刷胶封口。
    He sealed the gummed flap of the envelope.

# 八十六、宽　松

## 汉语关键词
宽松、宽松政策

## 英语关键词
spacious, commodious, relax, relaxed, ease, easy, loose, free from worry, free from restraint, loose-fitting, loose and comfortable, ample, well off, loose policy, easy policy, relaxed policy, liberal policy, lenient policy

## 句　子

为对抗世界范围的金融危机,中国政府决定采取适度宽松的货币政策。

## 100个热门话题汉译英

### ● 误 译

To combat the worldwide financial crisis, the Chinese Government has decided to adopt a moderately flexible monetary policy.

### ● 正 译

To combat the worldwide financial crisis, the Chinese Government has decided to adopt a moderately easy monetary policy.

### ● 解 释

flexible 的意思是"灵活的"或"变通的"。flexible policy 是"弹性的政策",与 rigid policy(刚性的政策)及 inflexible policy(僵硬的政策)相对立。而"宽松的政策"有"更自由、更少控制或限制"的意思,是与"紧缩的政策"相对而言的。英语中表示"紧缩政策"概念的说法有 tight policy(紧缩的政策), tightened policy(从紧的政策), strict policy(严格的政策), restricted policy(限制性政策)等。英语中表示"宽松政策"的说法有 loose policy, easy policy, relaxed policy, liberal policy, lenient policy 等。例如:

1. 这位专家认为弹性的政策应时时处处存在,直至达到最终目的。
   The expert holds that a flexible policy should be in place at any period until this ultimate is attained.
2. 这种刚性、僵硬的政策给许多小企业造成了过度的困难。
   This rigid, inflexible policy caused undue hardship to many small enterprises.
3. 政府坚持紧缩的货币政策以应对通货膨胀。
   The government maintained a tight monetary policy to combat inflation.
4. 一些经济学家预测在下一年度,由于实行从紧政策,银行提供的货币供应和新的贷款将会减少。
   Some economists predicted that in the coming year, with a tightened policy, both the money supply and new loans released by banks would be reduced.
5. 这位专家指出有两种主要的政策可以提高社会福利,即严格政策与宽松政策。
   The expert points out that there are two main policies to increase the welfare of the society, which are strict policy and loose policy.

6. 这个新的限制性政策将导致市场的萎缩。
   The new restricted policy will result in the shrinking of the market.
7. 这个经济学家认为通货膨胀在宽松的货币政策下比在紧缩政策下要高。
   The economist thinks that inflation is higher under the loose monetary policy than under the tight policy.
8. 报纸报导由于宽松的货币政策，通货膨胀正在全球，尤其是在美国增长。
   The newspaper reports that inflation is rising globally because of an easy monetary policy, especially in the United States.
9. 宽松的政策允许这些外国人和海外华人的大陆被抚养者可以申请在香港居住。
   The relaxed policy allows the Mainland dependants of these foreigners and overseas Chinese to apply to reside in Hong Kong.
10. 在美国，年轻人更可能支持宽松的移民政策。
    In the United States, young people are more likely to support a liberal policy on immigration.
11. 对贪腐采取宽大政策会导致无法控制的后果。
    A lenient policy of corruption may result in an uncontrollable consequence.

"宽松"的第一个意思是"宽敞，不拥挤"。英语可以译为 spacious, commodious。例如：

14. 搬走几件旧家具，屋里显得宽松多了。
    With a few pieces of used furniture moved away, the room looked more spacious.
15. 列车开动以后，拥挤的车厢略微宽松了一些。
    When the train started moving, the crowded carriage became a bit more commodious.
16. 这间教室坐20人比较宽松。
    The classroom allows twenty people to sit comfortably.

"宽松"的第二个意思是指"环境、氛围或心情松快,不紧张"。英语可以译为 relaxed, easy, loose, free from worry, free from restraint。例如:

17. 改革开放以后,我国的经济政策宽松了。
    Since we began to make the reform and open up to the outside world, the economic policy of our country has become loose.
18. 你们能否把付款条件对我们放宽松一点?
    Will you make your payment terms a little easier for us?
19. 我们的目的是使我们的师生能在宽松和谐的环境里表现出更高水平。
    Our purpose is to empower teachers and students to perform at a higher level in a relaxed and harmonious environment.
20. 这是课外在宽松环境里与其他课程师生见面的好机会。
    This is a good opportunity to meet faculty and students from other courses in relaxed circumstances outside class.
21. 这一解释使她心情宽松了。
    1) The explanation made her free from worry.
    2) The explanation took the weight of her worry away.
22. 她听了同事们劝慰的话,心里宽松多了。
    Hearing the advice from her colleagues, she got free from restraint.

"宽松"的第三个意思是指"使心情松快"。英语可以译为 to relax, to ease。例如:

23. 让我们宽松一下紧张情绪。
    1) Let's relax ourselves.
    2) Let's ease our tension.

"宽松"的第四个意思是指"衣服肥大舒松"。英语可以译为 loose-fitting, loose and comfortable。例如:

24. 他身穿宽松、舒适的衣服和鞋。
    He wears loose-fitting, comfortable clothes and shoes.
25. 现在紧身衣服和宽松衣服都流行。
    Both close-fitting and loose-fitting clothes are in fashion now.

26. 她正在挑选宽松的棉布衣服。
    She was choosing loose-fitting clothes made from cotton.
27. 她在夏天穿宽松的衣服。
    She wore loose garments in summer.

"宽松"的第五个意思是"经济宽裕"。英语可以译为 ample, well off。例如:
28. 孩子们都工作了,老两口的日子也就宽松了。
    Since their children have all got their jobs, the old couple are now living an ample life.
29. 工资提高了,老百姓手头宽松多了。
    1) As the people have had their wages raised, they have more money to spend.
    2) As the people have had their wages raised, they have become better off.
30. 我们的生活不是很宽松,但我们很知足。
    Although we are not well off now, we are very contented.

# 八十七、包　　袱

● 汉语关键词

包袱、抖包袱、包袱皮儿、甩包袱、包袱底儿

● 英语关键词

cloth wrapper, bundle, bundle wrapped in a cloth, load, load on one's mind, burden, mental burden, hindrance, millstone round one's neck, suspending joke, cast off a burden, abandon a burden, get a load off one's back, display a suspending joke, crack a suspending joke, reveal a suspending joke, family valuables, unseemly secret, unique skill

● 句　子

说这段相声时,两位演员不断地抖包袱,逗得观众捧腹大笑。

### 误 译

In the comic dialogue, the two performers continuously unfolded the cloth wrapper, which made the audience convulse with laughter.

### 正 译

In the comic dialogue, the two performers continuously revealed suspending jokes, which made the audience convulse with laughter.

### 解 释

to unfold the cloth wrapper 是"抖包袱"的字面意思,即"打开包袱"。在相声语言里,"抖包袱"比喻"揭示事先埋下的伏笔,以笑料逗听众开心",应译为 to display a suspending joke, to crack a suspending joke, to reveal a suspending joke。

"包袱"的第一个意思是"包衣服等东西用的布",也称"包袱皮儿"。英语可以译为 cloth wrapper。例如:

1. 小女孩抱着一个洋娃娃,裹在一个包袱皮儿里。
   The little girl carried a doll in her arms, which was tucked in a cloth wrapper.
2. 在肮脏的包袱里有三双穿过的草鞋。
   In the soiled cloth wrapper, there were three pairs of worn straw shoes.

"包袱"的第二个意思是"包有衣物等的布包儿"。英语可以译为 bundle。例如:

3. 他试图努力打开包袱。
   He tried hard to untie the bundle.
4. 她手上拎着一个红包袱。
   She carried a red bundle in her hand.
5. 他把包袱放在桌子上。
   He placed the bundle down on the table.

"包袱"的第三个意思是比喻"精神负担"。英语可以译为 load, load on

one's mind, mental burden。例如:
6. 他顾虑重重,背着沉重的思想包袱。
   1) With endless worries, he has a heavy load on his mind.
   2) With endless worries, he is weighed down by a mental burden.
7. 她甩掉了思想包袱。
   She abandoned her mental burden.
8. 我劝你放下思想包袱,轻装前进。
   I advise you to get the load off your back and make progress with ease and confidence.

"包袱"的第四个意思是比喻"使人沮丧、压抑或引起忧虑的事物"。英语可以译为 burden, hindrance, millstone round one's neck。"甩包袱"可以译为 to cast off a burden, to abandon a burden, to get a load off one's back。例如:
9. 他希望卸掉这个包袱。
   He hoped to get rid of the burden.
10. 你不应把赡养父母看成是包袱。
    You shouldn't consider supporting your parents as a burden.
11. 她很高兴甩掉了这个包袱。
    She was glad to be relieved of this burden.
12. 你不要把成绩当成阻碍前进的包袱。
    You mustn't turn your merits into a hindrance to your progress.
13. 她的懒丈夫是她的一个包袱。
    Her lazy husband is a millstone round her neck.

"包袱"的第五个意思是指"相声、快书等曲艺中的笑料"。英语可以译为 suspending joke。例如:
14. 这个喜剧演员善于抖包袱。
    The comedian is good at cracking suspending jokes.

"包袱底儿"的第一个意思是指"家庭常年不动用的或最贵重的东西",也称"家底儿"或"箱子底儿"。英语可以译为 family valuables。例如:

15. 老妇人向子女们亮了包袱底儿。
    The old woman showed her children their family valuables.

"包袱底儿"的第二个意思是比喻"隐私"。英语可以译为 unseemly secret。例如：

16. 她总爱打听同事们的包袱底儿。
    She is always fond of inquiring about the unseemly secret of her colleagues.
17. 他喜欢在自己的博客里抖一些电影明星的包袱底儿。
    He likes to reveal the unseemly secret about some film stars in his blog.
18. 别揭人家包袱底儿。
    Don't expose the unseemly secret about other people.

"包袱底儿"的第三个意思是比喻"最拿手的绝技或过硬本领"。英语可以译为 unique skill。例如：

19. 他在比赛中亮出了自己的包袱底儿。
    He showed his own unique skill in the contest.
20. 在魔术表演中，魔术师在观众面前抖搂了他的包袱底儿。
    In the magic show, the magician performed his unique skill in front of the audience.

# 八十八、突　　破

## 汉语关键词
突破、突破口、突破领域

## 英语关键词
break, breach, break through, breakthrough, hit, point of breach, point of penetration, breakthrough point, area of breakthrough

## 句　子
这个港口的集装箱年吞吐量已突破一百万箱。

# 100个热门话题汉译英
Chinese-English Translation of 100 Hot Topics

### 误 译

The annual handling capacity of shipping containers in this port has breached one million containers.

### 正 译

1) The annual handling capacity of shipping containers in this port has breached one million.

2) The annual handling capacity of shipping containers in this port has breached the million mark.

### 解 释

"突破一百万箱",实际上指的是"突破百万大关",不必译出"箱"字。译为 to breach one million, to break one million, to hit one million 或 to breach the million mark, to break the million mark, to hit the million mark 均可。

"突破"的第一个意思是"集中兵力向一点进攻或反攻,打开缺口",为军事用语。英语可以译为 to break, to breach, to break through。例如:

1. 红军突破了敌人无数次的包围和封锁,直至最后到达陕北。
   The Red Army broke through countless enemy encirclements and blockades until they finally reached northern Shaanxi.
2. 我方坦克突破了敌人的防线。
   Our tanks breached the enemy defences.
3. 示威者试图突破警察的封锁线。
   The demonstrators tried to break through the police cordon.
4. 敌人突破我们阵地的企图最终失败了。
   1) The enemy's attempt to break our position finally failed.
   2) The enemy's attempt to breach our position finally failed.
5. 敌军企图突破城墙。
   The enemy soldiers attempted to breach the walls of the city.

"突破"的第二个意思是"冲破障碍或难关"。动词可以译为 to break,

to breach, to break through;名词可以译为 breakthrough。例如:
6. 这个协议将突破实现自由贸易的障碍。
   This agreement will break through the obstacles to free trade.
7. 迈开第一步将使你能够突破障碍,引导你实现你平生的梦想。
   Taking that first step will enable you to break through your obstacles and lead you towards accomplishing your life's dreams.
8. 当他学习在公众面前讲话时,他突破了重重障碍。
   1) When he learned to speak in public, he broke through barrier after barrier.
   2) When he learned to speak in public, he broke through one barrier after another.
9. 你们应该足够坚决以突破这些条条杠杠。
   You should be resolute enough to break through these regulations and restrictions.
10. 科学家们说,他们在防治癌症方面正开始有所突破。
    Scientists say they are beginning to break through in the fight against cancer.
11. 我国科学家在各个研究领域都有突破。
    The scientists of our country have made a breakthrough in various fields of research.
12. 一项技术突破使得调查人员能够跟踪嫌疑人的活动情况。
    A technological breakthrough enabled investigators to track the movements of the suspects.
13. 双方在会谈与谈判中寻求外交突破。
    Both sides sought a diplomatic breakthrough in their talks and negotiations.
14. 他们正试图为达到他们的目的而做出突破性进展。
    They are trying to make breakthrough progress towards their objectives.

"突破"的第三个意思是"超过某个界限"。英语可以译为 to break, to breach, to hit。例如:
15. 他善于搞技术革新,屡屡突破生产定额。
    As he is good at making technological innovations, he has frequently

hit the production quota.
16. 2007年，中国香槟酒消费量突破66万瓶的记录。
    In 2007, Chinese consumption of champagne hit the record of 660 thousand bottles.
17. 2004年，中国汽车销量突破百万大关。
    1) In 2004, China's car sales broke one million.
    2) In 2004, China's car sales breached the million mark.
    3) In 2004, China's car sales hit the million mark.
18. 美国人口官方统计已突破3亿。
    America's population has officially hit three hundred million.

"突破口"或"突破点"的第一个意思是"在敌方防御阵地上打开的缺口"，为军事用语。英语可以译为 point of breach, point of penetration。例如：
19. 这位指挥官选择城墙西南角作为进攻的突破口。
    The commander chose the southwest corner of the city wall as the point of breach for the attack.
20. 这里就是据信罗马人攻破这座古城城墙的突破口。
    It was the point of penetration where the Romans are believed to have broken through the wall of the ancient city.

"突破口"或"突破点"的第二个意思是比喻"完成任务或解决问题最有利的入手处"。英语可以译为 breakthrough point。例如：
21. 解放思想的突破口是深入贯彻落实科学发展观。
    The breakthrough point for emancipating the mind is to apply the Scientific Outlook on Development thoroughly.

"突破领域"可以译为 area of breakthrough。例如：
22. 由于目前许多儿童失学，这个非洲国家的主要突破领域是初等教育。
    As a lot of children are missing from school currently, the major area of breakthrough in this African country is primary education.

## 八十九、山　　寨

### 汉语关键词
山寨、山寨工厂、山寨手机

### 英语关键词
mountain village, mountain hamlet, stockaded mountain village, fortified mountain village, fenced mountain hamlet, mountain stronghold, mountain fastness, knockoff factory, shoddy factory, emulational, an imitation of, shoddy, knockoff, ripoff, pirate, unlicenced

### 句　子
这些手机是一家山寨工厂生产的。

### 误　译
These mobile phones were made by a cottage factory.

### 正　译
1) These mobile phones were made by a knockoff factory.
2) These cell phones were produced by a shoddy factory.

### 解　释
香港将"山寨工厂"译为 cottage factory，指的是中、小型企业在住宅楼宇或简陋建筑物内设置的非正规厂房内的工厂。这个词来自 cottage industry，原指英国产业革命时家庭小规模制作，主要是生产纺织品。香港将 cottage industry 译为"山寨工业"，实指小企业经营的作坊工业，与国内的"山寨工业"无关。同样，香港将 cottage factory 译为"山寨工厂"，实指小规模作坊，与国内的"山寨工厂"无关。国内的"山寨工厂"指"有嫌疑仿冒或伪造著名品牌商品的生产厂家"，应译为 knockoff factory, shoddy factory。

"山寨"的第一个意思是泛指"山村"。英语可以译为 mountain village, mountain hamlet。例如：
1. 当喜讯传到苗族山寨时，村民们奔走相告。
When the good news spread to the mountain village of the Miao ethnic

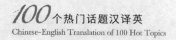

group, the villagers ran around passing on the message.
2. 她大学毕业后,自愿到贵州西部的一个山寨当小学教师。
After she graduated from the university, she volunteered to act as a primary school teacher in a mountain village in the west of Guizhou Province.
3. 在山寨入口处,一群当地的少女,边唱民歌,边向旅游者敬献她们自制的米酒。
At the entrance of the mountain village, a group of local young girls, singing folk songs, offered tourists rice wine brewed by themselves.
4. 这个山寨非常小,因此村民们彼此很熟悉。
The mountain hamlet is so small that the villagers know each other very well.

"山寨"的第二个意思是"筑有栅栏等防守工事的山庄"。英语可以译为 stockaded mountain village, fortified mountain village, fenced mountain hamlet。例如:
5. 村民们坚守山寨,抵御强盗的入侵。
   1) The villagers held their stockaded mountain village against the invasion of the bandits.
   2) The villagers held their fortified mountain village against the invasion of the bandits.
   3) The villagers held their fenced mountain hamlet against the invasion of the bandits.

"山寨"的第三个意思是"旧时绿林好汉占据的山中营寨"。英语可以译为 mountain stronghold, mountain fastness。例如:
6. 寨主在大厅摆酒席,宴请来山寨访问的绿林好汉。
The brigade chief held a grand banquet in the great hall, in honour of the outlaw heroes who were visiting the mountain stronghold.
7. 官军向位于山顶的盗匪山寨发动了进攻。
The government army launched an offensive against the bandits' mountain

fastness, which was located on the mountaintop.
8. 盗匪们撤回到他们的山寨中准备过冬。
   The bandits withdrew to their mountain fastness for the winter.

"山寨"的第四个意思是指"有嫌疑仿冒或伪造著名品牌商品的生产厂家"。英语可以译为 knockoff factory, shoddy factory。例如：
9. 这种相机是山寨厂生产的。
   1) This kind of camera was made in a knockoff factory.
   2) This kind of camera was produced in a shoddy factory.

"山寨"的第五个意思是指"仿制、粗制滥造或盗版现象"。人们对"山寨"有不同理解，因而有不同译法。强调"仿制的"，译为 emulational 或 an imitation of; 强调"粗制滥造的"，译为 shoddy, knockoff, ripoff; 强调"盗版的"，译为 pirate, unlicenced。例如：
10. "中国山寨电视"正在筹备一个山寨版春节晚会。
    CHINA COUNTRYSIDE TV (CCSTV, for short) is making plans for a spring festival gala, which will be an imitation of the CCTV Spring Festival Gala.
11. 许多平民百姓喜欢看山寨明星的表演。
    1) Many ordinary people enjoy the performance given by those star imitators.
    2) Many ordinary people enjoy the performance given by those celebrity imitators.
12. 根据保守估计，山寨机已占据我国三分之一的手机市场销售份额。
    According to a conservative estimate, emulational cell phones have had a one-third share of the domestic market.
13. 山寨机因价格低廉和功能齐全而受到农民工的青睐。
    Emulational mobile phones have won the favour of the rural migrant workers for their low prices and all necessary functions.
14. 这个顾客投诉说他刚买的山寨机因质量低劣而死机了。
    1) The customer complained that the shoddy mobile phone he had just

bought went dead because of poor quality.
2) The customer complained that the knockoff mobile phone he had just bought went dead because of poor quality.
3) The customer complained that the ripoff mobile phone he had just bought went dead because of poor quality.
15. 没有人知道这个山寨手机是哪里制造的。
1) Nobody knows where this pirate cell phone was made.
2) Nobody knows where this unlicenced cell phone was produced.

# 九十、跳 水

### ● 汉语关键词
跳水、跳台跳水、跳板跳水、双人跳水、花样跳水

### ● 英语关键词
jump into the water, dive into the water, jump into the water to commit suicide, dive into the water to commit suicide, diving, platform diving, springboard diving, synchronized diving, plummet, dive, take a dive, nose-dive, take a nose-dive

### ● 句 子
这名游泳者跳进水里,脚先入水。

### ● 误 译
The swimmer dived into the water feet first.

### ● 正 译
The swimmer jumped into the water feet first.

### ● 解 释
汉语的"跳水"作"跳入水中"解时,感兴趣的是出发动作,即脚跳起离开地面,而不管哪个身体部位先入水,相当于英语的 to jump into the water。而 to dive 的意思是 to jump into water with your head and arms

going in first,强调"头和双臂先入水"。to dive 与 feet first 毫不相干。

"跳水"的第一个意思是"跳入水中"。英语可以译为 to jump into the water, to dive into the water。例如:
1. 这个青年因跳水救一个快淹死的小孩而受到表扬。
   The young man was praised for jumping into the water to save a drowning child.
2. 当这位游泳运动员在比赛中跳水进入游泳池时,他抢跳了。
   When the swimmer dived into the swimming pool in a competition, he beat the pistol.

"跳水"的第二个意思是特指"跳入江河湖海自杀",可以具体说"跳江"、"跳河"、"跳湖"或"跳海"。英语可以译为 to jump/dive into the water/river/lake/sea to commit suicide。例如:
3. 当我桥上散步时,忽然听见求救声:"有人跳水啦!"
   When I was walking on the bridge, I suddenly heard a cry for help, "Someone has jumped into the water to commit suicide!"
4. 报载,昨晚一个失业工人跳海了。
   The newspaper reported that an unemployed worker jumped into the sea to commit suicide last night.

"跳水"的第三个意思是一种"水上体育运动项目"。英语可以译为 diving。例如:
5. 竞技跳水是奥运会正式竞赛项目之一,包括跳台跳水和跳板跳水。
   Athletics diving is one of Olympic Games official competition projects, including platform diving and springboard diving.
6. 同组的两名跳水运动员在3米跳板或10米跳台上用相同或相似的跳水动作表演。
   The two divers of a team perform either on the 3-metre springboard or the 10-metre platform, using the same or similar dives.
7. 双人跳水(花样跳水)之所以独特,是因为它的特点是由两名跳水运动员构成一队。
Synchronized diving is unique because it features two divers as a team.

"跳水"的第四个意思是比喻"价格、指数、利润等急剧下降"。英语可以译为 to plummet, to dive, to take a dive, to nose-dive, to take a nose-dive。例如：

8. 最近股价跳水,达到历史最低点。
Share prices have recently plummeted to an all-time low.
9. 由于商务活动急剧减少,本市一些高档酒店价格跳水。
As a result of the rapid decrease of commercial activities, the prices of some high-rating hotels in this city have plummeted.
10. 由于西瓜价格跳水,瓜农遭受惨重损失。
As the prices of watermelons plummeted, the melon farmers suffered a severe damage.
11. 这位专家指出:如果我们现在不下决心整顿房地产市场,房价将会大幅跳水。
The expert points out that if we don't make our determination to straighten out the real estate market, the housing prices will plummet by large margin.
12. 问题奶粉事件造成乳制品价格集体跳水。
The event of the problematic milk powder has caused the prices of dairy products to plummet collectively.
13. 国际市场的铁矿石价格已经大幅跳水。
In the international market, the prices of iron ores have plummeted.
14. 这座别墅以跳水价售出。
The villa was sold out at a plummeted price.
15. 如果石油生产商在短期内开采过多的自然资源,其结果将是导致跳水价格。
If oil producers extract too much of their natural resources in a short time, the result would be a plummeted price.

16. 2008年,上证综指从6,124点跳水,一路跌到1,665点。
    In 2008, Shanghai Composite Index dived from 6,124 points all the way down to 1,665 points.
17. 石油业的利润最近跳水了。
    The profits in oil industry have recently taken a dive.
18. 这家公司首席执行官被捕后股票跳水。
    The share price of the company nose-dived after its CEO was arrested.
19. 今天,股票市场跳水,下跌了125点。
    Today the stock market took a nose-dive and dropped 125 points.

# 九十一、慈 善

● 汉语关键词

慈善、慈善事业、慈善行为、善举、慈善活动、慈善工作、慈善团体、慈善机构、慈善组织、慈善学校、慈善商店、慈善家、慈善演出、义演、慈善捐款、善款、慈善拍卖、义拍、慈善义卖活动、义卖

● 英语关键词

tender, benevolent, charitable, philanthropic, charity, philanthropy, charitable act, charity activity, charity work, charitable society, charitable institution, philanthropic institution, charitable organization, philanthropic organization, charity school, charity shop, thrift shop, philanthropist, charity performance, charitable donations, charity auction, charity sale

● 句 子

他在30年的慈善生涯中不断地给有困难的人捐款。

● 误 译

In his 30 years' charitable career, he has continuously taken donations to those people in difficulties.

● 正 译

In his 30 years' charitable career, he has continuously made donations to those people in difficulties.

### ● 解 释

　　to make a tour 与 to take a tour 的意思相同。但是 to make donations 与 to take donations 的意思相反。前者的意思为"捐款",是"给予"。而后者的意思为"接受捐款",不是"给予"。表示"捐款"的说法有 to give money, to offer money, to donate money, to make donations, to give donations, to offer donations。

　　"慈善"的第一个意思是"对人关怀,富有同情心"。英语可以译为 tender, benevolent, charitable, philanthropic。例如:
1. 她心地慈善,乐善好施。
   1) She is tender-hearted, being glad to do good things for the people in need and give them alms.
   2) She is benevolent-minded, being glad to do good things for the people in need and give them alms.
2. 他是慈善心肠与商业头脑的完美结合。
   1) He is a perfect blend of a charitable heart and a business head.
   2) He is a perfect blend of a philanthropic heart and a business head.

　　"慈善"的第二个意思是"帮助穷人的精神、行为或事业"。英语可以译为 charity, philanthropy。例如:
3. 慈善始于家庭。
   Charity begins at home.
4. 慈善在我国已成为一种新的趋势。
   Philanthropy has become a new trend in our country.
5. 她出于慈善之心而关怀孤儿。
   She cared for the orphans out of charity.
6. 他出于慈善之心给老乞丐施舍了一些钱。
   He gave the old beggar some money because of charity.

7. 他们打着慈善的幌子干着骗人的勾当。
   They cheated people under the veil of charity.
8. 当我听说这个骗子正企图打着慈善的幌子掩饰他的臭名昭著的行动时,我真的失去了所有的耐性。
   I really lost all patience when I heard the swindler attempting to veil his infamous conduct under the mask of charity.

"慈善事业",可以译为 charity, philanthropy。例如:
9. 慈善事业依靠自愿捐赠。
   Charities rely on voluntary donations and contributions.
10. 由于中国愈加繁荣,中国人民愈加热衷于志愿服务和慈善事业。
    The Chinese people are keener on volunteer services and charity as China is becoming more prosperous.
11. 这对老夫妇定期为慈善事业捐款。
    The old couple regularly give money to charity.
12. 她献身于慈善事业。
    She committed herself to philanthropy.

"慈善行为"或"善举",可以译为 charity, charitable act。例如:
13. 许多有需要的家庭受益于他的善举。
    Many families in need benefit from his charity.
14. 他的善举受到网民们的赞扬,被全国主要报纸和网站刊载。
    His charitable act was hailed by netizens and carried by major newspapers and Websites across the country.

"慈善活动",可以译为 charity activity。例如:
15. 大多数慈善活动是由志愿者而不是由政府发起的。
    Most of the charity activities were initiated by volunteers rather than the government.

"慈善工作",可以译为 charity work。例如:
16. 他把大部分时间都奉献给了慈善工作。
    He dedicated most of his time to charity work.
17. 任何一个普通人作为志愿者都可以参与慈善工作。
    Any ordinary person can join in charity work as a volunteer.

"慈善团体",可以译为 charity, charitable society。例如
18. 这个慈善团体是个非营利性组织
    This charity is a nonprofit organization.
19. 红十字会是个国际性慈善团体。
    The Red Cross is an international charity.
20. 他创办了这个慈善团体以纪念他已故的妻子。
    He founded the charitable society in memory of his late wife.

"慈善机构",可以译为 charitable institution, philanthropic institution。例如:
21. 慈善机构旨在帮助穷人、病人和有困难的人。
    The charitable institution is intended to help people who are poor, sick and in difficulties.

"慈善组织",可以译为 charitable organization, philanthropic organization。例如:
22. 在一个慈善组织的支助下,他完成了大学的学习。
    Supported by a charitable organization, he finished his university studies.
23. 这些地震灾民从几个慈善组织收到了捐款和衣服。
    These earthquake victims received money and clothes from several philanthropic organizations.

"慈善学校",可以译为 charity school。例如:
24. 这个孤儿被送往一所慈善学校学习。
    The orphan was sent to study at a charity school.

"慈善商店",可以译为 charity shop(英), thrift shop(美)。例如:
25. 他把他的摄象机送给了当地的慈善商店。
   1) He gave his video camera to the local charity shop.
   2) He gave his video camera to the local thrift shop.

"慈善家",可以译为 philanthropist。例如:
26. 这位慈善家定期给慈善机构捐款。
   The philanthropist makes regular donations to charity.

"慈善演出"或"义演",可以译为 charity performance。例如:
27. 这位歌星参加了国际演艺家为救济饥荒进行筹款而举行的义演。
   The pop singer attended a charity performance given by international entertainers to raise money for famine relief.

"慈善捐款"或"善款",可以译为 charitable donations。例如:
28. 中国政府正在考虑对慈善捐款减税,以与国际惯例接轨。
   The Chinese government is considering tax breaks on charitable donations in line with international practice.

"慈善拍卖"或"义拍",可以译为 charity auction。例如:
29. 这个慈善机构将举行义拍来帮助地震灾民。
   The philanthropic organization will hold a charity auction in aid of the earthquake victims.

"慈善义卖活动"或"义卖",可以译为 charity sale。例如:
30. 昨天,这个慈善机构为地震灾区举办了一场慈善义卖活动。
   Yesterday, the philanthropic institution launched a charity sale for the quake-jolted areas.

# 九十二、护　　航

> 汉语关键词

护航、保驾护航、保驾

> 英语关键词

escort, convoy, protect, guarantee, escort the emperor, help

> 句　子

30年来,我国立法机构制定了一系列法律为改革开放护航。

> 误　译

Over the last 30 years, the legislature of our country has made a series of laws to escort the reform and opening-up to the outside world.

> 正　译

Over the last 30 years, the legislature of our country has made a series of laws to guarantee the implementation of the reform and opening-up policies.

> 解　释

这里的"护航"是比喻意义,指"保证"或"保障",应译为 to guarantee。而 to escort 的意思是 to go with sb to protect or guard them,即"护送"或"护卫",其宾语是人或交通工具,而不是抽象的事物。例如:

1. 总统在一组保镖的护卫下到达会议室。

The President arrived at the conference room, escorted by a group of bodyguards.

"护航"的第一个意思是"护送船只或飞机航行"。英语可以译为 to escort, to convoy。例如:

2. 中国政府将派海军舰艇前往亚丁湾、索马里海域执行护航任务。

The Chinese government will deploy naval ships to the Gulf of Aden and the waters off the Somalia coast for escorting operations.

3. 中国三艘海军舰艇将为中国船只和替国际组织运送人道主义救济

物资的船只护航,并执行反海盗巡逻任务。
The three Chinese naval ships will escort Chinese ships as well as ships carrying humanitarian relief materials for international organizations, and conduct anti-piracy patrols.

4. 这艘运兵船由两艘军舰护航。
   1) The troop ship had an escort of two warships.
   2) The troop ship was escorted by two warships.
   3) The troop ship was convoyed by two warships.
5. 这艘商船由一艘驱逐舰护航。
   1) This merchant ship had an escort of a destroyer.
   2) This merchant ship was escorted by a destroyer.
   3) This merchant ship was convoyed by a destroyer.
6. 这些船只将为运送联合国粮食援助到非洲国家的货轮护航。
   The ships will escort cargo vessels carrying UN food aid to the African country.
7. 这架总统专机由喷气式战斗机护航。
   The special plane for the President was escorted by jet fighters.
8. 这艘日本护航舰安排好与中国进行互访。
   1) The Japanese escort ship was scheduled to make a reciprocal visit to China.
   2) The Japanese convoy ship was scheduled to make a reciprocal visit to China.
   3) The Japanese convoying ship was scheduled to make a reciprocal visit to China.

"护航"的第二个意思是"保护或保障一种事物",也可以说"保驾护航"。英语动词可以译为 to protect, to guarantee;名词可以译为 guarantee。例如:
9. 发展农村经济,我们需要稳定的社会秩序为其保驾护航。
   To develop rural economy, we need a stable social order as its guarantee.
10. 不断改进的信息技术为互联网的正常运转保驾护航。
    The ever-improving information technology guarantees the normal

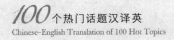

operation of the Internet.

11. 你们真是幸运,有这样医德高尚而且医术精湛的医生为你们的健康保驾护航。

You are really fortunate to have such doctors with high morality and consummate skill to protect your health.

12. 我们公司具有一支优秀的专业团队,为客户资产安全保驾护航,帮助客户实现增长财富的梦想。

Our company has an excellent professional team to protect the safety of our clients' assets and help them to realize their dream of increasing wealth.

"保驾"的原义是"护卫皇帝"。英语可以译为 to escort the emperor。例如:

13. 这位将军与御林军为皇帝保驾,去到皇家猎苑。

The General and the imperial guards escorted the emperor to the royal hunting ground.

现在,"保驾"用来泛指"保护或帮助某人"。英语可以译为 to escort, to help。例如:

14. 放心吧! 我一路上会给你保驾的。

Don't worry. I'll escort you all the way there.

15. 你开车时有老李保驾,怕什么?

What do you have to fear with Mr Li to escort you when you drive?

16. 有全家人为你保驾,你一定会成功的。

You will certainly succeed, with your whole family to help you.

# 九十三、团　圆

### 汉语关键词
团结、团圆、团圆节、团圆饭、团团、团团包围、团团围住、团团转

### 英语关键词
get united, get reunited, be reunited, have a reunion, reunion, Mid-Autumn Festival, Moon Festival, family reunion dinner, round, ball, surround completely, encircle tightly, cluster around, press around, crowd around, swarm around, walk around, run around, scurry around

### 句　子
在分别30年以后,这位老人与他的住在台湾的弟弟团圆了。

### 误　译
After they had been separated for 30 years, the old man got united with his brother who lived in Taiwan.

### 正　译
After they had been separated for 30 years, the old man got reunited with his brother who lived in Taiwan.

### 解　释
"团圆"指的是"散而复聚",to get reunited 的意思是 to have two or more people brought together again after they have been separated for a long time,为正确译法。而 to get united 的意思是 to join together politically or by shared aims,即"团结"。例如:

1. 让我们团结一致,战胜金融危机。
   Let's get united as one to win over the financial crisis.

"团圆"的第一个意思是"家庭成员又聚在一起"。英语动词可以译为 to have a reunion, to be reunited, to get reunited; 英语名词可以译为 reunion。例如:

# 100个热门话题汉译英
Chinese-English Translation of 100 Hot Topics

2. 春节前,千百万农民工回到故乡与家人团圆。
   Before the Spring Festival, millions of rural migrant workers go back to their hometowns to have a reunion with their families.
3. 父母与失散的孩子们团圆了。
   The parents were reunited with their lost children.
4. 他抱着有朝一日全家团圆的希望。
   He cherished a hope that some day his whole family would be reunited.
5. 战后,这个老兵与妻子和家人团圆了。
   After the war, the veteran soldier got reunited with his wife and family.
6. 我们被骨肉团圆的激情场面感动。
   We were moved by the emotional reunion between the parents and their children.
7. 传统上,春节是个家人团圆的日子。
   The Spring Festival was traditionally a day of family reunion.
8. 母子团圆的感人场面是难以忘怀的。
   The touching reunion between mother and son is unforgettable.

"团圆节",就是"中秋节"。英语可以译为 Mid-Autumn Festival, Moon Festival。例如:

9. 今晚,他全家人聚在一起过团圆节。
   Tonight, his whole family gathered together to celebrate the Moon Festival.
10. 根据传统,人们在团圆节要吃月饼。
    According to the tradition, people would eat moon cakes during the Mid-Autumn Festival.

"团圆饭",可以译为 family reunion dinner。例如:

11. 除夕之夜,我们围坐在桌前吃团圆饭。
    On the New Year's Eve, we sat round the table to have family reunion dinner.

"团圆"的第二个意思是"圆形的"。英语可以译为 round。例如:
12. 这个人团圆脸,大眼睛。
    This man has a round face, with big eyes.
13. 团圆的月亮挂在天空。
    The round moon was hanging in the sky.

"团团"的第一个意思是"圆形的"。英语可以译为 round。例如:
14. 这个孩子团团的小脸,十分可爱。
    With a little round face, the child is very lovely.

"团团"的第二个意思是"球形的东西"。英语可以译为 ball。例如:
15. 他把信揉成一个团团。
    He crumpled the letter into a ball.
16. 她把毛线绕成一个团团。
    She rolled the wool into a ball.
17. 她把面揉成一个团团。
    She kneaded the dough into a ball.

"团团"的第三个意思是形容"旋转或围绕的样子"。"团团包围"或"团团围住",可以译为 to surround completely, to encircle tightly, to cluster around, to press around, to crowd around, to swarm around。例如:
18. 一群记者把这位官员团团围住,向他提问题。
    A group of reporters surrounded the official completely and asked him questions.
19. 愤怒的人群把肇事者的小汽车团团围住。
    The angry crowd encircled the delinquent's car tightly.
20. 粉丝们把他们崇拜的著名电影明星团团围住。
    1) The fans clustered around the famous film star that they worshipped.
    2) The fans pressed around the famous film star that they worshipped.
    3) The fans crowded around the famous film star that they worshipped.
21. 激动的人群将获胜者团团围住。
    The excited crowd swarmed around the winner.

"团团转"的意思是"来回转圈儿,多用来形容忙碌、焦急的样子"。英语可以译为 to walk around, to run around, to scurry around。例如:
22. 他在房间里团团转,不知道怎么办才好。
   He walked around in the room, not knowing what to do.
23. 小朋友们在做游戏,围着老师团团转。
   The children were playing games, walking around their teacher.
24. 为筹备新年晚会,大家从早到晚忙得团团转。
   Everybody has been running around from morning till night, busy with preparing for the New Year's party.
25. 我由于试图照顾好每个孩子而忙得团团转,变得越来越累。
   I grew wearier as I scurried around, trying to care for each child.

# 九十四、折　　腾

● 汉语关键词

折腾、不折腾、被折腾

● 英语关键词

flip-flop, toss and turn, toss about, fool around, muck around, mess about, cause physical or mental suffering, get sb down, plague, torment, be hard hit, suffer, struggle, get sidetracked, not get sidetracked

● 句　子

中国股市稳健发展需要不折腾。

● 误　译

The steady development of China's stock market requires that we should not flip-flop.

● 正　译

The steady development of China's stock market requires that we should not get sidetracked.

● 解 释

to flip-flop 的意思是 to suddenly change one's position or opinion on a political issue,指"突然改变政治立场或观点",与股市无关。例如:
1. 这个政客被指责在若干重大问题上出尔反尔。
   The politician was accused of flip-flopping on several major issues.

"折腾"的第一个意思是"翻过来倒过去"。英语可以译为 to toss and turn, to toss about。例如:
2. 他折腾了大半夜,睡不着觉。
   He tossed and turned restlessly for most of the night, unable to go to sleep.
3. 你凑合着睡一会儿。别来回折腾了。
   Just try to get off to sleep for a while. Don't toss and turn restlessly.
4. 他躺在床上,折腾了一宿。
   Lying in bed, he tossed about all night.

"折腾"的第二个意思是"反复做某事",也可以说"瞎折腾"。英语可以译为 to fool around, to muck around, to mess about。例如:
5. 别瞎折腾了。你会摔个狗啃泥的。
   Stop fooling around! You could bite the dust.
6. 谁在折腾这个手机?它已经坏了。
   Who's been mucking the mobile phone around? It is already damaged.
7. 别瞎折腾了,先干完你的工作。
   Stop messing about — finish your work first.

"折腾"的第三个意思是"折磨"。英语动词可以译为 to cause physical or mental suffering, to get sb down, to plague;名词译为 torment。"被折腾",可以译为 to be hard hit, to suffer。例如:
8. 慢性病真是折腾人。
   1) A chronic disease can cause physical or mental suffering.

2) A chromic disease can be such a torment.
9. 牙痛折腾死我了!
   A toothache has got me down.
10. 化脓的伤口已经折腾我好几天了。
    The festering wound has plagued me for several days.
11. 你这一整天净用这样傻里傻气的问题来折腾我!
    You've been plaguing me with such silly questions all day!
12. 附近工地的噪声可把小区的居民折腾苦了。
    The noises from the nearby construction site have badly plagued the inhabitants of this residential area.
13. 这些年我们为了钱,被折腾得够呛。
    We've been really hard hit for money these years.
14. 你知道我心里在怎样折腾。
    You know how my mind is suffering!
15. 我太老了,经不起这种折腾了。
    I am too old to stand the torment.
16. 她说她再经不起折腾了。
    She said she couldn't stand the torment any more.
17. 他不得不忍受精神紧张、抑郁和焦虑的折腾。
    He had to endure the torment caused by stress, depression and anxiety.

"折腾"的第四个意思是"挣扎"或"奋斗"。英语可以译为 to struggle。例如:
18. 人的一辈子啊,其实就是为了生活而折腾,也同时被生活所折腾。
    In his lifetime, a person is actually struggling for survival and is plagued by life at the same time.

"不折腾"的意思很微妙,有"不乱做,不瞎搞,不翻来覆去,不做无用之功,不没事找事,不走岔路"等含义,很难在英语中找到对应词。这里姑且利用《中国日报》的译法 not to get sidetracked。例如:

19. 我们必须不动摇、不懈怠、不折腾,坚定不移地推进改革开放,坚定不移地走中国特色社会主义道路。
We must not sway back and forth, relax our efforts or get sidetracked, but firmly push forward the reform and opening-up as well as adhere to socialism with Chinese characteristics.

to get sidetracked 的意思为 to get off track,即"脱离正常的路径",有"折腾"的含义。在下面的原文中,to get sidetracked 可以译为"折腾":
20. The boys get sidetracked more while the girls are more confident.
男孩子们比较爱折腾,而女孩子们比较自信。
21. He does not let himself get sidetracked by fads and trends.
他不让自己受时髦和时尚东西的折腾。
22. I always get sidetracked. Sometimes we get going for a while and then something — a hubby on a business trip, a sick child or unexpected houseguests — gets us off track.
我总是被折腾。有时候,我们刚干了一会儿事情,接着有件事 — 出差途中的丈夫、生病的孩子、或者家里的不速之客 — 把我们折腾一番。

# 九十五、着　　陆

> 汉语关键词

拖累、着陆、软着陆、硬着陆、

> 英语关键词

drag down, land, touch down, landing, touchdown, make a soft landing, take a soft landing, make a soft touchdown, soft landing, make a hard landing, take a hard landing, hard landing

> 句　子

美元硬着陆可能拖累全球经济复苏。

# 100个热门话题汉译英
### Chinese-English Translation of 100 Hot Topics

● 误 译

A hard landing of the US dollar may well drag the global economic recovery.

● 正 译

A hard landing of the US dollar may well drag down the global economic recovery.

● 解 释

to drag 的意思是"拖",表达不了"拖累"的比喻意义。to drag sth down 的意思是 to bring sth to a lower social or economic level,具有"拖累"的含义。

"着陆"的意思是"飞行器从空中到达陆地,或航天器降落到地面或其他星球表面上"。英语动词可以译为 to land, to touch down。英语名词可以译为 landing, touchdown。例如:

1. 这位飞行员驾驶飞机安全着陆。

   The pilot landed the plane safely.

2. 这位飞行员试图驾驶严重损坏的飞机着陆。

   The pilot tried to land his crippled plane.

3. 这位飞行员设法让滑翔机在一个安全的地方着陆。

   The pilot managed to land the glider on a safe place.

4. 这架飞机安全着陆时,我感到十分放心。

   I was quite relieved when the plane landed safely.

5. 8个小时之后,这架飞机在纽约机场着陆。

   Eight hours later, the plane touched down at New York airport.

6. 这位飞行员作了一个完美的着陆。

   1) The pilot made a perfect landing.

   2) The pilot made a textbook landing.

7. 尽管天气不好,这位飞行员仍顺利着陆。

   Despite the bad weather, the pilot made a smooth landing.

8. 这些宇航员成功地在月球着陆。

   These astronauts made a successful landing on the moon.

9. 这位飞行员被迫紧急着陆。
   The pilot was forced to make an emergency landing.
10. 这位飞行员不得不在雾中盲目着陆。
    The pilot had to make a blind landing in the mist.
11. 我们遭遇液压系统故障,请求优先着陆。
    We have hydraulic trouble and request a priority landing.
12. 这架飞机着陆之前在机场上空盘旋。
    The plane circled the airport before landing.
13. 这架飞机在着陆时爆炸了。
    When landing, the aircraft exploded.
14. 由于天气恶劣,着陆延误了半个小时。
    The landing was delayed for half an hour because of the bad weather.
15. 当这架航天飞机和它的6名乘员安全着陆时,他们深深地松了一口气。
    They breathed a deep sigh of relief as the space shuttle and its six crew touched down safely.
16. 我们很快就要着陆。请您系好安全带。
    We shall be landing shortly. Please fasten your seatbelts.
17. 人类很有可能不久将在火星上着陆。
    It's quite possible that man will soon land on Mars.
18. 这位飞行员驾驶他的严重损坏的飞机在机场安全着陆。
    The pilot guided his crippled airplane to a safe landing in the airport.
19. 1969年7月20日,阿波罗号航天飞船首次登月着陆被载入史册。
    On July 20, 1969, history was made with the first Apollo moon landing.

"软着陆"的第一个意思是"航天器利用一定装置,改变运行轨道,逐渐减低降落速度,最后不受损坏地降落到地面或其他星球表面上"。英语可以译为 to make a soft landing, to take a soft landing, to make a soft touchdown。例如:

20. 这个降落舱利用降落伞减低下落速度,使它能在干燥地面软着陆。
    The descent module uses parachutes to slow its fall, enabling it to

# 100个热门话题汉译英
Chinese-English Translation of 100 Hot Topics

  make a soft landing on dry land.
21. 降落伞和气垫能帮助着陆装置软着陆。
  Parachutes and aircushions will help the lander make a soft touchdown.
22. 这个航天器成功地在火星软着陆。
  The spacecraft succeeded in making a soft touchdown in Mars.

  "软着陆"的第二个意思是比喻"采取稳妥的措施使某些重大问题和缓地得到解决"。英语动词可以译为 to make a soft landing。英语名词可以译为 soft landing。例如：
23. 我们必须扩大内需，以实现经济的软着陆。
  We must boost domestic demand so as to make a soft landing in economy.
24. 这个亚洲国家的经济正走向软着陆。
  The Asian country is on track to achieve a soft landing in economy.
25. 中国政府已采取实现经济软着陆的必需步骤。
  The Chinese government has taken the steps needed to engineer a soft landing for the economy.

  "硬着陆"的第一个意思是"飞行器不经减速控制而以高速度降落到地面上"。英语动词可以译为 to make a hard landing, to take a hard landing。英语名词可以译为 hard landing。例如：
26. 这架直升机在山顶硬着陆。
  1) The helicopter made a hard landing on the top of the mountain.
  2) The helicopter took a hard landing on the top of the mountain.
27. 星期一上午，当一架小型飞机在这个国际机场硬着陆时，有两人幸存。
  Two people survived when a small airplane made a hard landing at the international airport on Monday morning.

  "硬着陆"的第二个意思是比喻"采取过急、过猛的措施较生硬地解决某些重大问题"。英语动词可以译为 to make a hard landing, to take a hard landing。英语名词可以译为 hard landing。例如：

28. 这场金融危机可能引发全球性经济硬着陆。
    The financial crisis may trigger a global hard landing in economy.
29. 重大股市泡沫破灭可以使得经济硬着陆。
    The bursting of a major stock bubble can lead to a hard landing of the economy.
30. 高通货膨胀使得经济更容易遭受硬着陆。
    High inflation makes the economy more vulnerable to a hard landing.
31. 经济预言家暗示美国经济硬着陆有50%的可能性。
    Economic forecasters have suggested a 50% chance that the US economy could have a hard landing.

# 九十六、春雨贵如油

## 汉语关键词

人工雨、人工增雨、人工降雨、实施人工增雨、耕云播雨、播云

## 英语关键词

artificial rain, man-made rain, artificial rainmaking, artificial precipitation, artificial rain production, rain enhancement, prepare an artificial rain precipitation, carry out artificial precipitation, cloud seeding, seed clouds

## 句 子

春雨贵如油。

## 误 译

Spring rain is as expensive as oil.

## 正 译

Spring rain is as precious as (edible) oil.

## 解 释

expensive 的意思是 costing a lot of money，即"昂贵"，需要花许多钱才

能买到。而 precious 的意思是 valuable or important and not to be wasted，即"宝贵"或"珍贵"，指有价值、或重要而不可浪费。农谚"春雨贵如油"的意思是指春雨因稀少而宝贵，而且是无价的，应当译为 precious，而不宜译为 expensive。例如：

1. 淡水在干旱地区是一种宝贵的商品。

   Fresh water is a precious commodity in drought-affected areas.

   传统上，"贵如油"的"油"原指"食用油"，而不指"当作燃料的油"。而 oil 的意思是 a thick liquid that is found in rock underground，即"石油"或"原油"，是燃料或化工原料。当然，oil 还有另外一个意思，是 a smooth thick liquid that is made from plants or animals and is used in cooking，即"食用油"，一般前面要加上修饰词。例如：edible oil/cooking oil（食用油），peanut oil（花生油），soybean oil/soya oil/soy oil（大豆油），sesame oil（香油），olive oil（橄榄油），vegetable oil（植物油）。在燃料匮乏的现代社会，认为春雨如同石油一样宝贵，将"油"译为 oil，达到简练效果，也未尝不可。

   我国采用人工增雨的方法，缓解旱情。"人工雨"，英语可以译为 artificial rain, man-made rain。例如：

2. 到 2010 年，我国人造雨量可望达到每年 500 亿吨。

   By 2010, the volume of artificial rain is expected to reach 50 billion tons a year in our country.

3. 市政府将求助于人工降雨，以使城市凉爽。

   The municipal government will resort to man-made rain to cool down the city.

   "人工增雨"或"人工降雨"，英语可以译为 artificial rainmaking, artificial precipitation, artificial rain production, rain enhancement。例如：

4. 这些科学家开发了一项通过在大气层实施人工闪电来制造人工降雨的新技术。

   These scientists have developed a new technology for artificial rainmaking through artificial lightning in the atmosphere.

5. 由于人工增雨,这个干旱地区昨天得到了一些雨水。
   Thanks to an artificial precipitation, this drought-stricken area received some rain yesterday.
6. 这位专家指出:人工增雨使用的化学剂能够影响气候模式、生态系统、水源和土壤。
   The expert pointed out that the chemicals used in the artificial rain production could affect climatic patterns, ecosystem, water sources and the soil.
7. 这些科学家正在研究播云对降雨和防雹的效果。
   These scientists are doing research on the effects of cloud seeding for rain enhancement and hail suppression.
8. 在这些干旱地区采取了人工增雨的行动。
   Rain-enhancing practices were adopted in these drought-stricken regions.
9. 该地区的这一部分在星期日白天有厚云层,有利于实施诱雨措施。
   This part of the area saw thick clouds during Sunday daytime, which is favourable for rain-inducing measures.
10. 中国政府已实施人工方式在干旱省份造雨。
    The Chinese government has employed artificial means to create rains in drought-stricken provinces.

"实施人工增雨",英语可以译为 to prepare an artificial rain precipitation, to carry out artificial precipitation。例如:

11. 他们正在准备人工增雨,以在这个干旱地区制造阵雨。
    They are preparing an artificial rain precipitation to create showers in the drought-hit area.
12. 地方政府正在进行人工增雨,以缓解缺水状况,并保证人与牲畜的饮用水。
    The local government is carrying out artificial precipitation to alleviate water shortage and ensure drinking water for both people and livestock.
13. 政府正计划在这些干旱地区实施人工增雨,以缓解严重旱情。
    The government is planning to employ artificial means to cause rainfall

in the drought-affected areas to ease the serious drought.

汉语有"耕云播雨"的说法,比喻"人工降雨"。英语也有 cloud seeding, to seed clouds 的说法,译为"播云"。例如:

14. 自从20世纪40年代中期,科学家们就一直努力实施播云和人工降雨。
Scientists have been trying to seed clouds and produce rain since the mid-1940s.

15. 如果天气状况不利,我们就将不得不因涉及的巨大成本而推迟播云。
If the weather is not favourable, then we'll have to postpone the cloud seeding because of the huge cost involved.

# 九十七、抄　底

### 汉语关键词

抄底、触及底线、抄底者、抄底价、抄底游

### 英语关键词

touch the bottom line, fish the bottom, snap up bargains, bottom-fisher, bargain-hunter, lowest price, rock-bottom price, take a tour at a rock-bottom price, take a rock-bottom price tour

### 句　子

这位股评家警告股民们不要抄底,因为股市仍然价格贵。

### 误　译

The stock market analyst warned the investors not to touch the bottom line because the stock market was still expensive.

### 正　译

The stock market analyst warned the investors not to fish the bottom because the stock market was still expensive.

● 解　释

　　to touch the bottom line 的意思是"触及底线",指触及原则、规则、规定或数额的最低限度,与股民以最低价买股票没有关系。例如:
1. 他的言论因给历史人物抹黑和严重歪曲事实而触及人们道德价值观的底线。
   His remarks have touched the bottom line of people's moral values by smearing historical characters and grossly distorting the truth.
2. 规则是当价格触及底线时买入或补仓,而当价格触及顶线时卖出或卖空。
   The rule is to buy or cover short when the prices touch the bottom line and sell or sell short when prices touch the top line.
3. 这些钢铁供应商深信价格已经触及底线,所以他们囤积不卖以期市场回暖。
   These iron and steel suppliers believe the price has already touched the bottom line, and so they hold off sales in anticipation of the market warming up.
4. 这本书的作者说在他的国家里,生产力已经触及底线,而贫穷已经达到了顶点。
   The author of the book said that productivity had touched the bottom line and poverty had reached its peak in his country.

　　"抄底"的意思与股市投资有关,指"在价格最低的时候买入股票"。英语可以译为 to fish the bottom。本来,to fish the bottom 的意思是"在水底捕鱼",其比喻意义是 to attempt to buy stocks at or near their lowest price,即"企图以最低价买股票",相当于"抄底"。例如:
5. 我用鱼钩钓水底的鱼,用鸡肝作饵。
   I fished the bottom with a hook, using chicken liver as bait.
6. 当这个公司的股票跌到最低价时,这些股民抄了底。
   When the stocks of the company fell to their lowest prices, these investors

fished the bottom.

"抄底",还可以译为 to snap up bargains。例如:
7. 这些日本投资者最近当楼价下跌时在美国楼市抄底。
These Japanese investors have recently snapped up bargains in U. S. housing market when prices were falling down.

"抄底者",英语可以译为 bottom-fisher, bargain-hunter。例如:
8. 作为一个抄底者,这个股民一直在最近急剧跌价的股票中寻找低价股票。
As a bottom-fisher, the investor has been looking for bargains among stocks whose prices have recently dropped dramatically.
9. 作为一个真正忠实的抄底者,他有耐心等待到股票降到最低价再反弹。
As a truly dedicated bargain hunter, he has the patience to wait until stocks fall to their bottom prices before turning up.

"抄底价",就是"最低的价格",即"超低价"。英语可以译为 lowest price, rock-bottom price。例如:
10. 由于许多外国航空公司和饭店在全球金融衰退中开始降价,一些中国人利用这个机会以抄底价到海外旅游。
As many airline companies and hotels in foreign countries have started to cut their prices amid the global financial downturn, some Chinese take advantage of the opportunity to embark on overseas travel at the lowest price.
11. 在金融危机时,这个中国投资者在美国以抄底价买了一座别墅。
During the financial crisis, the Chinese investor bought a villa at a rock-bottom price in the United States.

"抄底游",英语可以译为 to take a tour at a rock-bottom price, to take a rock-bottom-price tour。例如:

12. 在淡季里,他去欧洲"抄底游"。
    During the slack season, he took a tour in Europe at a rock-bottom price.
13. 现在外币贬值,机票降价,正是"抄底游"的好时候。
    As foreign currencies are now depreciating and air fares are lowering, it's good time to take a rock-bottom-price tour.
14. 最近几个月,日本和韩国的一些旅行社来华推广"抄底游"项目。
    In recent months, some travel agencies from Japan and Korea have been to China to promote a rock-bottom-price travel programme.

# 九十八、代　言

## ● 汉语关键词
代言、代言人、品牌代言人、喉舌

## ● 英语关键词
speak on behalf of sb, endorse, endorse a brand, endorse a product, become the face of a brand, spokesperson, spokesman, spokeswoman, spokespeople, prolocutor, mouthpiece, voice, brand spokesperson, brand ambassador, brand prolocutor

## ● 句　子
名人代言"问题食品"将承担连带责任。

## ● 误　译
Those famous people who speak on behalf of problematic food shall bear joint liabilities.

## ● 正　译
1) Those celebrities who endorse problematic food shall bear joint liabilities.

2) Those celebrities who endorse problematic food shall undertake joint liabilities.

3) Those celebrities who endorse problematic food shall be jointly liable.

# 100个热门话题汉译英
Chinese-English Translation of 100 Hot Topics

## ● 解 释

to speak on behalf of sb 的意思是"代表某人说话"。这里的"代言"的特殊含义是"明星代表某一品牌或产品的形象,做广告宣传"。to endorse 的意思是 to say in an advertisement that you use and like a particular product so that other people will want to buy it,正是"在广告中代言"的特殊含义。famous people 泛指"著名的人",而代言的名人基本上是明星,英语用 celebrity 表示。

"代言"的第一个意思是"代表某一阶层或团体发表言论或说话"。英语可以译为 to speak on behalf of sb。例如:
1. 这个学者实际上是为少数专业大户代言,而不是代表普通农民的利益。
   The scholar actually speaks on behalf of a few large family-based special-line enterprises, rather than representing the interests of common farmers.

"代言"的第二个意思是"代表某一品牌或产品的形象,在广告中加以宣传"。英语可以译为 to endorse a brand, to endorse a product, to become the face of a brand。例如:
2. 当购买一种产品时,有些顾客想知道是否有位名人代言这种品牌。
   While buying a product, some customers want to know whether a celebrity endorses the brand.
3. 这位著名演员说,"如果我不亲自使用一种产品,我决不会为它代言。"
   The famous actor said, "I won't endorse a product if I don't use it personally."
4. 我不知道究竟有多少名人真正使用他们代言的产品。
   I wonder how many celebrities actually use the products they endorse.
5. 这位影星代言乳品广告,赚了不少钱。
   The film star endorsed a dairy product, and made a lot of money.
6. 名人得到几百万美元来为一个品牌代言。
   Celebrities are paid millions of dollars to become the face of a brand.

"代言人"的第一个意思是"代表某一阶层或团体发表言论或说话的人",即"喉舌"。英语可以译为 spokesperson, spokespeople, prolocutor, mouthpiece, voice。例如:

7. 由于某些小区业主委员会成员即是物业管理公司工作人员,业主委员会实际上变成物业管理公司代言人。

   As the members of the estate proprietors' committees in some residential areas are staff members of the property management companies, the estate proprietors' committees have actually become spokespeople of the property management companies.

8. 学生会是广泛范围学生的代言人。

   The students' association is the prolocutor of a wide range of students.

9. 这家报纸只不过是某些有钱人的代言人。

   The newspaper is only a mouthpiece of certain rich people.

10. 工会应该成为员工的代言人。

    The trade union should be the voice of the staff members.

"代言人"的第二个意思是"为企业或组织的赢利性或公益性目标而进行信息传播服务的特殊人员",即"形象代言人"。英语可以译为 spokesperson, spokesman, spokeswoman, spokespeople。例如:

11. 这位体育明星充当了我们产品的代言人。

    The sports star acted as the spokesperson of our product.

12. 作为篮球运动的代言人,他在杂志和电视上的数十个广告中亮相。

    As a basketball spokesman, he was featured on dozens of ads in magazines and on TV.

13. 这个模特作为一个世界著名品牌的代言人惊艳登台亮相。

    As the spokeswoman of a world famous brand, the model stroke a pose on the stage, which made people pleasantly surprised.

14. 耐克怎么总是可以签下最红的明星作为名人代言人?

    How does Nike always sign the biggest stars as celebrity spokespeople?

"品牌代言人",可以译为 brand spokesperson, brand ambassador,

brand prolocutor。例如：

15. 香港动作片超级明星成龙为一种乌发洗发水充当品牌代言人。
    Hong Kong action superstar Jackie Chan acts as the brand spokesperson of a hair dyeing shampoo.
16. 这家公司通过使用品牌代言人达到了一些明确的目标。
    The company achieved some clear-cut goals by using a brand ambassador.
17. 现在一些广告商和代理商倾向于使用虚拟品牌代言人，而不是名人来代言。
    Now a few advertisers and agencies tend to use virtual brand prolocutors instead of celebrities to endorse a product.

# 九十九、申　报

### 汉语关键词
申报、报关、报税、申报财产、申报户口

### 英语关键词
submit a proposal, declare, make a declaration, declare to the customs, declare to the tax office, declare one's property, apply for, apply for residence registration

### 句　子
这个地方政府发布了一项规定，要求县级官员申报个人财产。

### 误　译
The local government issued a rule that required county-level officials to report their personal property.

### 正　译
The local government issued a rule that required county-level officials to declare their personal property.

## 解 释

to report 的意思是 to give people information about sth that you have seen, heard, done, etc.,即"报告所见、所闻或所做之事",与个人财产无关。而"申报财产"指"向上级或有关部门报告和说明个人财产状况",英语要用 to declare 表示。

"申报"的第一个意思是"向上级或有关部门递交建议报告,以争取获准"。英语可以译为 to submit a proposal to higher authorities or to a concerning department。例如:
1. 分公司必须在年底之前向总公司申报预算。
   The subsidiaries must submit a budget proposal to the general company by the end of the year.
2. 你必须使用这种表格申报项目。
   You must use this form to submit a proposal for the project.
3. 这位科学家正在准备申报一项国家自然基金项目。
   The scientist is making a preparation to submit a proposal for a project supported by the National Natural Sciences Fund.

"申报世界遗产"的意思是"提交提名建议将文化或自然遗产列入《世界遗产名录》",简称"申遗",英语可以译为 to submit a nomination proposal for sth to be considered for inscription on the World Heritage List。例如:
4. 这个亚洲国家已将这座有一千多年历史的古庙申报世界遗产。
   This Asian country has submitted a nomination proposal for the old temple with a history of over one thousand years to be considered for inscription on the World Heritage List.

"申报"的第二个意思是"向海关或税务部门报告情况,或向有关部门报告个人财产情况"。英语可以译为 to declare, to make a declaration。"报关"是 to declare to the customs。"报税"是 to declare to the tax office。"申报财产"是 to declare one's property。例如:
5. 你有什么东西要申报吗?
   Have you got anything to declare?

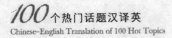

6. 他书面申报了在国外购买的全部商品。
   He made a written declaration for all the goods he had bought abroad.
7. 未携带须申报货物者,沿绿色标记通行。
   1) Follow the green signs if you haven't any goods to declare.
   2) Follow the green signs unless you have goods to declare.
8. 我的助手通常代表我进行入口/出口申报。
   My assistant usually makes an import/export declaration on my behalf.
9. 他申报了他去年的全部收入。
   He declared all he had earned in the previous year.
10. 公民应向税务部门如实申报个人收入。
    Citizens must honestly declare their personal income to the tax office.
11. 数年前中国官员开始申报财产,只是申报情况从未公开。
    Chinese officials began to declare their assets years ago, but the declarations have never been made public.
12. 新任命和将调职的官员需要在刚上任或刚离职时申报财产。
    Those officials who are newly appointed or to be transferred to other posts are supposed to declare their property as soon as they take or leave office.

"申报"的第三个意思是"向上级或有关部门报告情况并提出申请"。英语可以译为 to apply for。"申报户口"是"申请户籍",英语可以译为 to apply for residence registration。例如:

13. 你有资格申报项目经费。
    You are eligible to apply for the project grant.
14. 通过互联网、传真或其他方式申报户口者根据要求须提交相关信息。
    Those who apply for residence registration through the Internet, fax or any other means shall submit the relevant information according to the requirements.
15. 如果你在有效时间之内到中国其他地区,没有必要重新申报户口。
    It is not necessary to re-apply for residence registration if you go to other regions of China within the validity time.

## 一〇〇、民　　生

### 汉语关键词
民生、民生工程、生活、生命、性命

### 英语关键词
life, lives, people's life, people's well-being, project for people's well-being, people's livelihood

### 句　子
我们的政府官员应该关注民生。

### 误　译
Our government officials should be concerned with people's lives.

### 正　译
Our government officials should be concerned with people's life.

### 解　释
当 life 表示"生活"的意思时,是不可数名词,仅有单数形式,没有复数形式。"民生"应译为 people's life。当 life 表示"生命"或"性命"的意思时,是可数名词,一个人一条命,不仅有单数形式,也有复数形式。people's lives 指"人们的性命"。

"民生"的第一个意思是"人民的生计或生活状况"。英语可以译为 people's life, people's well-being。例如:
1. 农业的发展关系到国计民生。
   The development of agriculture is closely related to the national economy and people's well-being.
2. 大部分财政收入将用于改善民生。
   Most of the revenue will go to the improvement of people's life.
3. 我们必须做出更大努力以改善民生。
   We must make more efforts to improve people's well-being.

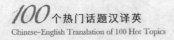

4. 解放前,民生凋敝。
   1) Before liberation, the people lived a destitute life.
   2) In the pre-liberation days, the people lived in destitution.
5. 这个黑社会组织已给本地区的民生和治安造成了恶劣影响。
   The gangdom organization has produced abominable influence upon the people's life and public security in this area.
6. 经过多年努力,我市已建成了食品、化妆品、洗涤品、纺织品、服装、皮鞋、玩具、和眼镜等民生产品制造基地。
   Through many years' hard work, we have built up bases in our city for manufacturing such products for people's life as food, cosmetics, detergent products, textiles, garments, leather shoes, toys and glasses.
7. 市质量监察局昨天公布了最近对汽车配件、装饰材料、燃气用具和木制家具等类民生产品抽查结果。
   Yesterday, the Municipal Bureau of Quality Supervision issued the results of random inspection on such products for people's well-being as car accessories, furnishing materials, gas appliances and wooden furniture.
8. 劳动就业、社会保障、医疗卫生、教育收费、安全生产、食品安全、司法公正、收入分配、企业改制、城市拆迁和环境污染是普通群众和媒体经常谈论的民生话题。
   Labour and employment, social security, medical care and health service, education and tuition, safety in production, food safety, judicial justice, income and distribution, enterprise restructuring, urban house demolition and relocation, and environmental pollution are topics about people's well-being, which are frequently talked about by the ordinary people and media.

"民生工程",英语可以译为 project for people's well-being。例如:
9. 民生工程涉及教育、就业、医疗、住房、社区服务、饮水、农村养老和信息等方面。
   The projects for people's well-being are concerned with education,

employment, medical care, housing, community service, drinking water supply, pension systems in rural areas and information transmission.

有人以为 civil 是"平民的", engineering 是"工程",就将"民生工程"译为 civil engineering,这是错误的。civil engineering 的意思是 a professional engineering discipline that deals with the design, construction and maintenance of the physical and naturally built environment, including works such as bridges, roads, canals, dams and buildings,即"土木工程"。

"民生"的第二个意思是"人民维持生活的办法和门路"。英语可以译为 people's livelihood。例如:

10. 市政府已推出和实施一系列涉及民生的工程。
    The municipal government has put forward and carried out a series of projects concerning people's livelihood.
11. 发展经济和改善民生是政府的义不容辞的责任。
    The development of economy and the improvement of people's livelihood are the bounding duties of the government.
12. 就业是民生之本。
    Employment is vital to people's livelihood.
13. 经济的迅速发展为政府改善民生提供了保证。
    The rapid development of economy has provided a guarantee for the government to improve people's livelihood.
14. 孙中山所倡导的三民主义由民族主义、民权主义和民生主义构成。
    The Three People's Principles put forward by Dr Sun Yat-sen was composed of Nationalism, Democracy and People's Livelihood.

# 100个热门话题汉译英
Chinese-English Translation of 100 Hot Topics

# 汉语关键词索引

## A

按揭 ànjiē 24

## B

八卦 bāguà 19
八卦新闻 bāguà xīnwén 19
八卦杂志 bāguà zázhì 19
摆架子 bǎijià·zi 57
绑匪 bǎngfěi 28
绑架 bǎngjià 28
绑架者 bǎngjiàzhě 28
绑票 bǎng//piào 28
包袱 bāo·fu 87
包袱底儿 bāo·fudǐr 87
包袱皮儿 bāo·fupír 87
保驾 bǎo//jià 92
保驾护航 bǎo jià hù háng 92
报关 bào//guān 99
报税 bàoshuì 99
暴风雪 bàofēngxuě 46
暴光 bào//guāng 73
暴雪 bàoxuě 46
曝丑 bào//chǒu 73
曝光 bào//guāng 73
被潜规则 bèi qiánguīzé 42
被折腾 bèi zhēteng 94
飙车 biāochē 35
飙升 biāoshēng 35

飙戏 biāo//xì 35
飙涨 biāozhǎng 35
播云 bōyún 96
不相信 bù xiāngxìn 54
不信任 bú xìnrèn 54
不折腾 bù zhēténg 94

## C

猜测 cāicè 54
彩信 cǎixìn 20
舱外航天服 cāngwài hángtiānfú 78
草根 cǎogēn 49
草根工业 cǎogēn gōngyè 49
草根阶层 cǎogēn jiēcéng 49
草根文化 cǎogēn wénhuà 49
草根艺人 cǎogēn yìrén 49
草根性 cǎogēnxìng 49
插足 chāzú 31
查帖子 chá//tiě·zi 1
柴鸡蛋 cháijīdàn 71
畅销书排行榜 chàngxiāo shū páihángbǎng 52
抄底 chāo//dǐ 97
抄底价 chāodǐjià 97
抄底游 chāodǐyóu 97
抄底者 chāodǐzhě 97
炒股 chǎo//gǔ 8
炒股者 chǎogǔzhě 8
炒基金 chǎo//jījīn 8

成双的 chéngshuāngde 74
承包 chéngbāo 81
承包人 chéngbāorén 81
承包商 chéngbāoshāng 81
承包制 chéngbāozhì 81
承担 chéngdān 81
持枪杀手 chíqiāng shāshǒu 45
重建 chóngjiàn 50
出轨 chū//guǐ 59
出轨行为 chūguǐ xíngwéi 59
出专辑 chū//zhuānjí 3
触及底线 chùjí//dǐxiàn 97
传播 chuánbō 32
慈善 císhàn 91
慈善工作 císhàn gōngzuò 91
慈善活动 císhàn huódòng 91
慈善机构 císhàn jīgòu 91
慈善家 císhànjiā 91
慈善捐款 císhàn juānkuǎn 91
慈善拍卖 císhàn pāimài 91
慈善商店 císhàn shāngdiàn 91
慈善事业 císhàn shìyè 91
慈善团体 císhàn tuántǐ 91
慈善行为 císhàn xíngwéi 91
慈善学校 císhàn xuéxiào 91
慈善演出 císhàn yǎnchū 91
慈善义卖活动 císhàn yìmài huódòng 91
慈善组织 císhàn zǔzhī 91

## D

打工 dǎ//gōng 13
打工妹 dǎgōngmèi 13
打工仔 dǎgōngzǎi 13

打工族 dǎgōngzú 13
打假 dǎjiǎ 53
大地震 dàdìzhèn 61
大雪 dàxuě 46
代考者 dàikǎozhě 15, 45
代谢障碍 dàixiè zhàngài 76
代言 dàiyán 98
代言人 dàiyánrén 98
代养 dàiyǎng 69
单个的 dāngède 74
单号 dānhào 74
单日 dānrì 74
单数 dānshù 74
倒计时 dàojìshí 23
倒数读秒 dàoshǔ dúmiǎo 23
道德破产 dàodé pòchǎn 77
抵押品 dǐyāpǐn 28
抵制 dǐzhì 68
地震 dìzhèn 61
地震断层 dìzhèn duàncéng 64
地震灾区 dìzhèn zāiqū 61
第三党 dìsāndǎng 31
第三方 dìsānfāng 31
第三者 dìsānzhě 31
第一 dìyī 62
第一地点 dì yī dìdiǎn 62
第一时间 dì yī shíjiān 62
典礼主持人 diǎnlǐ zhǔchírén 30
电视主持人 diànshì zhǔchírén 30
奠基石 diànjīshí 48
冻雨 dòngyǔ 46
抖包袱 dǒu//bāo·fu 87
短信 duǎnxìn 20

# 100个热门话题汉译英
Chinese-English Translation of 100 Hot Topics

断层 duàncéng 64
断层带 duàncéngdài 64
断层地震 duàncéng dìzhèn 64
断层作用 duàncéng zuòyòng 64
对接 duìjiē 51

## E

扼杀 èshā 68
恶搞 ègǎo 38
恶搞文化 ègǎo wénhuà 38
恶搞者 ègǎozhě 38
恶魔 èmó 60

## F

发飙 fābiāo 35
发短信 fā//duǎnxìn 20
发烧 fā//shāo 4
发烧友 fāshāoyǒu 4
发生 fāshēng 61
发帖子 fā//tiě·zi 1
反洗钱 fǎn xǐqián 75
泛滥 fànlàn 72
方丈 fāngzhàng 29
房地产泡沫 fángdìchǎn pàomò 14
房奴 fángnú 24
非上市公司 fēishàngshì gōngsī 40
分包 fēnbāo 81
粉丝 fěnsī 5
封禁 fēngjìn 68
封口 fēng//kǒu 85
封口费 fēngkǒufèi 85
封杀 fēngshā 85
峰会 fēnghuì 47

福利事业 fúlì shìyè 56
复原 fù//yuán 50

## G

概念 gàiniàn 33
干涉 gānshè 67
干预 gānyù 67
高峰 gāofēng 47
高峰会议 gāofēng huìyì 47
高峰期 gāofēngqī 47
高峰时间 gāofēng shíjiān 47
个人拓展 gèrén tuòzhǎn 32
跟帖子 gēn//tiě·zi 1
耕云播雨 gēng yún bō yǔ 96
工程 gōngchéng 11
公害 gōnghài 71
公用事业 gōngyòng shìyè 56
公众形象 gōngzhòng xíngxiàng 55
功能性障碍 gōngnéngxìng zhàng'ài 76
拱顶石 gǒngdǐngshí 48
狗仔队 gǒuzǎiduì 19
股民 gǔmín 8
股市泡沫 gǔshì pàomò 14
观 guān 33
观点 guāndiǎn 33
观念 guānniàn 33
广播主持人 guǎngbō zhǔchírén 30

## H

海底断层 hǎidǐ duàncéng 64
海峡两岸 hǎixiá liǎng'àn 83
海啸 hǎixiào 82
海选 hǎixuǎn 10

航天服 hángtiānfú 78
喉舌 hóushé 98
忽悠 hūyou 21
忽悠一下 hūyōu yīxià 21
互联网泡沫 hùliánwǎng pàomò 14
护航 hùháng 92
花样跳水 huāyàng tiàoshuǐ 90
怀疑 huáiyí 54
环境危机 huánjìng wēijī 80
换客 huànkè 12
恢复 huīfù 50
回帖子 huí//tiě・zi 1
婚庆主持人 hūnqìng zhǔchírén 30
火枪手 huǒqiāngshǒu 45
火上加油 huǒ shàng jiā yóu 65
火上浇油 huǒ shàng jiāo yóu 65

## J

奇数 jīshù 74
基层 jīcéng 49
基层民众 jīcéng mínzhòng 49
基金 jījīn 8
基石 jīshí 48
计时 jìshí 23
计时工资 jìshí gōngzī 23
计时收费 jìshí shōufèi 23
继承 jìchéng 27
继承传统 jìchéng//chuántǒng 27
继承王位 jìchéng//wángwèi 27
继任 jìrèn 27
继任者 jìrènzhě 27
加油 jiāyóu 65
加油加醋 jiā yóu jiā cù 65

加油添醋 jiā yóu tiān cù 65
加油站 jiāyóuzhàn 65
假 jiǎ 53
假货 jiǎhuò 53
架子 jià・zi 57
奖牌排行榜 jiǎngpái páihángbǎng 52
接班 jiē//bān 27
接班人 jiēbānrén 27
接触 jiēchù 51
接轨 jiē//guǐ 51
节目主持人 jiémù zhǔchírén 30
金融海啸 jīnróng hǎixiào 82
金融危机 jīnróng wēijī 80
经济海啸 jīngjì hǎixiào 82
经济泡沫 jīngjì pàomò 14
经济危机 jīngjì wēijī 80
精神破产 jīngshén pòchǎn 77
精神障碍 jīngshén zhàng'ài 76
救 jiù 63
救荒 jiù//huāng 63
救火 jiù//huǒ 63
救急 jiù//jí 63
救险 jiùxiǎn 63
救灾 jiù//zāi 63
拘留 jūliú 28
拘押 jūyā 28

## K

看法 kànfǎ 33
看帖子 kàn//tiě・zi 1
考试作弊 kǎoshì zuòbì 15
考试作弊者 kǎoshì zuòbìzhě 15
科学发展观 kēxué fāzhǎnguān 33

# 100个热门话题汉译英
Chinese-English Translation of 100 Hot Topics

啃老族 kěnlǎozú 7
空巢 kōngcháo 6
空巢家庭 kōngcháo jiātíng 6
空巢老人 kōngcháo lǎorén 6
空巢者 kōngcháozhě 6
空巢综合症 kōngcháo zōnghézhèng 6
宽松 kuānsōng 86
宽松政策 kuānsōng zhèngcè 86
狂飙 kuángbiāo 35

## L

理财 lǐ//cái 9
理财顾问 lǐcái gùwèn 9
理财计划 lǐcái jìhuà 9
理财师 lǐcáishī 9
理念 lǐniàn 33
连接 liánjiē 51
联系 liánxì 51
粮食危机 liángshí wēijī 80
两岸 liǎng'àn 83
两岸关系 liǎng'àn guānxì 83
两岸四地 liǎng'àn sìdì 83
临时工 línshígōng 13
领养 lǐngyǎng 69
流行歌曲排行榜 liúxíng gēqǔ páihángbǎng 52
流行音乐排行榜 liúxíng yīnyuè páihángbǎng 52
笼养鸡蛋 lóngyǎng jīdàn 71
乱涂 luàntú 2
乱写 luànxiě 2

## M

漫游 mànyóu 22
漫游费 mànyóufèi 22
没有架子 méiyǒu jià·zǐ 57
民生 mínshēng 100
民生工程 mínshēng gōngchéng 100
名列榜首 mínglìe bǎngshǒu 52
名列第一 mínglìe dìyī 52
名列首位 mínglìe shǒuwèi 52
名帖 míngtiě 1
摩擦 mócā 58
摩擦力 mócālì 58
摩擦音 mócāyīn 58
墓碑 mùbēi 48
墓脚基石 mùjiǎo jīshí 48
墓石 mùshí 48

## N

拿架子 ná jià·zi 57
能源危机 néngyuán wēijī 80
农民工 nóngmíngōng 13

## O

偶数 ǒushù 74

## P

排行榜 páihángbǎng 52
盘存 páncún 43
盘点 pándiǎn 43
盘货 pán//huò 43
盘库 pán//kù 43
盘账 pán//zhàng 43
泡沫 pàomò 14
泡沫经济 pàomò jīngjì 14
膨胀 péngzhàng 44

· 336 ·

拼车 pīnchē 37
拼车服务 pīnchē fúwù 37
拼车服务公司 pīnchē fúwù gōngsī 37
拼车伙伴 pīnchē huǒbàn 37
拼车族 pīnchēzú 37
拼车族车道 pīnchēzú chēdào 37
品牌代言人 pǐnpái dàiyánrén 98
瓶颈 píngjǐng 41
破产 pò//chǎn 77

## Q

潜规则 qiánguīzé 42
枪手 qiāngshǒu 15，45
侵扰公共利益罪 qīnrǎo gōnggòng lìyì zuì 71
清除 qīngchú 2
情感破产 qínggǎn pòchǎn 77
请帖 qǐngtiě 1
取缔 qǔdì 68

## R

热疾病 rèjíbìng 17
热射病 rèshèbìng 17
热虚脱 rèxūtuō 17
人才断层 réncái duàncéng 64
人才危机 réncái wēijī 80
人格障碍 réngé zhàng'ài 76
人工降雨 réngōng jiàngyǔ 96
人工雨 réngōngyǔ 96
人工增雨 réngōng zēngyǔ 96
人口膨胀 rénkǒu péngzhàng 44
人事地震 rénshì dìzhèn 61
人事海啸 rénshì hǎixiào 82

人体写真 réntǐ xiězhēn 25
人质 rénzhì 28
认同危机 rèntóng wēijī 80
认养 rènyǎng 69
日射病 rìshèbìng 17
软着陆 ruǎnzhuólù 95

## S

散养鸡蛋 sǎnyǎng jīdàn 71
散发 sànfā 2
桑拿日 sāngnárì 16
桑拿天 sāngnátiān 16
桑拿浴 sāngnáyù 16
桑拿浴室 sāngnáyùshì 16
晒 shài 36
晒成绩单 shài//chéngjīdān 36
晒工资 shài//gōngzī 36
晒秘密 shài//mìmì 36
晒生活 shài//shēnghuó 36
山寨 shānzhài 89
山寨工厂 shānzhài gōngchǎng 89
山寨手机 shānzhài shǒujī 89
善举 shànjǔ 91
善款 shànkuǎn 91
上市 shàng//shì 40
上市公司 shàngshì gōngsī 40
上市股票 shàngshì gǔpiào 40
射击手 shèjīshǒu 45
申报 shēnbào 99
申报财产 shēnbào//cáichǎn 99
申报户口 shēnbào//hùkǒu 99
生活 shēnghuó 100
生命 shēngmìng 100

# 100个热门话题汉译英
Chinese-English Translation of 100 Hot Topics

生态海啸 shēngtài hǎixiào 82
生态危机 shēngtài wēijī 80
神枪手 shénqiāngshǒu 45
石油危机 shíyóu wēijī 80
实施人工增雨 shíshī réngōng zēngyǔ 96
事业 shìyè 56
事业单位 shìyè dānwèi 56
事业费 shìyèfèi 56
事业心 shìyèxīn 56
视觉形象 shìjué xíngxiàng 55
释放人质 shìfàng//rénzhì 28
收养 shōuyǎng 69
手机漫游 shǒujī mànyóu 22
疏导 shūdǎo 70
赎金 shújīn 28
甩包袱 shuǎibāo·fú 87
双倍的 shuāngbèide 74
双重的 shuāngchóngde 74
双号 shuānghào 74
双人的 shuāngrénde 74
双人跳水 shuāngrén tiàoshuǐ 90
双日 shuāngrì 74
双数 shuāngshù 74
撕票 sī//piào 28
搜索 sōusuǒ 66
搜索飞行 sōusuǒ fēixíng 66
搜索工具 sōusuǒ gōngjù 66
搜索枯肠 sōusuǒ kūcháng 66
搜索引擎 sōusuǒ yǐnqíng 66

## T
踏足 tàzú 31
太空服 tàikōngfú 78

太空行走 tàikōng xíngzǒu 78
谈话秀 tánhuàxiù 11
跳板跳水 tiàobǎn tiàoshuǐ 90
跳水 tiàoshuǐ 90
跳台跳水 tiàotái tiàoshuǐ 90
帖子 tiě·zi 1
听觉障碍 tīngjué zhàng'ài 76
通货膨胀 tōnghuò péngzhàng 44
突破 tūpò 88
突破口 tūpòkǒu 88
突破领域 tūpò lǐngyù 88
突破瓶颈 tūpò//píngjǐng 41
图像时代 túxiàng shídài 55
团队拓展 tuánduì tuòzhǎn 32
团结 tuánjié 93
团团 tuántuán 93
团团包围 tuántuán bāowéi 93
团团围住 tuántuán wéizhù 93
团团转 tuántuánzhuàn 93
团圆 tuányuán 93
团圆饭 tuányuánfàn 93
团圆节 tuányuánjié 93
拖累 tuōlèi 95
脱口秀 tuōkǒuxiù 11
拓展 tuòzhǎn 32
拓展训练 tuòzhǎn xùnliàn 32

## W
网络海选 wǎngluò hǎixuǎn 10
网络游戏作弊 wǎngluò yóuxì zuòbì 15
网上交易中心 wǎngshàng jiāoyì zhōngxīn 12
网上以物易物 wǎngshàng

yǐ wù yì wù 12
危机 wēijī 80
危机处理 wēijī chùlǐ 80
危机点 wēijīdiǎn 80
危机干预 wēijī gānyù 67
危机感 wēijīgǎn 80
危机意识 wēijī yìshí 80
违章 wéi//zhāng 39
违章建筑 wéizhāng jiànzhù 39
违章开车 wéizhāng kāichē 39
违章作业 wéizhāng zuòyè 39
文化断层 wénhuà duàncéng 64
文学形象 wénxué xíngxiàng 55
问题 wèntí 79
问题儿童 wèntí értóng 79
问题奶粉 wèntí nǎifěn 79
无障碍 wúzhàng'ài 76
无障碍环境 wúzhàng'ài huánjìng 76
无障碍设施 wúzhàng'ài shèshī 76

## X

洗 xǐ 75
洗钱 xǐ//qián 75
洗桑拿浴 xǐ//sāngnáyù 16
下水 xià//shuǐ 84
下水道 xiàshuǐdào 84
下水道系统 xiàshuǐdào xìtǒng 84
下水管 xiàshuǐguǎn 84
项目主持人 xiàngmù zhǔchírén 30
小广告 xiǎoguǎnggào 2
小康 xiǎokāng 34
小康人家 xiǎokāng rénjiā 34
小康社会 xiǎokāng shèhuì 34

写真 xiězhēn 25
写真集 xiězhēnjí 25
心境障碍 xīnjìng zhàng'ài 76
心理干预 xīnlǐ gānyù 67
心理疏导 xīnlǐ shūdǎo 70
心理障碍 xīnlǐ zhàng'ài 76
信心危机 xìnxīn wēijī 80
信用危机 xìnyòng wēijī 80
行为越轨 xíngwéi yuèguǐ 59
行走 xíngzǒu 78
行走江湖 xíngzǒu//jiānghú 78
形象 xíngxiàng 55
形象代言人 xíngxiàng dàiyánrén 55
形象年龄 xíngxiàng niánlíng 55
形象设计师 xíngxiàng shèjìshī 55
形象思维 xíngxiàng sīwéi 55
性命 xìngmìng 100
性障碍 xìngzhàng'ài 76
修复 xiūfù 50
选美 xuǎn//měi 10
选美比赛 xuǎnměi bǐsài 10
选秀 xuǎn//xiù 10
选秀节目 xuǎnxiù jiémù 10
学习障碍 xuéxí zhàng'ài 76
雪灾 xuězāi 46

## Y

言语障碍 yányǔ zhàng'ài 76
妖魔 yāomó 60
妖魔化 yāomóhuà 60
衣裳架子 yīshang jià·zi 57
遗产 yíchǎn 26
疑惑 yíhuò 54

# 100个热门话题汉译英
## Chinese-English Translation of 100 Hot Topics

以物易物 yǐ wù yì wù 12
义工 yìgōng 18
义卖 yìmài 91
义拍 yìpāi 91
义务 yìwù 18
义演 yìyǎn 91
艺术形象 yìshù xíngxiàng 55
音乐节目主持人 yīnyuè jiémù zhǔchírén 30
英雄形象 yīngxióng xíngxiàng 55
硬着陆 yìngzhuólù 95
游戏作弊 yóuxì zuòbì 15
娱乐八卦 yúlè bāguà 19
语言障碍 yǔyán zhàng'ài 76
越轨 yuè//guǐ 59
运动成绩排行榜 yùndòng chéngjī páihángbǎng 52

## Z

灾区 zāiqū 46
造假 zàojiǎ 53
造假术 zàojiǎshù 53
造假行为 zàojiǎ xíngwéi 53
造假账 zào//jiǎzhàng 53
张贴 zhāngtiē 2
障碍 zhàng'ài 76
障碍比赛 zhàng'ài bǐsài 76
障碍赛跑 zhàng'ài sàipǎo 76
障碍物 zhàng'àiwù 76
折腾 zhēteng 94
整修 zhěngxiū 50
政治地震 zhèngzhì dìzhèn 61

政治海啸 zhèngzhì hǎixiào 82
政治破产 zhèngzhì pòchǎn 77
政治危机 zhèngzhì wēijī 80
知识断层 zhīshí duàncéng 64
职业杀手 zhíyè shāshǒu 45
志愿者 zhìyuànzhě 18
制止 zhìzhǐ 68
智力破产 zhìlì pòchǎn 77
中暑 zhòngshǔ 17
主持 zhǔchí 29
主持典礼 zhǔchí//diǎnlǐ 29
主持电视节目 zhǔchí//diànshì jiémù 29
主持公道 zhǔchí//gōngdào 29
主持公正 zhǔchí//gōngzhèng 29
主持会议 zhǔchí//huìyì 29
主持婚礼 zhǔchí//hūnlǐ 29
主持人 zhǔchírén 30
主持日常工作 zhǔchí//rìcháng gōngzuò 29
主持小组讨论会 zhǔchí//xiǎozǔ tǎolùnhuì 29
主持宴会 zhǔchí//yànhuì 29
主持正义 zhǔchí//zhèngyì 29
住持 zhùchí 29
住房危机 zhùfáng wēijī 80
专辑 zhuānjí 3
追星 zhuīxīng 5
追星族 zhuīxīngzú 5
捉刀代笔者 zhuōdāo dàibǐzhě 45
着陆 zhuó//lù 95
作弊 zuò//bì 15
作秀 zuò//xiù 11

# 英语关键词索引

## A

abandon a burden 87
abbot 29
abduct 28
abductor 28
abusive imitation 38
across the Taiwan Straits 83
act 35
act as host 29
act as host at a banquet 29
act improperly 59
add highly-coloured details to sth 65
adopt 69
adoption 69
adore a star 5
adult dependent child 7
adultery 59
advance 27
album 3
all of a sudden 21
alter sb into a demon 60
ample 86
an imitation of 89
anchor 30
anchorman 30
anchorperson 30
anchorwoman 30
anti-money laundering 75

appear on the market 40
apply for 99
apply for residence registration 99
area of breakthrough 88
arise 61
artificial precipitation 96
artificial rain 96
artificial rain production 96
artificial rainmaking 96
artistic image 55
assume great airs 57

## B

ball 93
bamboozle 21
ban 68
ban sb from entering a contest 68
bankruptcy 77
bargain-hunter 97
barrier 76
barrier-free 76
barrier-free environment 76
barrier-free facilities 76
barter A for B 12
battery egg 71
be against regulations 39
be available on the market 40
be awash with 72
be deluged with 72

be derailed 59
be docked on 51
be docked with 51
be doubtful about 54
be doubtful if 54
be doubtful that 54
be doubtful whether 54
be doubious about 54
be dubious of 54
be easy of approach 57
be employed 13
be exploded 77
be flooded with 72
be fond of gossip 19
be forced to share a casting couch with sb 42
be fuel to sth 65
be geared to 51
be gossipy 19
be hard hit 94
be haughty in one's manner 57
be hired 13
be in charge of 29
be in charge of day-today work 29
be in flood 72
be infatuated with 4
be involved in 31
be listed 40
be mistrustful of 54
be modest and unassuming in one's manner 57
be Number One on the list 52
be obsessed with 4, 5

be on top of the list 52
be ranked first 52
be responsible for 29
be reunited 93
be sceptical about 54
be sceptical of 54
be skeptical about 54
be skeptical of 54
be suspicious about 54
be suspicious of 54
be top of the list 52
be top on the list 52
beat one's brain over sth 66
beauty contest 10
beauty pageant 10
become compatible with 51
become impoverished 77
become integrated with 51
become the face of a brand 98
before we realized it 21
benevolent 91
best-seller list 52
big earthquake 61
blizzard 46
bogus 53
boomerang child 7
boomerang kid 7
both banks 83
both sides 83
both sides of the Straits 83
bottleneck 41
bottom-fisher 97
boycott 68

brand ambassador 98
brand prolocutor 98
brand spokesperson 98
breach 88
break 88
break in a continuum 64
break in continuity 64
break open the bottleneck 41
break out 61
break the regulation 39
break through 88
break through the bottleneck 41
breakthrough 88
breakthrough point 88
broaden 32
brush 58
bubble 14
bubble economy 14
bundle 87
bundle wrapped in a cloth 87
burden 87
buy and sell stocks 8

## C

cage-free egg 71
captor 28
capture 28
career 56
carpool 37
carpool buddy 37
carpool lane 37
carpool partner 37
carpooling 37

carpooling service 37
carry forward 27
carry on 27
carry on sb's unfinished work 27
carry out a salvage operation 63
carry out artificial precipitation 96
cast off a burden 87
casting couch 42
casual labourer 13
casual worker 13
cause 56
cause physical or mental suffering 94
chair 29
chair a group discussion 29
chair a meeting 29
change sb into a demon 60
channel 70
charge by the hour 23
charitable 91
charitable act 91
charitable donations 91
charitable institution 91
charitable organization 91
charitable society 91
charity 91
charity activity 91
charity auction 91
charity performance 91
charity sale 91
charity school 91
charity shop 91
charity work 91
charts 52

chase a star 5
chat show 11
cheat 15
cheating 15, 53
cheating in exam 15
check accounts 43
cheer sb on 65
cheer up 65
China's mainland, Taiwan, Hong Kong and Macao 83
clash 58
close one's door to further compromise 85
close one's mouth about 85
cloth wrapper 87
clothes-horse figure 57
cloud seeding 96
cluster around 93
collapse from sunstroke 17
comb a place for sth 66
come first 52, 62
come in 40
come on 65
come to naught 77
come to sb's rescue 63
commit an act of decency 59
commit an act of indiscretion 59
commit an act of transgression 59
commodious 86
compere 30
compulsory 18
concept 33
conception 33

confidence crisis 80
connect 51
contact 51
continue the work left by sb 27
contract 81
contracting 81
contracting responsibility system 81
contractor 81
convert sb into a demon 60
convoy 92
cook the accounts 53
cook the books 53
cornerstone 48
cost of roaming 22
count by time 23
count down 23
count the time 23
countdown 23
counterfeit 53
crack a suspending joke 87
crack down on 53
crack shot 45
credibility crisis 80
crisis 80
crisis awareness 80
crisis interference 67
crisis intervention 67
crisis management 80
crisis point 80
cross-Straits 83
cross-Straits relations 83
crowd around 93
crust fault 64

cudgel one's brain for sth 66

## D

danger 80
declare 99
declare one's property 99
declare to the customs 99
declare to the tax office 99
dedication to one's work 56
demon 60
demonize 60
derail 59
develop 32
development 32
devotion to one's work 56
dilate 44
direct 29, 70
disaster-affected area 46
disaster-attacked area 46
disaster-hit area 46
disaster-plagued area 46
disaster-stricken area 46
disc jockey 30
disclose 36
discontinuity 64
disobey the regulation 39
disorder 76
display a suspending joke 87
distribute 2
dive 90
dive into the water 90
dive into the water to commit suicide 90
diving 90

divulge 36
do a show 11
do a wedding ceremony 29
do casual work 13
do justice 29
do manual work 13
do odd jobs 13
do part-time work 13
do temporary work 13
do unskilled work 13
dock on 51
dock with 51
double 74
doubt if 54
doubt that 54
doubt whether 54
downstream 84
drag down 95
drain 84
draw a portrait 25
dredge 70
drive a car at top speed 35
drive against traffic regulations 39
drive sb out of the entertainment business 68
duty 18

## E

earthquake 61
earthquake fault 64
earthquake-battered area 61
earthquake-hit area 61
earthquake-jolted area 61

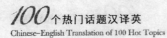

earthquake-stricken area 61
ease 86
easy 86
easy policy 86
ecological crisis 80
ecological tsunami 82
economic bubble 14
economic crisis 80
economic tsunami 82
Eight Hexagrams 19
Eight Trigrams 19
either bank 83
either side 83
election through direct voting 10
emcee 30
emotional bankruptcy 77
employed worker 13
empty nest 6
empty nest elderly 6
empty nest family 6
empty nest syndrome 6
empty nester 6
emulational 89
encircle tightly 93
endorse 98
endorse a brand 98
endorse a product 98
energy crisis 80
engage in evil doing 84
engineering 11
enlarge 32
enter stock fund market 8
entertainment gossip 19

enthusiast 4
entrails 84
environmental crisis 80
escapade 59
escort 92
escort the emperor 92
EVA spacesuit 78
even day 74
even number 74
exam cheat 15
exam imposter 15
examine 43
examine accounts 43
exceed the bounds 59
exceed the limits 59
exchange A for B 12
expand 32, 44
expert marksman 45
expose 36, 73
expose one's defects or shortcomings 73
exposure 73
expressive 55
extend 32
extensive audition 10
extinguish a fire 63

**F**

fairly well-off 34
fairly well-to-do 34
fairly well-to-do family 34
fake 53
fake examinee 15
fakery 53

fall into evil ways 84
fall through 77
false 53
family of moderate means 34
family reunion dinner 93
family valuables 87
-fancier 4
fault 64
fault earthquake 64
fault zone 64
faulting 64
fenced mountain hamlet 89
fight a fire 63
filling station 65
financial adviser 9
financial advisor 9
financial crisis 80
financial plan 9
financial planner 9
financial planning 9
financial tsunami 82
first 62
first audition 10
fish the bottom 97
flap 85
flicker 21
flip-flop 94
flood 72
foam 14
foamy economy 14
follow around a star 5
food crisis 80
fool around 94

footing stone 48
footstone 48
forbid sb to participate in a contest 68
force of friction 58
force out 68
forge 53
forged 53
forgery 53
fortified mountain village 89
foster 69
foundation 48
foundation stone 48
frame 57
framework 57
fraud 53
free from restraint 86
free from worry 86
free the hostage 28
free-range egg 71
freezing rain 46
fricative 58
friction 58
frictional force 58
frozen rain 46
fuel 65
functional disorder 76

# G

game cheating 15
gap in a continuum 64
gap in continuity 64
gas station 65
get a load off one's back 87

get geared to 51
get integrated with 51
get into the water 84
get involved in 31
get involved in one's marriage 31
get reunited 93
get rid of 2
get sb down 94
get sidetracked 94
get united 93
get wild 35
ghostwriter 45
give a show 11
glue 2
go 65
go against regulations 39
go bankrupt 77
go beyond the limits 59
go crazy 35
go from place to place 78
go into bankruptcy 77
go into the water 84
go mad 35
go off the rails 59
go public 40
go to the market 40
gossip 19
gossip magazine 19
gossip news 19
gossipy magazine 19
gossipy news 19
grass roots 49
grass roots level 49

grass-rooted culture 49
grass-roots character 49
grass-roots entertainer 49
grass-roots industry 49
great earthquake 61
groupie 5
guarantee 92
guide 70
guide by persuasion 70
gunman 45

# H

hand out 2
happen 61
hard landing 95
hatchet man 45
have a fever 4
have a mistrust of 54
have a reunion 93
have a sauna 16
have a sauna bath 16
have doubts that 54
hazard 71
headstone 48
heal 85
heal over 85
heal up 85
hearing disorder 76
heat exhaustion 17
heat illness 17
heat prostration 17
heat-related illness 17
heatstroke 17

heavy snow 46
height 47
help 92
help sb to cope with an emergency 63
help sb to tide over a crop failure 63
heritage 26
heroic image 55
hidden rule 42
hindrance 76,87
hired labourer 13
hit 88
hit man 45
hit parade 52
hoax 38
hoaxer 38
hold sb 28
hold sb prisoner 28
hoodwink 21
host 29,30
host a dinner party 29
host a television programme 29
host a television show 29
hostage 28
hostage-taker 28
hostess 30
housing crisis 80
huge earthquake 61
hunt for 66
hurricane 35
hush money 85

I

icy rain 46

identity crisis 80
idolize a star 5
illegal ad 2
illegal ad poster 2
image 55
image age 55
image designer 55
image spokesman 55
image spokeswoman 55
impediment 76
inflation 44
inherit 27
inheritance 26
initial audition 10
insolvency 77
integrate 51
intellectual bankruptcy 77
interfere 67
Internet audition 10
Internet bubble 14
intervene 67
inundate 72
invest in mutual fund 8
invest in stock market 8
invitation 1
invitation card 1
issue 79
issue an album 3

J

jerk sb around 21
juggled culture 38
jump (off) the rails 59

jump into the water 90
jump into the water to commit suicide 90
jump the track 59

## K

keep in line with 51
keep quiet about 85
keep silent about 85
key 79
keystone 48
kidnap 28
kidnapper 28
kill the hostage 28
knockoff 89
knockoff factory 89

## L

land 95
landing 95
language barrier 76
large earthquake 61
large-scale audition 10
latent rule 42
launch 84
launch an album 3
launder 75
launder money 75
lay bare 36, 73
lay bare one's private secret 36
lead 70
learning disorder 76
legacy 26
lenient policy 86
liberal policy 86
life 100
lighten up 65

link 51
link up with 51
list of best-sellers 52
list of best-selling books 52
listed company 40
listed share 40
listed stock 40
literary image 55
lives 100
load 87
load on one's mind 87
loose 86
loose and comfortable 86
loose policy 86
loose-fitting 86
lowest price 97
lubricate 65

## M

maintain justice 29
maintain righteousness 29
major earthquake 61
make a declaration 99
make a hard landing 95
make a show 11
make a soft landing 95
make a soft touchdown 95
make a spacewalk 78
make an extra effort 65
make an inventory of 43
make fake things 53
make financial planning 9
make investments in stock market 8
make stock investment 8
-manic 4
man-made rain 96

manual labourer 13
manual worker 13
marksman 45
massive audition 10
massive earthquake 61
master of ceremonies 30
medal rankings 52
medal standings 52
medal table 52
medal tally 52
meddle 67
menace 80
mental burden 87
mental disorder 76
mental interference 67
mental intervention 67
mess about 94
metabolic disorder 76
microphone jockey 30
Mid-Autumn Festival 93
millstone round one's neck 87
mischievous distortion 38
mishap 79
mistrust 54
moderate prosperity 34
moderately prosperous 34
moderately prosperous society 34
moderately well-off 34
moderately well-off family 34
moderately well-to-do 34
money laundering 75
mood disorder 76
Moon Festival 93
moral bankruptcy 77
mortgage 24
mortgage slave 24

most important 62
most significant 62
mount the high horse 57
mountain fastness 89
mountain hamlet 89
mountain stronghold 89
mountain village 89
mouthpiece 98
move into the water 84
muck around 94
multimedia message 20
music charts 52
musketeer 45
mutual fund 8

N

name card 1
nature of grass roots 49
neck of a bottle 41
NEET 7
NEET group 7
nip 68
nose-dive 90
not get sidetracked 94
nude photography 25

O

obligation 18
obstacle 76
obstacle race 76
obstacle-free 76
obstacle-free environment 76
obstacle-free facilities 76
obstruction 76

occur 61
odd day 74
odd number 74
odd-job boy 13
odd-job girl 13
odd-job man 13
odd-jobber 13
offal 84
oil 65
oil crisis 80
online barter 12
online barterer 12
online bartering 12
online exchange 12
online exchanger 12
online game cheating 15
online swap 12
online swapper 12
open a new topic 1
open the bottleneck 41
operate against regulations 39
operating expenses 56
outline 57
outlook 33
outward bound 32
overflow 72
overstep the bounds 59

## P

paint a portrait 25
paparazzi 19
paparazzo 19
part-time worker 13

paste 2
peak 47
peak period 47
people's life 100
people's livelihood 100
people's well-being 100
perform a wedding ceremony 29
peril 80
person in charge of a programme 30
person in charge of a project 30
personal development 32
personality disorder 76
personnel earthquake 61
personnel tsunami 82
persuade by reason 70
petrol station 65
philanthropic 91
philanthropic institution 91
philanthropic organization 91
philanthropist 91
philanthropy 91
-phile 4
photo of a person 25
pick stocks 8
pirate 89
place first 52
plague 71,94
platform diving 90
play a role 35
play up 65
plummet 90
point 79
point of breach 88

point of penetration 88
political bankruptcy 77
political crisis 80
political earthquake 61
political tsunami 82
pop charts 52
population expansion 44
portrait 25
portray sb 25
pose 11
post a new topic 1
posture 57
pour oil on the flames 65
powerful earthquake 61
practical joke 38
prepare an artificial rain precipitation 96
preside over 29
preside over a ceremony 29
preside over a group discussion 29
preside over a meeting 29
preside over a wedding ceremony 29
press around 93
primary 62
primary place 62
primary time 62
private company 40
problem 79
problem child 79
problem milk powder 79
problematic 79
problematic child 79
problematic milk powder 79
professional master of wedding ceremonies 30
professional presider of wedding ceremonies 30
programme compere 30
project 11
project for people's well-being 100
prolocutor 98
protect 92
proxy examinee 15, 45
psychological counseling 70
psychological disorder 76
psychological interference 67
psychological intervention 67
psychological persuasion 70
public company 40
public harm to the environment 71
public hazard 71
public image 55
public institution 56
public nuisance 71
public plague 71
public utilities 56
publicize 36
publish an album 3
pursue a star 5
put on a show 11
put on airs 57
put out a fire 63
put up 2

# Q

question 79
questionable 79

# 100个热门话题汉译英
Chinese-English Translation of 100 Hot Topics

## R

rack 57
rack one's brain for sth 66
rain enhancement 96
ramble 22
rank first 52
rankings 52
ransom 28
reach epidemic levels 72
reach epidemic proportions 72
read a thread 1
real estate bubble 14
rebuild 50
rebuilding 50
reconstruct 50
reconstruction 50
recover 50
recovery 50
reestablish 50
reestablishment 50
refuel 65
regulate 70
rehabilitate 50
rehabilitation 50
relations between China's mainland and Taiwan 83
relations between the two sides of the Straits 83
relax 86
relaxed 86
relaxed policy 86
release an album 3

release the hostage 28
relieve famine 63
remove 2
reply to a topic 1
rescue 63
restoration 50
restore 50
reunion 93
reveal 36
reveal a suspending joke 87
reveal one's private secret 36
reveal one's real life 36
reveal one's real-life situation 36
reveal one's real-life story 36
reveal one's salary 36
reveal one's school report 36
review 43
ride the high horse 57
ridematching service 37
ripoff 89
rise drastically 35
rise rapidly 35
rise sharply 35
roam 22
roaming 22
roaming charge 22
roaming call 22
roaming fee 22
rock-bottom price 97
rocket up 35
root for sb/sth 65
round 93
rub 58

run a fever 4
run around 93
run off the lines 59
run off the rails 59
run up sky high 35
rural migrant worker 13

## S

sauna 16
sauna bath 16
sauna day 16
sauna weather 16
save 63
Scientific Outlook on Development 33
scout around 66
scouting flight 66
scribble 2
scurry around 93
seal 85
seal sb's mouth 85
search 66
search engine 66
search for 66
search one's mind for sth 66
search tool 66
seed clouds 96
seismic fault 64
send a short message 20
sense of crisis 80
serious environmental pollution 71
serious pollution to the environment 71
set foot at 31
set foot in 31

set foot on 31
set it as the maximum limit 85
sewer 84
sewer pipe 84
sewer system 84
sewerage 84
sexual disorder 76
sham 53
share the ride in a carpool 37
sharpshooter 45
shelf 57
shoddy 89
shoddy factory 89
shoot sky high 35
short message 20
shoulder of a neck 41
show 11
shut one's door to further negotiation 85
shut one's mouth about 85
single 74
skeleton 57
sketch a picture 25
skyrocket 35
sleet 46
small ad 2
snap up bargains 97
snow disaster 46
snow havoc 46
snowstorm 46
soak in water 84
soar 35
soft landing 95
something wrong 79

spacesuit 78
spacewalk 78
spacious 86
speak on behalf of sb 98
speak with a tone of finality 85
special issue 3
speech disorder 76
speed for the thrill of driving fast 35
speed for the thrill of it 35
spiritual bankruptcy 77
spokesman 98
spokespeople 98
spokesperson 98
spokeswoman 98
spoofing culture 38
spread 32
spread in an unchecked way 72
spread unchecked 72
springboard diving 90
stage a show 11
stance 57
stand 57
stand for fair play 29
stand on one's dignity 57
star chaser 5
star fan 5
star pursuer 5
star-struck fan 5
steeplechase 76
stick 2
stock fund 8
stock investor 8
stock market bubble 14

stock picker 8
stock trader 8
stockaded mountain village 89
stocktaking 43
struggle 94
subcontract 81
submarine fault 64
submit a proposal 99
substitute examinee 15, 45
substitute testee 15, 45
succeed 27
succeed to the crown 27
succeed to the throne 27
successor 27
suddenly 21
suffer 94
suffer from a collapse from sunstroke 17
suffer from heatstroke 17
summit 47
summit conference 47
summit meeting 47
sunstroke 17
surround completely 93
suspect 54
suspending joke 87
swap A for B 12
swarm around 93
sway 21
swell 44
switch over to 51
synchronized diving 90

**T**

take a dive 90

take a hard landing 95
take a nose-dive 90
take a photo of sb 25
take a picture of sb 25
take a rock-bottom price tour 97
take a sauna 16
take a sauna bath 16
take a soft landing 95
take a spacewalk 78
take a tour at a rock-bottom price 97
take an inventory of 43
take care of 29
take care of day-today work 29
take care of the routines 29
take charge of 29
take charge of day-to-day work 29
take in and bring up 69
take in and provide for 69
take inventory 43
take place 61
take sb hostage 28
take stock 43
take the carpool 37
talent crisis 80
talent search 10
talent show 10
talent-search show 10
talk show 11
team development 32
television host 30
tell the time 23
temporary worker 13
tender 91

text message 20
the other man 31
the other woman 31,
thing 79
thinking in terms of images 55
third party 31
threat 80
thrift shop 91
tidal wave 82
time-rate wage 23
top the list 52
torment 94
toss about 94
toss and turn 94
touch down 95
touch the bottom line 97
touchdown 95
trade A for B 12
trade stocks 8
traffic peak 47
transform sb into a demon 60
transgress the bounds of decency 59
travel peak 47
travel to live 78
travel to survive 78
trouble 79
true description 25
true-to-life depiction 25
true-to-life portrayal 25
tsunami 82
turn sb into a demon 60
TV anchor 30
TV anchorperson 30

# 100个热门话题汉译英
Chinese-English Translation of 100 Hot Topics

two banks 83
two sides 83
two sides of the Taiwan Straits 83

## U

unauthorized building 39
unauthorized building works 39
unauthorized construction 39
unauthorized house 39
unchecked spread 72
unchecked spreading 72
underlying rule 42
undertake 81
undertaking 56
unique skill 87
unlicenced 89
unlisted company 40
unseemly secret 87
unspoken rule 42
uphold justice 29

## V

very strong wind 35
video game cheating 15
view 33
view a topic 1
viewpoint 33
violate the regulation 39
visual image 55
vivid 55

voice 98
voluntary 18
voluntary work 18
voluntary worker 18
volunteer 18
volunteer work 18
volunteer worker 18

## W

walk 78
walk around 93
walk in space 78
wander 22
wash 75
way 57
website barterer 12
welfare services 56
well off 86
well-off 34
well-to-do 34
whirlwind 35
widen 32
work against regulations 39
work part-time jobs 13
work temporary jobs 13
work with added vigour 65

## Z

zealot 4